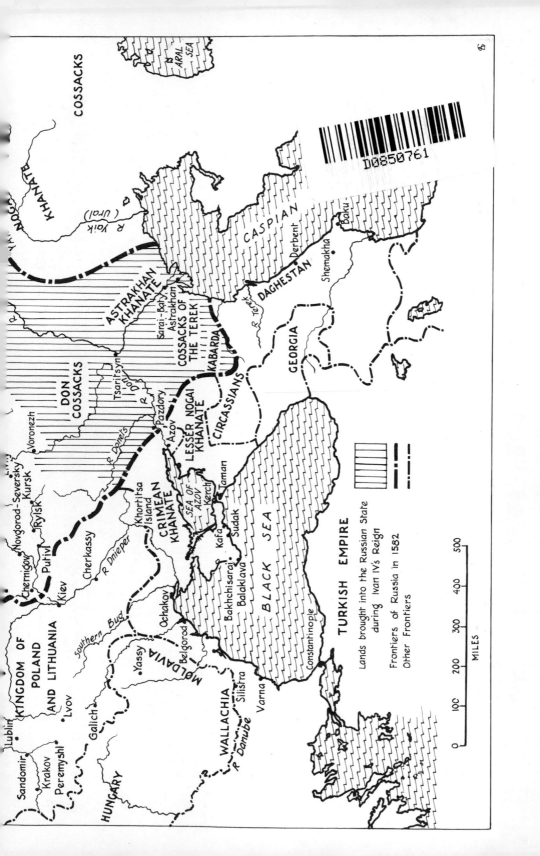

COSSACKS

KHANATE

NOGAI

R Yaik (Ural)

ARAL SEA

CASPIAN

Derbent

DAGHESTAN

Shemakha

Baku

GEORGIA

R Terek

ASTRAKHAN KHANATE

Sarai-Baty
Astrakhan

COSSACKS OF THE TEREK

KABARDA

CIRCASSIANS

DON COSSACKS

Voronezh

Tsaritsyn

R Don

Pazdory

Azov

LESSER NOGAI KHANATE

Kursk

Rylsk

Khortitsa Island

SEA OF AZOV

Taman

Kerch

R Donets

CRIMEAN KHANATE

Kafa

Sudak

BLACK SEA

Novgorod-Seversky

Chernigov

Putivl

Kiev

Cherkassy

R Dnieper

Ochakov

Bakhisaraj

Balaklava

Lublin

KINGDOM OF POLAND AND LITHUANIA

Lvov

Galich

Southern Bug

Belgorod

Yassy

MOLDAVIA

Silistra

WALLACHIA

R Danube

Varna

Constantinople

TURKISH EMPIRE

Sandomir

Krakov

Peremyshl

HUNGARY

Lands brought into the Russian State during Ivan IV's Reign

Frontiers of Russia in 1582

Other Frontiers

0   100   200   300   400   500

MILES

Boris Godunov, the chief minister and favorite of Ivan the Terrible, and later Tsar of Russia, is known in the West mainly as the hero of Mussorgsky's famous opera and of Pushkin's tragedy, on which the opera is based. Boris is usually depicted as a despot, evil and scheming, dedicated to the single-minded pursuit of supreme power and the establishment of his own dynasty on the throne of Russia, a man capable of the murder of a nine-year-old child, the legitimate heir Dmitri, in order to gain the throne for himself.

Ian Grey does not, however, accept this harsh assessment of Boris. He traces his life as Boris gradually and peacefully made himself indispensable to Ivan the Terrible and his son Fedor, eventually becoming Tsar himself, on Fedor's death from illness.

The first years of Boris's reign were successful, but slowly the power of rival families, the Romanovs and the Belskys, grew. The pressure mounted against Boris as the famine of 1602 caused the deaths of half a million people in Moscow alone, but he managed to remain in power throughout his lifetime. But after Boris's death the opposition proved too strong for the Godunov family, and his son Tsar Fedor was murdered. The years following Fedor's death were years of killing and internal war, surpassing even the horrors of the reign of Ivan the Terrible.

Ian Grey has written a fascinating and sympathetic biography. He sees Boris Godunov as a man who was too lenient in an age when brutality and murder were the norm, as a man who acted too lightly and too late, with the result that his dynasty failed to establish itself on the throne of Russia.

Born in New Zealand, Ian Grey served on the Russian front during World War II, and then went to London to work on the Russian information desk of the Foreign Office. He is now Editor of Publications for the Commonwealth Parliamentary Association in London. Ian Grey is well known for his many books on key figures in Russian history, most notably for his biographies of Peter the Great, Ivan the Terrible, and Catherine the Great.

BORIS GODUNOV

BORIS GODUNOV
The Tragic Tsar

by

Ian Grey

CHARLES SCRIBNER'S SONS
NEW YORK

To Joe and Marie

in friendship

Printed in the United States of America
Library of Congress Catalog Card Number   72-11119
SBN 684-13339-3 (cloth)

Contents

Illustrations

Acknowledgments

* Ashmolean Museum, Oxford.

All other photographs: Novosti Press Agency, Moscow.

† Photograph by Y. Kaplun, V. Vdovin.

Preface

THE SIXTEENTH CENTURY IS A FASCINATING PERIOD IN RUSSIAN history and it is not really remote from the present. Walking in the Kremlin and especially visiting the Novodevichy Monastery and the Troitsa Monastery in Zagorsk where cathedrals are open for services, one may feel that the sombre spirit of the century is still alive and relevant to the understanding of Russia today.

Sixteenth-century Russia was dominated by Tsar Ivan IV, the Terrible, and to a far lesser extent by Boris Godunov. The treatment of both Tsars by historians has followed a more or less set pattern. Tsar Ivan has been portrayed as a cruel tyrant who established in the Oprichnina a model of brutal security forces outside the law which has been continued in the Soviet Union. Boris has been described as a ruthless, power-hungry usurper. Both portrayals are misleading, but only comparatively recently have historians questioned them. Reappraisals are hampered by the dire lack of materials, but there is, I believe, evidence enough, although often only circumstantial, to support the approach that certain historians have suggested and I have sought to follow.

In my study of Ivan the Terrible, published in 1964, I attempted to portray him not as a monster but as a tormented human being whose crimes and malevolence have been greatly exaggerated. I persist in thinking that Ivan has been the victim of calumny. It is, for example, significant that notwithstanding Prince Kurbsky's campaign of vilification against his former master, there was strong support in Poland-Lithuania for Ivan to be King and, indeed, he could have been King of Poland-Lithuania had he so wished. Likewise, it is noteworthy that few Russian troops defected to Lithuania, although, following defeat by Stefan Batory, they might have been expected to be in fear of the anger of their dread Tsar.

This attempt to scrape away the accumulated calumnies of

Boris Godunov and to portray him as an able and also an honest and even humane ruler who suffered a cruel fate and who has been maligned by generations of historians may be criticised. The reader must judge for himself.

In transliterating Russian words I have broadly followed the system of the British Academy. Also except where it might cause confusion as, for example, in using Pyotr for Peter, I have retained the Russian forms of Christian names and have avoided translating Mikhail into Michael, Ivan into John and so forth. Dates are given according to the old style or Julian Calendar which in the sixteenth and seventeenth centuries was ten days behind the new style or Gregorian Calendar.

I would like to express my appreciation for the help and facilities I have received in the London Library, the British Museum and also the Lenin Library and from friends in the British Embassy in Moscow. To Mrs Jakki Becker who typed the final text and to Miss Helen Roy who made the Index I give my thanks. To my wife, Winsome, I am, as always, indebted for patience and support. I am also grateful to my daughter, Catherine, just for being there.

London, March 1973.

PROLOGUE

The Enigma

BORIS GODUNOV REMAINS ONE OF THE ENIGMAS OF RUSSIAN history. So many of his contemporaries, like subsequent historians, appeared determined to charge him with evil motives and sinister deeds. Ivan Timofeev, a *dyak* or senior Muscovite official, who wrote on the period in his *Annals,* tried to portray him, and confessed finally that he could not understand him or make up his mind whether the good or evil was predominant in his character.[1] Such ambivalence was typical of contemporary attitudes towards Boris. Political factors and the paucity of reliable information on sixteenth-century Russia combined to obscure further the man and his rule. But it is clear, notwithstanding these obstacles, that Boris has been misrepresented and treated by most historians with extraordinary prejudice and even malice.

Russian historians in the seventeenth and eighteenth centuries did not hesitate to condemn him. They followed the chronicles of the times, written by the monks, and the *Zhitie* or official biography which was endorsed by the Orthodox Church and, representing the "official truth", was beyond challenge. The Church was the main force in holding the young nation from final collapse during the anarchy of the Time of Troubles which followed the death of Boris Godunov. In this period and afterwards the Church gave its full support to the Romanov dynasty as the pivot of the nation and source of its stability. The Romanovs had been the bitter opponents of the Godunovs. It was thus a matter of loyalty to the Romanov dynasty to condemn Boris, and the Church, which dictated Russian opinion, was unsparing in its condemnation of the Godunovs.

The established portrait of Boris was set down most effectively by N. M. Karamzin in his massive *History of the Russian State,* the first eight volumes of which were published in 1816. Karamzin was the foremost writer and historian of his time, and he contributed significantly to the formation of the Russian literary language. He was an ardent champion of autocracy and of the Romanov dynasty, and he idealised old Russia. He was an able historian who read and researched widely, and had a lively feeling for the history of his country. His writings had immediate and lasting success. In 1803 Emperor Alexander I appointed him official historian. Bearing such imperial approval his books, and particularly the *History,* which was so persuasive in its magisterial and at times moving style, exercised tremendous influence. Of all his historical judgments, none has endured so strongly as his indictment of "the criminal ambition" of Boris, "this power-loving man", and he observed with relish that "the punishment of Heaven awaited him".[2]

In Western countries Boris Godunov is known as the ruthless and ill-fated Tsar of Mussorgsky's opera. The libretto of the opera was provided by Alexander Pushkin's drama, *Boris Godunov,* and Pushkin took his material from Karamzin's *History.* Indeed, both inside Russia and beyond its frontiers, Karamzin must bear special responsibility for the distorted portrayal of Boris which historians with only a few exceptions have followed until the present century.[3]

Boris Godunov has suffered, in fact, from consistent and unjust denigration. The gravamen of the charges against him has been that he so lusted after power and the throne that to attain them he resorted to deceit, violence, and crime, and in particular was guilty of the murder of a nine-year-old child, Tsarevich Dmitri, who was said to stand between him and the throne. It was even alleged that he was responsible for the deaths of Tsar Ivan IV, Tsar Fedor, and Tsaritsa Irina, his own sister. Karamzin repeated but did not endorse all of these allegations, but held Boris guilty of the murder of the Tsarevich. It is now generally accepted that Boris was not guilty of or involved in the death of the Tsarevich. Other accusations rest on flimsy evidence or no evidence at all.

In nineteenth-century Russia some re-examination of historical dogmas became permissible without implying disloyalty to the ruling dynasty or affront to the established Church. Certain historians took up the defence of Boris or at least denied that he had been guilty of the murder of the Tsarevich. It was significant, however, that the two greatest Russian historians, S. M. Solovyev and V. O. Klyuchevsky, remained unsympathetic. Klyuchevsky, for example, wrote that Boris "attracted by his presence, his intelligence, and his ability, but repelled by his failings of heart and conscience".[4] It is a judgment reflecting three centuries of calumniation, and not justified by the known facts about the man and his life.

The high intelligence and ability of Boris have been generally acknowledged. But there is ample evidence of his concern for the welfare of his people, especially the humble and oppressed, and for the nation. He strove to restore standards of conduct that had been debased in the reign of Ivan the Terrible. He acted humanely and honestly, pursuing sound policies with considerable success in external relations, but with less success in dealing with the intractable internal problems of the country. In his public and private life he was a man more deserving of popular respect and loyalty and especially of the approbation of the Church than Tsar Ivan the Terrible. Notwithstanding the savageries of his reign, however, Tsar Ivan remained for his subjects and in history a great autocrat, while Boris was to find himself betrayed by the people who had unanimously supported his election to the throne, and he has been execrated in history.

Boris reigned as Tsar for only a short time and his attempt to establish a dynasty failed. He became the victim of the turbulence of a period when Russia was struggling to survive as a nation. Indeed, for all the brilliance of his career and the sagacity and enlightenment of his rule, he appeared to be doomed from the outset, like the hero of a Greek tragedy. His undeserved fate placed Orthodox Christians in a dilemma. As a mediaeval morality play the tragic end and aftermath of the reign of Boris might have borne the title *The Triumph of Evil* and, since evil could not be allowed to triumph, they felt impelled to find or invent crimes, committed by Boris, to explain and justify "the punishment of Heaven" which clearly befell him.

Notes
1. Ivan Timofeev, *Vremennik* (Extracted from volume XIII of the *Russian Historical Library*. St. Petersburg, 1907) pp. 60, 83–87.
2. N. M. Karamzin, *History of the Russian State* (5th ed. St. Petersburg, 1842–43) X, III, Col. 136.
   Cited as "Karamzin" in subsequent notes.
3. N. Nisbet Bain in *Slavonic Europe* (Cambridge, 1908) and Stephen Graham in *Boris Godunov* (London, 1933) followed the practice of denigration. Nisbet Bain acknowledged, however, that Boris was "one of the greatest of the Muscovite Tsars".
   A more recent and not untypical reference to Boris is in W. H. Parker's *An Historical Geography of Russia* (London, 1968, p. 85) where he is described as "capable and cruel"; in his age he was remarkable for humanity rather than cruelty.

4. V. O. Klyuchevsky *Course of Russian History* (Moscow, 1956–59) II, pp. 24–25.

Cited as "Klyuchevsky" in subsequent notes.

CHAPTER 1

Aleksandrovskaya Sloboda
November 1581

THE GRIM TRAGEDY OF ONE DAY IN NOVEMBER 1581 SET BORIS
Godunov on the path to the throne of Russia. Long before this
time he had made his mark at court and had become the trusted
favourite of Tsar Ivan IV, the Terrible. He could look forward to
a brilliant career under Ivan and under his successor as chief
minister and the most powerful boyar in the land. But until the
events of this day he could never have dreamt that he, an
untitled boyar, might become Tsar.

For Tsar Ivan the year 1581 was one of bitter defeat and
personal suffering. Notwithstanding its savageries, his reign had
been a time of great achievements. The nation was more united
under his absolute rule. He had conquered Kazan and Astrakhan
and with his authority extending over the whole length of the
mighty Volga, the conquest and colonisation of Siberia had begun.
But in the west he had had to admit the failure of his long
struggle to secure access to the Baltic Sea. At this time of defeat
he committed an act of violence which placed his dynasty in
jeopardy.

During the autumn of 1581 Ivan had spent most of his time at
Aleksandrovsk. Hidden in dense forests some seventy miles north
of Moscow, this town was fortified by a moat and a stone wall
with ramparts. The approaches were closely guarded for a distance
of two miles on all sides and no one entered or departed without
his personal knowledge. He felt more secure in this gloomy retreat
than in Moscow and had come to regard it as his residence.

Tall and imperious, with a compelling aquiline face, forbidding
in expression, Ivan was a lonely mistrustful man. He inspired
reverence and fear in his people, but absolute power and the
position of Tsar, appointed by God, had isolated him. In this
solitude his fears for the survival of himself, his dynasty, and the
nation had become obsessive. In the last years of his reign,

however, he drew comfort from the companionship of two people —Tsarevich Ivan and Boris Godunov. He was rarely separated from the Tsarevich who was the son of Anastasia, his beloved first wife. At formal court occasions, when he accompanied his armies, and at such fearsome events as the execution of traitors and the massacres in Novgorod, the Tsarevich was at his side. He evidently craved his son's company, but also, following Muscovite practice, he was introducing him to the duties of the autocrat and accustoming the people to their future ruler. The security of the nation and, which was the same thing in the minds of the Russians, the security of the dynasty rested on his shoulders, for his brother, Tsarevich Fedor, was sickly and appeared to be mentally backward. Tsarevich Ivan had inherited his father's majestic presence and his ability; all saw in him the strong Tsar that Russia needed.

In November of this year Ivan waited impatiently in Aleksandrovsk for reports from his envoys. Stefan Batory, King of Poland, was laying siege to the frontier town of Pskov. The Poles had made no impression on its defences. Polish morale was low and an attack by the Russian army, standing nearby, would certainly have routed them. But Ivan was anxious to come to terms. He had already lost the two important towns of Polotsk and Velikie Luki, and he feared that Pskov would fall. He had therefore sent envoys to the Polish king with the offer to surrender all the Russian gains in Livonia in return for peace.

Under strain Ivan's intensely nervous nature became more unpredictable and dangerous. The smallest affront, the least disagreement could throw him into a violent rage. He then lost control of himself. All present, even those closest to him, went in danger of their lives.

At this time in Aleksandrovsk, Tsarevich Ivan approached his father about some matter, either bearing on the relief of Pskov or a domestic concern.[1] What he said is not known, but Ivan gave a roar of anger. He raised the iron-tipped staff which he always carried and lunged at his son. Boris Godunov quickly moved forward and warded off the blow. He was badly hurt. But his intervention merely added to the Tsar's fury. He struck again at his son and the iron top of the staff this time fractured his skull.

Slowly the Tsarevich sank to the ground. Blood began to flow from the wound. Ivan, his anger dispelled by shock and realisation of what he had done, knelt and took his son in his arms. With trembling fingers he tried to staunch the wound, but blood seeped over his hand and onto his robes. He called for doctors and began to weep convulsively. He muttered incoherent prayers that his son might live.

The Tsarevich had not lost consciousness. He begged his father not to give way to grief and kissed his hand. At this time father and son came closer together. But the Tsarevich was rapidly growing weaker. The doctors found that they could do nothing for him. Four days later he died.

Ivan was crazed with grief. The two people whom he had loved most in life were Anastasia, his first wife, and her son, Ivan, and both had died young. But his grief was now beyond endurance, for he had killed his son with his own hand. He had, moreover, destroyed his successor and possibly the last of his dynasty.

From Aleksandrovsk, clad in simple white robes of penitence, without any of the insignia of majesty, Ivan followed the coffin to Moscow. The body lay in state before the magnificent golden ikonostasis of the Arkhangelsky Cathedral where all the Muscovite Grand Princes had been laid to rest. Ivan kept vigil under the boding eyes of the Saviour and the Orthodox saints which peered from the numerous ikons, set into the ikonostasis and hanging on the walls, and also looked down from the bright frescoes painted on the columns which supported the high ceiling. The cathedral, illuminated by chandeliers and countless candles, was filled with the sonorous incantations of the priests and the choir. The Tsar appeared lost to his surroundings, but as the top was placed on the coffin, and it was lowered finally into the stone tomb, he gave a sudden cry and fell to the floor.

Ivan remained inconsolable. He wandered through the Kremlin Palace. He did not pause to pray before the ikons in the corners of the corridors and chambers, for his grief was beyond the intercession of saints. When he was exhausted he sank to the floor and slept where he lay. Servants, watching fearfully out of sight, then crept forward to cover him with furs.

On awakening he would begin his wandering anew, a lonely man, tortured by remorse. He summoned senior churchmen and boyars and told them that he would retire to a monastery and that, since his surviving son was incapable of ruling, they must choose another sovereign. But this proposal aroused general alarm. Not only the leading men of the realm but all Russians were convinced of the inviolability of the Rurikid succession; to choose a Tsar outside the dynasty was unthinkable. So strong was their opposition that Ivan bowed to the general will, and gradually the responsibilities of the throne drew him out of his grief.

In the meantime Boris Godunov had returned to Moscow from Aleksandrovsk, but he did not appear at court. All assumed that he was recovering from the wounds received while trying to defend the Tsarevich. But Fedor Nagoi, brother of the Tsar's seventh wife, insinuated that Boris stayed away because of his grief and anger.[2] Eager for the company of his favourite, Ivan called at Godunov's house to learn the truth. He found that Boris was indeed still recovering from his injury.[3] He embraced him warmly and showed him the greatest favour, not only from affection but probably also in gratitude for his brave attempt to save the Tsarevich, and to atone for the injuries which he himself had inflicted.

Boris now stood closer to the Tsar than ever before. He was ambitious and may have begun to think of the throne for himself, but this is doubtful. Tsar Ivan might have more children.[4] Tsarevich Fedor, although unlikely to live long, might produce an heir. Only if the dynasty died out would the way be clear for an outsider to occupy the throne, and then the obstacles were formidable. But there is no evidence to suggest that Boris was looking ahead and calculating so boldly at this stage. He had grown up under the rule of Tsar Ivan. He had served loyally and like all Russians he was devoted to the dynasty which had brought the Russian nation to birth. The death of Tsarevich Ivan nevertheless opened the way for Boris to mount the throne in years to come.

Notes

1. According to Karamzin's account the Tsarevich demanded to be allowed to take command of the Russian army and to relieve Pskov, thus saving the honour of the nation. Another account relates that the Tsar had chided and even struck his daughter-in-law, wife of the Tsarevich, who defended his wife and remonstrated with his father.

   This account of the death of Tsarevich Ivan is taken from Karamzin IX, VII, Cols. 208, 210–11. See also S. M. Solovyev, *History of Russia from earliest times* (Moscow, 1959–66) III, V, p. 703.

   Cited as "Solovyev" in subsequent notes.

2. Karamzin, *loc. cit.*

3. The Tsar, finding that Fedor Nagoi had lied out of malice, ordered Stroganov, who was skilled in medicine, to inflict on him the same wound as Boris had suffered and to stitch him up in the same way. *Ibid.*

4. Tsarevich Dmitri Ivanovich, the Tsar's son by his seventh wife, was born on 19 October in the following year.

CHAPTER II

The Godunovs

BORIS GODUNOV WAS BORN AND GREW TO MANHOOD IN THE REIGN of Ivan the Terrible. His career began early, but it was already in the period when through fear and depravity the Tsar had debased court life and engulfed the country in terror. Boris first came to prominence under auspices reflecting this dark side of the Tsar's rule. In 1570 at the age of about twenty, he married Maria, a daughter of Grigori Malyuta, the trusted favourite and executioner of the Tsar.[1] Malyuta had served in humble posts at court and had begun to rise in the Tsar's favour only a few years earlier.

In a time of bloodshed and terror, Malyuta impressed the Tsar by his unquestioning loyalty and his zeal in carrying out orders. He could be counted on to execute, and to destroy the property of, nobles who incurred the Tsar's disfavour. He would bring their wives and daughters to court to serve in orgies and to gratify the lusts of the Tsar and his associates. He was prepared to strangle the deposed Metropolitan with his own hands. A few weeks later he distinguished himself in the massacres in Novgorod, directed personally by the Tsar. In May 1570 Malyuta was raised to the rank of *Dumny Dvoryarnin* and appointed to be in personal attendance on the Tsar.

As the son-in-law of Malyuta, Boris was soon one of the leading young men at court. It is possible, however, that he had begun to attract notice before his marriage. Although only of medium height, he was strikingly handsome with a dignified presence and great charm. He possessed a natural courtesy and was always correct in bearing, showing appropriate subservience to his Tsar and respect to the princes and boyars. The result was that, at a court divided by suspicions, jealousies, and factions, which were held in check only by fear of the Tsar, he was generally liked and respected.

Boris was, however, more than a model courtier. He possessed
high intelligence and ability, and his interests were wide. Moreover, although an *Oprichnik,* he evidently managed to avoid taking
part in the debauchery and savageries without losing the goodwill
and trust of the Tsar. In attempting to defend the Tsarevich
from his father's anger he had not only incurred physical harm,
but had risked the disfavour of the Tsar which usually spelt death.
It can only be assumed that the Tsar recognised in him a young
man of remarkable character and that, trusting him, he did not
demand the subservience that he required of others.

Boris had become a member of the Tsar's personal suite soon
after his marriage to Malyuta's daughter. He was *Druzhka,* a best
man, at the Tsar's marriage to Marfa in October 1571. More
important was his appointment as *Kravchy,* an office of great
trust. The *Kravchy* waited on the Tsar at table. It was he who
took each dish from the *Stolnik* (steward) and tasted it before
placing it before the Tsar.

Poison was a common method of disposing of enemies at this
time. Ivan III had arrested several "evil women" during a dynastic
crisis, for they had been visiting his wife and were found to be
carrying poisonous herbs. Their purpose was not clear, but he had
them pushed through holes in the ice of the Moskva River and
drowned as a warning to others. Ivan the Terrible himself was
convinced that enemies at court were watching for an opportunity
to poison him. It was rumoured that Anastasia and Marfa, his
first and third wives, had been poisoned, and he himself appeared
to believe it. The office of *Kravchy* was thus far more than a
formal honour.

Unlike others who gained Ivan's favour only to lose it and
suffer the penalties of his mistrust, Boris became closer to the
Tsar. Jerome Horsey, the English agent, wrote that the Tsar had
adopted Boris "as his third son".[2] In 1580 the Godunovs were
set above other princely and boyar families at court by the
marriage of Irina, the sister of Boris, to Tsarevich Fedor, the
Tsar's second son. On this occasion Boris was elevated to the rank
of boyar and the whole Godunov family was honoured as part of
the Tsar's family.

The Godunovs were of Tatar origin, as were a number of
eminent Russian families.[3] In their struggle against the Tatar
Khanates, the Grand Princes of Moscow had sought, often with
considerable success, to gain the allegiance of the Tatar princes
and clans on whose support the Khans depended. Among the first
of the Tatar princes to swear allegiance to Moscow and to settle
there was the Murza Chet. About 1330 he entered the service of

Grand Prince Ivan Kalita. He was converted to Christianity and baptised with the name of Zakhary. Among his descendants were the Godunovs who served the Muscovite Grand Princes faithfully for over two hundred years. They belonged to the small circle of untitled families of boyars and senior officials whose service to successive Grand Princes contributed to the expansion of Muscovy and the creation of the Russian nation.

The bonds between the Muscovite rulers and these families were strong. Grand Prince Dmitri Donskoi acknowledged the debt which Moscow owed to its boyars, when he said to them " . . . you are not to be called boyars, but princes of my realm", and on his deathbed he called on his sons to treat them as brothers.[4] But they had not held their special position without strong challenges.

In the early period of its history, Muscovy had been one of a number of principalities, each with its own Grand Prince, serving princes, and boyars. As Moscow extended its power in the fifteenth century, it absorbed the other principalities. The princely families and their retainers then faced the choice of seeking refuge in Lithuania or finding service in Moscow, and most chose this latter course. The procedure then was that they swore an oath of loyalty and the Grand Prince restored their estates as patrimonial holdings in return for their service as his subjects.

Cherishing memories of their past independence and power, most of these princes hated their new subservient position. They served, but with reluctance, and a number subsequently defected to Lithuania. In Moscow they held themselves aloof. They considered themselves to be superiors of all but the Grand Prince himself. They always demanded precedence at court and in military service over the Muscovite serving princes and boyars. In time the practice developed of granting to the most eminent princes the rank of boyar and to lesser princes the rank of *Okolnichy,* the grade next below boyar. But this did not merge the princes and boyars into one serving class for many decades. Relying on the genealogical lists, carefully maintained at court, the princes continued to demand precedence, especially over the untitled Muscovite boyars. In the fifteenth century they evolved a system of seniority, known as *Mestnichestvo,* which fixed immutably the order of precedence among the princely and boyar families. Descendants of the ruling princes formed the most senior class; next came the Muscovite boyars, who were followed in seniority by the lesser princely families. This system was applied strictly to official appointments, for no prince or boyar would accept a civil or military office lower in the hierarchy than an office held by one of his forebears. The system was negative and restrictive in that birth alone, and not ability, experience, or seniority in service, determined appointments to high office; it shackled the power of the Grand Prince to make suitable appointments and it imposed burdens on the country.

The Muscovite boyars were not submerged, however, by the influx of princes into Moscow in the sixteenth century. The old boyar families took pride in their long service to the Grand Prince. They had taken an active part in the conquest and annexation of the principalities of these princes who now patronised them. The Grand Princes, aware of the reluctant loyalty of many of the newcomers, continued to depend on their own boyars. The names of the leading untitled Muscovite boyar families—Morozov, Saltykov, Shein, Zakharin, Sheremetev, Buturlin, Saburov, Pleshcheev, Romanovich-Yuriev—recurred in every decade.

The continued prominence of these boyar families was the more remarkable, because so many of the proud princely clans declined. The practice of providing equal patrimonial estates for all the sons of each generation, a practice eschewed by the Muscovite families, had by the fifteenth century led to the fragmentation of many princely estates. The English ambassador, Giles Fletcher, noted that petty princes were "so many that the plenty maketh them cheap: so that you shall see dukes glad to serve a mean man for five or six rubles or marks a year; and yet they will stand highly upon their *bestchest* or reputation of their honours".[5]

The Godunovs belonged to this inner circle of trusted servants of the Muscovite Grand Princes. They were, however, humble in status, and did not attain boyar rank until the reign of Ivan the Terrible. Indeed, they apparently served worthily but without distinction, and the name of Godunov might well have faded from the pages of history, but for the remarkable career of Boris Godunov.

Notes

1. *Voprosy Istorii*, No. 2, (1966), pp. 210–12.
2. R. Hakluyt, *The Principal Navigations, Voyages, Traffiques, and Discoveries of the English Nation* (Dent Edition, London, 1927) II, p. 269.
3. G. Vernadsky, *The Tsardom of Moscow 1547–1682* (New Haven, 1969) I, p. 7.
4. Klyuchevsky, II, p. 158.
5. E. A. Bond (ed.), *Russia at the close of the 16th century* (Hakluyt Society, London, 1856) p. 38.

CHAPTER III

Muscovy

MUSCOVY WAS IN A FERMENT THROUGHOUT THE SIXTEENTH CENTURY. The Russian people had moved rapidly towards nationhood. They needed a period of peace and stability to enable the Muscovite Grand Prince to establish his authority, to create a new administrative system, to integrate the new society, and to develop the economy.

Far from having such a respite, the people found themselves under greater strains. Wars, natural calamities, internal conflicts, and periods of terror led to general disorder. The country was beset by enemies and, lacking natural frontiers, except in the Arctic north, it was vulnerable. In pursuit of security the Grand Princes were forced to embark on a policy of expansion. Unlike the peoples of Western Europe, the Russians found themselves committed to creating a nation and an empire at the same time. This double process aggravated their predicament. By the end of the sixteenth century the young nation was near to collapse and disintegration.

Tsar Ivan IV, the Terrible, played a significant part in the dual process of nation and empire-building and also in bringing the country near to disaster. Boris Godunov provided a period of stability, when Muscovy began to recover, but the period was cut short by internal crises. The Russians faced special problems, which no ruler alone could resolve, for they stemmed from the early history of the country.

Kievan Rus, which endured for some three and a half centuries, had been the first stage in the movement of the Russian people towards political unity. The city of Kiev on the Dnieper River became the centre of a loose federation of princely city-states. In the tenth and eleventh centuries Grand Princes Vladimir (978–1015) and Yaroslav (1019–1054) brought Kiev to the zenith of its power and splendour. Vladimir embraced Orthodox Christianity and ordered the conversion of his people. It was a momentous event. Orthodox Christianity was soon permeating the lives of the Russian people. It exerted a powerful influence in moulding their outlook and national character and in forging the nation.

Grand Prince Vladimir married the sister of the Byzantine Emperor, Basil II, and this, too, was a significant event. Byzantium was for all Russians the immensely rich and imperishable bastion of civilisation. Their prosperity depended upon trade with Constantinople. Byzantine influence was predominant in every field of Russian life. The Grand Princes in Kiev and the minor princes of every city-state sought to emulate the splendour of Constantinople. Grand Prince Yaroslav engaged Greek builders to erect the Cathedral of St. Sofia and other fine buildings in Kiev. A library and theological school were attached to the cathedral. The Monastery of the Caves and other monasteries were soon developing spiritual and cultural traditions which were to guide Russians in centuries to come. Kiev grew into a large and magnificent city, advanced beyond other European cities at this time as a centre of civilisation and trade. But the splendour was soon to pass.

By the beginning of the twelfth century Kievan Rus was in decline. It covered an immense area, extending from a frontier about a hundred miles to the south of the city northwards to the Arctic Ocean. The dynasty of Rurik whose Grand Princes had held the federation together had become too numerous and divided. The princes warred among themselves, struggling for power and petty independence.

Obsessed with trade and dynastic rivalries, the princes and people could not remain united even for their own defence. In destructive waves the Pechenegs, Cumans, and other Asiatic nomads swept in from the east. In the north, moreover, the Russians were coming under pressure from the Germanic tribes which were moving eastwards, pushing the Lithuanians and Letts before them.

In search of greater security the Russians began to leave the Kievan lands. Many went to Galicia and Belorussia which were to come under the rule of Poland-Lithuania. The main migration was, however, to the north-east, to the forest lands of the upper Volga and its tributaries. Here at first the Grand Princes of the principality of Rostov-Vladimir-Suzdal, known as Suzdalia, held the primacy over a number of independent principalities. The region of the upper Volga and Oka Rivers became the centre around which the Russian nation was to be formed. But this growth was checked by the catastrophe of the Mongol-Tatar invasion.

The nomadic invasions reached their climax in the thirteenth century when the Horde of Chingiz Khan swept in an irresistible destructive wave across Russia and into Western Europe. The Mongol cavalry was a formidable force. The hardy, slant-eyed horsemen were disciplined and lived for war. They advanced swiftly on their sturdy horses, loosing their iron-tipped arrows with deadly force and accuracy. They destroyed all in their path and then withdrew as suddenly as they had come. News of the scale and speed of their operations and the appalling devastation that they inflicted, spread throughout the civilised world. Mention of their name filled men with dread.

On the death of Chingiz Khan in 1227 the Mongol Empire was divided among his sons, each receiving his own *ulus* or regional khanate. Juji, eldest son of Chingiz Khan, had died and his son, Batu, inherited the Khanate of Kipchak, embracing the area to the west of the Irtysh River and the Aral Sea. Most of the region was as yet unconquered and in 1236 Batu set out with an army of fifty thousand strong. He passed through the Caspian Gate, south of the Ural Mountains, and then moved to the north-west.

The savage winter gripped the land, but the Mongols advanced, taking all in their path. The important town of Ryazan was destroyed. The chronicler recorded that "the prince with his mother, wife, and sons, the boyars and inhabitants, without regard to age or sex, were slaughtered with the savage cruelty of Mongol revenge . . . Priests were roasted alive, and nuns and maidens were ravished in the churches before their relatives. No eye remained open to weep for the dead."[1]

Continuing his advance in 1240, Batu razed to the ground the cities of Pereyaslavl and Chernigov. He sent envoys, demanding the surrender of Kiev. The governor of the city put the envoys to death. His action sealed the doom of the city. In December 1240 the Mongols took Kiev by storm. They massacred all forms of life and reduced the great city to ruins. Six years later, when the envoy of Pope Innocent IV passed through Kiev, he found only two hundred houses standing and "an innumerable multitude of men's skulls and bones".[2]

Batu ranged over the whole Russian plain. He was poised to advance into Western Europe when news reached him that the Great Khan, Ogadai, had died. He withdrew and set up his headquarters at Sarai on the lower Volga, some sixty-five miles north of Astrakhan. Here he created a city of tents which became legendary as the centre of the Khanate of Kipchak or the Golden Horde, so called after his own gold-embroidered tent. From Sarai,

Batu and his successors enforced their suzerainty over the Russian lands for more than two centuries.

The Russians were completely subservient to their Mongol overlords. The Grand Prince of Suzdalia answered to the Khan for the whole of north-east Russia. He travelled to Sarai and even on occasions to Karakorum, the capital of the Great Khan, to make obeisance and to obtain the *yarlyk,* the Mongol badge of authority without which he could not rule. Other princes also made the journey to Sarai to seek favour. The Khans were brutal masters, who exacted fullest obedience. Failure to pay the prescribed taxes or to deliver the full number of recruits and, worst of all, rebellion, brought prompt and savage punishments.

In the region of lakes and swamps to the north-west, Novgorod had escaped destruction. Batu had approached the city at a time of exceptional rains and, deterred by the swampy terrain, had turned back. The prince and people of Novgorod had made haste to swear allegiance, and he did not renew his attack.

The Khans always encouraged trade as a source of tribute. They recognised the value of Novgorod as a commercial centre, linked with the Baltic and with the Caspian Sea by the river route. For this reason they guaranteed the city's political and trading privileges, and throughout the period of the Mongol-Tatar domination, Novgorod flourished.

After trade, the Novgorodtsi valued their freedom and autonomy. The city had acknowledged the primacy of Kiev in the eleventh century, but had been quick to assert its independence as soon as Kiev's authority declined. The Novgorodtsi also took pride in their constitution which was republican and in some degree democratic. They claimed the right to choose their prince from among the princely families of Russia. Usually they elected the Grand Prince of Suzdalia and later of Moscow, since they were dependent on him for defence. Real power was vested, however, not in the prince but in the *veche* or assembly, in which all men of Novgorod could take part and vote, and in the Boyar Council. "Lord Novgorod the Great," as the people called their republic, became more prosperous and powerful. But it failed to develop military forces and, sited between the vigorous and growing powers of Lithuania and Moscow, its independence could not endure.

The Russian Orthodox Church also flourished during the Mongol-Tatar occupation. In the twelfth century certain Mongol and Turkish tribes had embraced Nestorian Christianity. The Khans themselves had shown such interest in Christianity at one time that Rome had entertained hopes of their conversion. Finally they had adopted Islam, but they always showed special favour to the Orthodox Church, protecting its rights by charter and exempting its lands from all interference and obligations to pay taxes.

In this privileged position the Orthodox Church became wealthy and a powerful landowner. Its lands attracted peasant labour. Its influence and authority expanded and, consistently supporting the Grand Princes, it promoted a sense of unity among the people.

At the same time the Church, isolated from outside influences and conceiving its mission to be the preservation of Orthodoxy in pristine purity, intensified the natural conservatism of the Russian people. Cut off from virtually all contact with the West, they were untouched by the Renaissance, the Reformation, the spirit of exploration and scientific discovery, which bore witness to the tremendous intellectual vitality of the Western peoples. The Orthodox Church and the Russian people cultivated a sense of spiritual and cultural self-sufficiency. This isolation and its stultifying consequences were major effects of the Mongol occupation, and were causes of the backwardness which was to plague Russia in succeeding centuries.

The great development during the Mongol occupation was, however, the dramatic and unexpected rise of Moscow. In the seventeenth century a Muscovite exclaimed: "What man could have divined that Moscow would become a great realm?" His comment reflected the surprise that many Russians felt as they looked back on this chapter in their history.

The first mention of Moscow is made in a chronicle which relates that in 1147 Grand Prince Yury Dolgoruky of Suzdalia sent an invitation to an ally: "Come to me, brother, in Moscow! Be my guest in Moscow!"[3] At this time Moscow was no more than a settlement of log huts. Nine years later Grand Prince Yury founded the town on its present site by building the first Kremlin, or fortress, surrounded by a pallisade of logs on the high ground between the Moskva and Neglinnaya Rivers.

In 1238 the Mongols captured Moscow. The chronicler relates that they "slaughtered all the inhabitants, from old men to infants at the breast; and they set fire to the fortress and the holy churches, and burned all the monasteries and villages".[4] The description suggests that Moscow had already become a large town, although still only a minor principality under the suzerainty of Vladimir-Suzdal.

Rising from the ashes of Mongol devastation, Moscow at once began to expand. In the first four years of the fourteenth century alone the extent of the principality increased almost three-fold. It continued to grow until within a short period it had established its ascendancy over all the principalities of the Russian plain, and become not only the centre but the chief driving force in creating the Russian nation.

The question was why Moscow should have attained primacy rather than Suzdalia, Rostov, Yaroslavl, or Nizhny Novgorod. The answer was that Moscow was favoured by several advantages. Foremost among them was its position in the region of the upper Volga and Oka Rivers at the centre of the network of rivers, which extended over the whole country. Moreover, the Moskva River which served as the main artery, linking the great river communication system, was already wholly within the principality at the beginning of the fourteenth century. A further important advantage was Moscow's natural defence system. The dense forest zone to the east of the city provided a barrier against attack. Indeed, throughout the fourteenth and fifteenth centuries, when other Russian towns suffered repeated Tatar onslaughts, Moscow was not attacked once from the east.[5]

Attracted by the greater security and by the growing importance of the principality, Russians of all classes made their way there. The inner Volga-Oka region was already well populated, compared with other parts of north-eastern Russia, and the further increases in population added to the strength of the principality.

Moscow was also fortunate in its Grand Princes. They do not emerge clearly as individuals from the surviving materials of these centuries, and historians have disputed their competence and leadership.[6] They nevertheless played an important part in the rise of Moscow. They were remarkable less for heroic deeds than for their opportunism, tenacity, and ruthless expansion of the principality. Ivan I, known as Kalita, or Money-Bag, because he was "wise and thrifty", was typical.[7] Usually recognised as the first of the great "gatherers of the Russian land", a title that is disputed,[8] Ivan Kalita was always carefully subservient to the Golden Horde and gained the confidence of the Khans. Earlier they had encouraged individual princes in north-east Russia in such manner as to ensure that no one became too powerful. The easterly expansion of Lithuania under the forceful rule of Grand Prince Gedimin led the Khan to treat the Grand Prince of Moscow as the senior prince on whom he could count to block the Lithuanian advance. Ivan Kalita was prompt to take advantage of this change in Mongol-Tatar policy to entrench the power of Moscow over other principalities.

Ivan Kalita also persuaded Metropolitan Peter, head of the Russian Church, to move from Vladimir and to reside in Moscow.

The Metropolitan and Ivan together laid the foundation stone of the Uspensky Cathedral within the Kremlin, and the Metropolitan "with his own hands built a stone grave for himself in the wall", where he was laid only four and a half months later.[9] From this time Moscow became the ecclesiastical centre of the country, and the authority of the Church greatly strengthened the position of the Muscovite Grand Prince. Finally, Ivan Kalita managed to ensure that his son should receive the Khan's *yarlyk* to rule as Grand Prince. Thus, while he did not himself add to the lands of Moscow, he prepared the way for his successors to establish the supremacy of Moscow.

During the fourteenth century the unity of the Horde was weakening and the Russians were more and more prepared to assert themselves. Their new attitude was demonstrated on the battle of Kulikovo Pole, fought on the banks of the Don in 1380, when Grand Price Dmitri gained a signal victory over the Khan's army. It gave rise to legends and the Grand Prince was always known as Dmitri Donskoi thereafter. Two years later the Tatars returned, destroyed Moscow, and massacred the inhabitants "until their arms wearied and their swords became blunt".[10] The Russians had proved to themselves at Kulikovo, however, that the Tatars were not invincible.

Grand Prince Ivan III, the Great, was the chief architect of the unification of Russia. The Italian traveller, Ambrogio Contarini, who visited Moscow about 1499, wrote that he was "tall, thin, and handsome", but he was also stooped and sometimes described as *Gorbaty*, the Hunchback.[11] His presence could be forbidding and women sometimes fainted on coming face to face with him.[12] Like his predecessors he was tenacious, ruthless, and an opportunist, but he worked on a bolder scale and he had the vision of a statesman. They had been primarily concerned with maintaining themselves and their heirs on the throne and with the aggrandisement of Moscow. Ivan saw beyond the principality. Throughout the forty-four years of his reign he devoted himself to creating a nation. As he envisaged it, the nation would embrace, under the rule of Moscow, not only the whole of north-eastern Russia but also all lands then under foreign rule inhabited by Orthodox Russians. He asserted boldly that "since olden times from our ancient forebears they have been part of our patrimony".[13]

At the time of his accession in 1462, Belorussia or White Russia in the west and much of the Ukraine including Kiev were in Lithuanian possession. Eastern Galicia was part of Poland. Extending southwards from Ryazan and Tula, the fertile steppelands formed a kind of no-man's-land, constantly overrun by the predatory Tatars of the Crimea and the lower Volga. Moreover, the four principalities of Yaroslavl, Ryazan, Rostov, and Tver and also the city-states of Novgorod, Pskov, and Vyatka remained independent of Moscow. The formidable task of bringing such vast territories under his rule was further complicated for Ivan by the fact that he had to be on guard against his own kinsmen and the princes generally, for they posed a threat to his throne and to the stability of Muscovy.

Ivan's first concern was to deal with the Tatars of the Khanate of Kazan. The Golden Horde had been weakened by internal discords and by the devastation inflicted by Tamburlaine, the great Asiatic conqueror. About 1445 the Horde had been shattered by the breakaway of the Khanates of Kazan and the Crimea, which pursued independent, often conflicting, policies. At that time the Khanate of Kazan, centred on the middle Volga some four hundred miles to the east of Moscow, was the most troublesome.

Soon after his accession, Ivan began preparations to capture Kazan. His three attempts to do so failed, but had the effect of deterring the Kazan Tatars from attacking Muscovy for some years. In 1479 the Tatars of the Golden Horde threatened Moscow. Ahmad, Khan of the Horde, claimed direct descent from Chingiz Khan and expressed his intention to enforce his suzerainty and collect tribute from the Grand Prince of Muscovy as in the days of the Horde's greatness. In 1480 he sent envoys who presented to Ivan the Khan's *yarlyk* or badge of authority to rule, and demanded tribute. Ivan was said to have spat on the yarlyk and thrown it to the ground. The incident is probably legendary. Since 1452 Moscow had ceased to pay tribute and to acknowledge the overlordship of the Khan. The incident and Ahmad's abortive campaign of 1480 against Muscovy are taken usually to symbolise the end of the Golden Horde's dominion over Russia.

Ahmad at once began new preparations for the conquest of Muscovy. But attacks by Tatars from the Crimea, led by Khan Haji Girei, founder of the great Girei dynasty, destroyed his army. This battle was the beginning of a savage enmity between the Golden Horde and the Crimean Khanate.

In 1472 Ivan proposed an alliance with the Khan of the Crimea, who had already rendered a service in defeating the Golden Horde. Several years elapsed before the Khan responded. The reason for the delay was that the Khan had been deposed. Sultan Mohammed II, the Conqueror (1451–81), ruled over the whole of Asia Minor and the Balkans, and threatened to dominate Eastern Europe and the Mediterranean. In 1475 his army occupied the Crimea as part of his policy of maintaining the Black Sea as a Turkish lake, a "virgin" undefiled by Christian ships. He had the Khan cast into prison, but in 1478 unexpectedly he restored him to his throne. At once the Khan responded to Ivan's earlier proposals and in April 1480 agreed an alliance against both Lithuania and the Golden Horde.

At this time the Khan of the Golden Horde and the Lithuanian Grand Prince were planning a joint attack on Muscovy. The Livonian Knights had invaded the Pskov region. Sedition had broken out in Novgorod and Ivan was faced with a revolt by his two brothers. The joint campaign against Muscovy proved abortive. The Crimean Khan invaded and devastated the Lithuanian territory of Podolia. Deprived of support from Lithuania, the Khan of the Golden Horde had to be content with plundering the towns of the upper Volga region. He then withdrew to Sarai. The Tatars of the Western Siberian Khanate and the Nogai Tatars joined forces and in 1481 they sacked Sarai, killing the Khan. The Golden Horde was soon to cease to exist.

The alliance with the Crimean Khan, which Ivan promoted with payments of money and gifts, suited his purpose. The Crimean Tatars made regular incursions into Lithuanian-held Ukraine, finding plentiful plunder in Kiev and other towns. They were eager, too, to take fair-headed captives, who were sold as slaves and sent to all parts of Asia Minor and the Mediterranean. The pressure of these attacks held Lithuania from invading Muscovy. The time was soon to come, however, when the Ukraine was part of Muscovy, and this was to involve Moscow in long conflict with the Crimea.

During these years Ivan brought under the rule of Moscow the independent principalities and the city-states. The principalities proved amenable. The Prince of Yaroslavl swore allegiance to him in 1463. Ivan married his sister, Anna, to the Prince of Ryazan which prepared the way for him to annex the principality. Rostov raised no real opposition to being absorbed into Moscow. But on learning that the Grand Prince of Tver was seeking alliance with Lithuania, Ivan annexed the principality by force.

The city-states of Vyatka, Pskov, and Novgorod presented special problems. Ivan's policy of unification demanded their absorption. Of more immediate concern, however, was the fact that each city-state could become a threat to Moscow. Pskov was an important defence outpost on the north-western frontier, but stood loyal to Moscow against attacks by the Teutonic Order and Lithuania. Ivan was content to leave the city independent for the time being. Vyatka posed a danger. Its people were unruly and hostile to Moscow. Situated on the upper reaches of the Vyatka

River to the north-east of Moscow, they threatened to join with the Tatars of Kazan against Muscovy. In 1489 Ivan took the city by force of arms. He had the leading men executed and resettled the whole population near Moscow where they could be kept under surveillance. Loyal Muscovites were sent to occupy their lands.

Novgorod was, however, of far greater importance. As a commercial centre the city-republic overshadowed Moscow and possession of Novgorod was crucial to Ivan's policies. For their part the Novgorodtsi had watched with misgiving the growth of Muscovy, seeing it as a threat to their wealth and independence. The boyars, merchants, and upper classes generally favoured a defensive alliance with Lithuania. The lower classes wanted good relations with Muscovy to ensure the ample supply of grain for bread. Ivan's father, Vasily II, had sent troops in 1456 to forestall any move by influential groups to join with Lithuania. The Novgorodtsi became increasingly restless. In 1471 the boyars gained the approval of the *veche*, the city assembly, for the severance of all ties with Moscow and the signing of an alliance with Grand Prince Casimir of Lithuania.

Ivan at once despatched troops, who captured the city. He showed lenience, allowing the Novgorodtsi to retain nominal independence. But the spirit of rebellion remained among them. In 1477 Ivan again had to take the city by force. This time he annexed its eastern dependencies and put an end to its independence, requiring all citizens to swear the oath of allegiance to him as their *Gosudar* or sovereign.

Ivan found now that annexation of Novgorod brought him into direct conflict with Sweden and the Baltic Knights. The Neva River, flowing from Lake Ladoga into the Gulf of Finland, was the natural trade route from central Russia. The Swedes and Novgodrodtsi had fought on past occasions for control of the Gulf. Ivan continued this struggle. In 1493 he formed an alliance with Denmark, Sweden's main enemy. Three times in the years 1495 and 1496 his armies invaded Sweden and Finland, but without decisive result. Sweden was torn by internal strife, however, and in 1497 sued for peace.

Casimir had died in 1492 and his son, Alexander, had succeeded as Grand Prince of Lithuania. He was young and unsure of himself, and desperately wanted peace with Muscovy. He was persuaded to agree to a treaty which would be confirmed by his marriage with Ivan's daughter, Elena. Ivan welcomed the treaty, especially as under its terms he acquired the important principality of Vyazma. But he also saw that the marriage would give pretext for war against Lithuania, when he was ready. He had made it a major condition of the agreement that his daughter should be free to observe the Orthodox faith without being subjected to pressures of any kind.

In 1499 Ivan seized on a report from Vilna that Elena and all Orthodox believers in Lithuania were being coerced into joining the Uniat Church.[14] Elena herself denied the truth of the report. Ivan insisted on making it the ground for declaring war. In 1500 his armies marched and under the armistice, concluded three years later, he gained extensive territories east of the Dniepr River. Before he could embark on the next stage in this recovery of the lands which he claimed as part of his patrimony, both Ivan and Alexander died.

Vasily III, the son and successor of Ivan, proved an energetic and decisive ruler. But he found his task more difficult. The Khanates of Kazan and the Crimea were preparing to act together against Muscovy. Moreover, in 1512 Mengli Girei, the Crimean Khan, and Sigismund Augustus, the successor to Alexander as Grand Prince of Lithuania and King of Poland, formed an alliance against Muscovy. A few years later the Crimean Tatars invaded Muscovy and reached the walls of Moscow. They could have captured the city itself, but withdrew on receiving enormous payments of treasure.

Notwithstanding the Tatar threats, Vasily invaded Lithuania in 1514 and achieved his immediate purpose of taking the key fortress-city of Smolensk. His armies then suffered severe defeat. In 1522, however, Vasily concluded a five-year armistice with Sigismund Augustus under which Smolensk and the surrounding territory remained part of Muscovy.

Ivan III's vision of the Russian nation involved more, however, than territorial expansion of Muscovy. It demanded the forging of a strong state, centralised on Moscow, and recognition of the absolute authority of the Grand Prince as autocrat. The current of events at this time enabled him to go far in elevating the position and power of the Grand Prince and the prestige of Moscow as the pillars of the emerging nation.

Ivan III's first wife, Maria, sister of the Grand Prince of Tver, died in 1467. She had borne a son, whom his father had recognised as his heir. The people of Moscow were nevertheless anxious that their Grand Prince should remarry. In an age when life was often cut short, the Tsarevich might die without leaving a successor. But Ivan, although only twenty-seven years old at this time, showed no impatience to remarry. Proposals came from Rome, however, which he could not ignore.

In February 1469 Ivan learnt that Pope Paul II offered him the

Monomakh. When he mobilised his army to attack Constantinople, Emperor Constantine Monomachus responded by sending the Greek Metropolitan to Kiev with rich gifts and the imperial crown to propose that all Orthodox Christians should live in peace "under the combined power of our Tsardom and of your great autocracy, 'Great Rus'."[17] Vladimir was then crowned anew with the crown of the Emperor and took the name of Monomakh. The *Shapka Monomakha* (Cap of Monomachus) was always used from this time in coronations of the Grand Princes and then the Tsars of Russia.

A further legend, which was to prove even more influential in establishing the authority of the Russian autocrat and the prestige of his capital, claimed that Moscow was the Third Rome. Constantinople had been the citadel of Orthodox Christianity, but the Greeks had betrayed their mission when at the Council of Florence in 1439 they had accepted union with the Church of Rome. Retribution had followed promptly in the conquest of Constantinople by the infidel Turks. Muscovy remained thereafter as the only independent Orthodox Christian Tsardom and the guardian of Orthodoxy.

Filofei, a monk in the Eleazar Monastery in Pskov, gave expression to this idea in a letter to Grand Prince Ivan III or to his son, Vasily III. He wrote:

> I wish to add a few words on the present Orthodox Empire of our ruler. He is on earth the sole Emperor [Tsar] of the Christians, the leader of the Apostolic Church which stands no longer in Rome or in Constantinople, but in the blessed city of Moscow. She alone shines in the whole world brighter than the sun . . . All Christian Empires are fallen and in their stead stands alone the Empire of our ruler in accordance with the prophetical books. Two Romes have fallen, but the third stands, and a fourth there will not be.[18]

This legend made a strong emotional appeal to the Russians who were devout and stirring with new nationalist loyalties. They readily accepted that their capital, Moscow was a holy city and that their ruler was divinely appointed, and they gave him their full obedience.

By the time of Vasily III, son of Ivan III, the power of the Grand Prince was already impressive. Herberstein, the imperial ambassador who visited Muscovy twice in Vasily III's reign, wrote that:

> In the sway which he [Vasily] holds over his people, he

surpasses all the monarchs of the whole world . . . He uses his authority as much over ecclesiastics as laymen, and holds unlimited control over the lives and property of all his subjects; not one of his counsellors has sufficient authority to dare to oppose him, or even differ from him, on any subject. They openly confess that the will of the prince is the will of God, and that whatever the prince does he does by the will of God . . .[19]

The princely caste resented the greatly enhanced authority and prestige of the Muscovite Grand Prince and their own position of humble subjects. Ivan III and Vasily III had held them firmly in check. At the first opportunity they rebelled.

Notes
1. Karamzin, III, Cols. 167–8.
2. John of Plano Carpini, *The Mongol Mission* (New York, 1955) p. 29.
3. Klyuchevsky, II, p. 6, quoting *Ipatevsky Chronicle* (St. Petersburg, 1871) p. 240.
4. J. L. I. Fennell, *The Emergence of Moscow* (London, 1968) p. 46.
5. M. N. Tikhomirov, *Russia in the 16th Century* (Moscow, 1962) p. 107.
6. See for example Klyuchevsky, II, pp. 49–53; J. L. I. Fennell, *op. cit.*, pp. 119–20.
7. J. L. I. Fennell, *op. cit.*, pp. 186, 193.
8. *Ibid.*
9. *Ibid.* pp. 191–2.
10. G. Vernadsky, *The Mongols and Russia* (New Haven, 1953) p. 266; *The Patriarch Nikon Chronicle* in *Polnoe Sobranie Russkikh Letopisei* (Moscow, 1862–1906) II, pp. 78–79.
11. Ambrogio Contarini, *Travels to Tana and Persia by Josafa Barbaro and Ambrogio Contarini* (Hakluyt Society, London, 1873) p. 163; Solovyev, III, V, p. 9.
12. Sigismund von Herberstein, *Notes upon Russia . . .* Translated and edited by R. H. Major (Hakluyt Society, London, 1851–52) I, p. 24.
13. Klyuchevsky, II, pp. 117–18.
14. A sect among the Orthodox which acknowledged the supremacy of the Pope, but retained Orthodox rites.
15. See Chapter VIII below.
16. Ian Grey, *Ivan III and the Unification of Russia* (London, 1964) pp. 171–4.
17. *Ibid.* p. 42.

18. N. Zernov, *The Russians and their Church* (London, 1945) p. 71.
19. Sigismund von Herberstein, *op. cit.*, pp. 2, 30, 32

CHAPTER IV

Ivan the Terrible
The Time of Reform and Conquest,
1530–1560

TSAR IVAN IV MADE AN EXTRAORDINARY IMPACT ON THE MINDS OF Russians and of many Europeans in his own and in later centuries. In the West his name conjured up the image of a savage tyrant whose reign was a long twilight of massacres, terror, and depravity. His own people did not regard him in this way, however, and the Western image of Ivan was neither true nor did it explain the impression that he has made in history.

Cruel despots were numerous in the sixteenth century. Ivan's contemporaries included Louis XI of France, Philip II of Spain, Richard III and Henry VIII of England, Cesare Borgia and his father, Pope Alexander VI, Christian II of Denmark, and Sigismondo Malatesta in Rimini, all of whose reigns were marked by grim deeds.

Ivan himself was a great Tsar who set his imprint on an age in Russian history, as Peter the Great did in a later century. To his subjects he was *Grozny,* the "awe-inspiring", of whom the Englishman, Anthony Jenkinson, wrote " . . . I think no prince in Christendom is more feared of his own than he is, nor better loved."[1] In a real sense he brought the Russian nation to birth and for his people he was the embodiment of the nation. But his greatness and achievement were marred by his excesses. Childhood sufferings, betrayals, obsessive mistrust, and the isolation of power distorted his outlook. In the later years of his reign he appeared at times to be close to madness, and he brought the country to the point of collapse.

Ivan was three years old in 1533 when his father, Vasily III, died suddenly. He succeeded to the throne under the regency of his mother, Elena Glinskaya. Aided by her lover, Prince Ivan Fedorovich Ovchina-Telepnev-Obolensky, she struggled to maintain the stability of the country and to carry on the policies of her husband. In particular she continued the vast programme of building churches and monasteries, launched by Vasily III, a devout man who believed fervently in the role of Muscovy as the citadel of Orthodox Christianity. But unrest was mounting among the princes and boyars. Elena crushed attempts by Princes Yuri and Andrei, her brothers-in-law and the uncles of Ivan, to seize power. More serious challenges were threatening when suddenly on 3 April, 1538, Elena died, presumably from poison. A few days later Obolensky was seized and cast into prison, where he starved to death.

A period of anarchy followed. The Boyar Duma took over the government. Two of its members, Princes Vasily and Ivan Shuisky, who were descended from the same Rurikid line as the ruling family, dominated the country for a time. Opposing them were the Belsky who drew support from princes of the Lithuanian Gedimin line and among the untitled boyars. Under the vicious rule of Vasily and then of Ivan Shuisky the Kremlin was the scene of violence and conspiracy, and the country veered towards anarchy.

Grand Prince Ivan, at the age of eight, had lost not only his mother but also his beloved governess, who was banished to the Arctic North by the Shuisky. For him this was a time of terror and humiliation. He sat upon the throne on formal occasions, resplendent in his robes, as he received the humble respect of his subjects and foreign ambassadors. At other times he suffered cruel neglect. He hated the Shuisky and went in fear for his life.

Some twenty years later, recalling his childhood, Ivan wrote:

What sufferings did I not endure through lack of clothing and through hunger! For in all things my will was not my own; everything was contrary to my will and unbefitting my tender years. I well recall one thing: whilst we [Ivan and Yuri, his younger brother] were playing childish games in our infancy, Prince Ivan Vasilievich Shuisky was sitting on a bench, leaning with his elbows on our father's bed and with his leg up on a chair; and he did not even incline his head toward us, either in parental manner or as a master . . . And who can endure such arrogance? How can I enumerate such countless sore sufferings as I put up with in my youth?[2]

Although so young, Ivan thought constantly of the time when he would assert his power. His formal education was neglected, but he was a precocious boy who absorbed all of the books of theology and history that he could find. He studied the Bible closely and drew from it confirmation of the divine authority for his position and power. He may also have had guidance and encouragement from Metropolitan Makari, who was to prove the outstanding churchman of the age.

Towards the end of December 1543, Ivan suddenly acted. He ordered the arrest of Andrei Shuisky, who was killed on the way to prison. His closest associates were banished to distant places. From this time, according to the chronicler, the boyars began to live in fear of their Grand Prince.[3]

During the next few years Ivan exercised power according to his own whim. Princes and boyars found themselves in favour one day and disgraced and banished on the next. It was in this period that he was said to have revealed his sadistic nature.[4] He was certainly emotionally insecure and mistrustful of all around him. He was to show, however, that he could give his trust to men who justified it and that he recognised the high responsibility of his office.

The year 1547 marked a turning-point in Ivan's life. At a solemn meeting of churchmen and boyars in the Kremlin, he announced his coronation when he would "assume the titles of our ancestors . . . and of our kinsman, Grand Prince Vladimir Vsevolodovich Monomakh". He declared also that he would take a wife.[5] On 16 January (1547) he was crowned in the Uspensky Cathedral with the magnificent ceremonial of the Orthodox Church. His coronation was, in fact, an exceptional occasion. For the first time the full regalia, which it was claimed had been received by the Grand Prince of Kiev from the Emperor Constantine Monomachus in the twelfth century, was used in the coronation of the Tsar. Predecessors had been crowned Grand Prince; Ivan was the first crowned Tsar of Russia.[6]

On 3 February Ivan married Anastasia Romanovna, the daughter of a deceased Okolnichy, named Roman Yurievich Zakharin-Yuriev, an untitled Muscovite boyar family which was to give Russia the Romanov dynasty.[7] Anastasia was a woman of piety, humility, and charity, the feminine virtues most prized by Orthodox Russians. The marriage nevertheless aroused hostility among the princely families. They recalled that the Tsar's grandfather, Ivan III, had married a Byzantine princess and that his father, Vasily III, had married the daughter of an eminent noble family. This critical attitude was expressed by Prince Semeon Lobanov-Rostovsky who wrote: "The sovereign offended us [the princely clans] by his marriage, by taking his boyar's daughter, his slave, for bride. And we have to serve her as if she were our sister."[8] But while the princes and boyars remained antagonistic, the people of Moscow developed a strong affection for this gentle young Tsaritsa.

At this time Moscow was already a vast city. Richard Chancellor, the English sea-captain who was received at Ivan's court, considered it to be "greater than London".[9] The imperial ambassador, Herberstein, who visited Russia in 1517–18 and again in 1526–27, wrote that the city with more than 41,500 houses was "scarcely credible" and that the Kremlin not only contained "the very extensive and magnificently built stone palace of the Prince" but also the grand timbered houses of the nobility and boyars and the Metropolitan and numerous churches.[10] The city was, however, crude and sprawling as a result of its rapid growth and also the frequent and hasty rebuilding of whole suburbs destroyed by fires.

On 12 April, 1547, a fire burnt out Kitai Gorod, the merchant quarter. A smaller fire occurred a few days later. But on 21 June fire broke out in the Arbat, a suburb to the west of the Kremlin. Strong winds carried the flames across the city, reducing most of it to ashes. Within the Kremlin the palace, treasury, armouries, the Metropolitan's palace, and other buildings suffered. Some 25,000 houses were destroyed and, in addition to heavy casualties, about 80,000 people were homeless. The Tsar and his family took refuge in the nearby village of Vorobievo.

The people of Moscow were stunned by the disaster. Popular opinion, inflamed by boyars hostile to the Glinsky family, began to accept that they had caused the fires by sorcery. A mood of hysteria developed and there was a growing demand for the blood of the Glinsky. Prince Yuri, the Tsar's uncle, was killed by an angry mob which ransacked his house and massacred his retainers. For two days the mob took over the city. A rumour that Prince Yuri's mother and brother had taken refuge with the Tsar in Vorobievo, sent the mob surging out to the village. Rioters surrounded the Tsar's residence, demanding that he hand over to them all members of the Glinsky family, and threatening to kill him if he refused. Ivan himself assured them that he was not hiding the Glinsky. But then he ordered his guards to seize and execute the leading rioters, and the rebellion was crushed.

Coronation and marriage, the Moscow fires, and the uprising against his own kinsmen, all happening within the first six months of 1547, made a profound impression on Ivan. A change in his outlook and behaviour appeared to date from this time. His enemies claimed that the miraculous intervention of God, especially in sending the priest, Silvestr, to guide him, was responsible for this transformation.[11]

Metropolitan Makari had sought to instruct and influence the young Tsar, and he probably played a part in the emergence at court about this time of a small group of able counsellors. To these few men Ivan gave his trust and they became known as the Chosen Council.[12] The leading members of this group were Silvestr, a stern and exceedingly devout priest, and Aleksei Adashev, a young courtier of remarkable ability. With the Metropolitan they planned reforms which called for co-operation between the Tsar, the Church, and the nation or land *(zemliya)*.

The need for reform was urgent. Boyar misrule during Ivan's minority had shaken the stability of the government. Reorganisation of the armed forces was essential for defence against the Tatars. Muscovy was no longer a principality but an emerging nation in which the base of the government had to be broadened. This was partially effected by extensive reforms and by the convening of the first *Zemsky Sobor* (Assembly of the Land).

This assembly, to which the people of the city and representatives from the towns had been summoned, took place on 27 February, 1549, on the Red Square. It was a dramatic occasion, dominated by the young Tsar. He spoke vehemently. He asked forgiveness for his failure to protect the interests of the people. He denounced the boyars for their unruly behaviour and threatened with severe punishment any who disobeyed him in the future. He proclaimed a new era of justice and reform.[13] His appeal to the people and his promise of better government aroused an enthusiastic response, and in his direct personal approaches he was always to be received with popular acclaim. The reforms that followed included the *Sudebnik,* providing a new legal code, the reorganisation of military service and of the civil administration, and the *Stoglav* which had far-reaching results in the management of church affairs. In fact, the assembly in the Red Square marked the beginning of a new drive to forge a strong centralised state.

At the root of the reforms was the problem of providing land to maintain the new class of gentry or serving officers on whom the military needs and stability of the country were coming to depend. The gentry could be counted on to serve the Tsar loyally without resenting or challenging his authority, as the princely caste was liable to do.

During 1549 measures curbing the powers of the boyars were introduced. The system of *Mestnichestvo*, which caused endless disputes, was to be set aside in future military campaigns. At the same time action was taken to strengthen the position of the gentry as the mainstay of the army. In October 1550 provision was made for a thousand chosen members of the gentry to be settled on lands near Moscow. They were to constitute a special guard on which the Tsar could call at any time. It was clearly intended that the "Thousanders", as they were called, would be on hand to suppress any challengers by powerful boyars.[14]

Grand Prince Ivan III had allotted to the gentry military fiefs, known as *pomestie,* which were estates granted to individual gentry officers in return for their services. He had converted state lands into *pomestie,* but as the numbers of the gentry grew, the need for more land became pressing. The church had been acquiring estates on a massive scale since the thirteenth century. Ivan III had taken over church and monastery lands in Novgorod and had proposed a general secularisation of church lands throughout Russia. Within the Church itself a strong minority group maintained that it was contrary to Orthodoxy for the Church and its monasteries to own vast estates. The majority opinion, expressed in the decision of the church assembly of 1503 to veto Ivan III's secularisation policy, held that the church estates must remain inviolable as they had been in the period of the Tatar yoke. Among those close to Tsar Ivan at this time, Metropolitan Makari stood strongly for the landowning rights of the Church, while Silvestr and Adashev favoured secularisation.

In this period of reform there was ardent debate not only about church lands but also on the relationship between Church and State. The view which was to gain widest support was forcefully expressed by Ivan Semenovich Peresvetov, a courtier who had served for a time with the Polish army and about 1538 had entered the Tsar's service. In two petitions to Tsar Ivan and in letters and treatises he asserted that Muscovy must be a strongly centralised state, ruled by an autocrat with absolute powers. He had been impressed by the Turkish system and emphasised that the Tsar must rule, as the Sultan ruled, without fear or thought for his powerful nobles and without the restraint or influence of the Church. He denounced "the magnates of the Russian Tsar (who) themselves grow rich and lazy and impoverish his realm and do not play the game of death against the foe, and thus betray God and their sovereign".[15]

Peresvetov was an impassioned champion of autocracy and also of equality and justice. He condemned all forms of slavery, including the partial slavery of serfdom which was already spreading insidiously in Muscovy. All men should be free, for only free people could labour and serve zealously. Justice was also needed and, according with the customs of the time, his conception of justice was harsh. Indeed, he wrote that "there cannot be a ruler without terror. Like a steed under the rider without a bridle, so is a realm without terror.''[16]

Peresvetov's ideas were of special importance, because they also reflected the desires of the gentry and the ordinary Muscovites. They wanted to be ruled by an autocrat who enforced justice, which meant in particular justice against the great magnates. They wanted a strong army which would defend the country against the predatory Tatars and other enemies. In his pleas for equality he was ahead of the time, but he was voicing an unspoken, half-realised aspiration of the people. Tsar Ivan probably studied Peresvetov's petitions closely. They expressed ideas close to his own, and some ten years later when he cast aside the influence of Silvestr and Adashev, he was to rule as the dread autocrat whom Peresvetov had envisaged.

Ambitious to make his mark as a great Tsar, Ivan had dreamt of the conquest of the Kazan Khanate. Nothing could be more popular with the Muscovites whose memories of sufferings at Tatar hands extended over generations. Russian prisoners in the city of Kazan alone were said to number 100,000, and the slave markets of the Mediterranean were crowded with fair Slavs, captured in Tatar raids. Moreover, the conquest of the Khanate was a sacred duty, for it would mean raising the Cross there in place of the Crescent.

Ivan was fifteen years old when he impatiently launched his first campaign against Kazan. It failed, as did two further attempts. In the campaign of 1551-52, however, Ivan's determination was crowned with victory, but only after savage fighting with terrible casualties on both sides. Ivan returned in triumph. The Russian people hailed him as the Tsar-Liberator. Already he had become a legendary hero and for Russians nothing could displace or overcloud his achievement.

The conquest of Kazan was a great victory, gratifying national pride. But it was also an event of outstanding importance in Russia's history. Through its emotional impact on the people, it gave them a sense of nationhood. Moreover, it removed the barrier to Russia's eastern expansion. The Khanate of Astrakhan at the mouth of the Volga was annexed soon afterwards, giving Moscow control over the whole length of the mighty river. The young nation was ready to surge eastwards. The conquest and colonisation of Siberia were soon to follow.

Boris Godunov was about one year old at the time of this historic event. As a boy, however, he would have listened to tales of the battle of Kazan and the prowess of the Tsar. Siberia gripped his imagination at an early age and as a young man he showed an intense interest in the eastward expansion, which he himself was to direct in the years to come.

Ivan's joy over the capture of Kazan was heightened by the news that reached him in Nizhni Novgorod on his journey back to Moscow that the Tsaritsa had borne him a son, to be christened Dmitri. His entry into the capital was an occasion of unprecedented fervour and acclaim. From this time Ivan became to be known as *Grozny* or "awesome" by his own people who revered him as the scourge of their enemies.

Ivan's elation was to be cut short. Many boyars had been opposed to the Kazan campaign. It had lasted too long, and they saw that the consolidation of Moscow's control over the Khanate would demand time and money. Rebellion among the Tatars confirmed them in their opposition to further efforts to hold the Khanate. The boyars were more interested in securing their privileges against the tide of reforms threatening to engulf them. They were anxious to get rid of Adashev and one group of boyars talked of replacing Ivan himself by his cousin, Prince Vladimir Staritsky.

On 1 March, 1553, Ivan fell ill. His condition declined rapidly, and the last rites were administered. His great anxiety was that all at court should swear allegiance to his son, Tsarevich Dmitri. He was taken by surprise by the furious quarrelling among the boyars, and he was overwhelmed to learn that a number were determined to swear allegiance to Prince Vladimir Staritsky, who could be expected to protect the rights of the princely class. Many boyars argued, too, that if Tsarevich Dmitri, a child, became Tsar, then his mother, Tsaritsa Anastasia, would be regent and power would fall into the hands of the Zakharin-Yuriev, who were merely untitled boyars.

Aleksei Adashev swore loyalty to the Tsarevich, but he shared the view of his father, who declared: "In allegiance to you and your son, Tsarevich Dmitri, we will kiss the cross, but we will not serve the Zakharini, Daniel and his brother. We have already witnessed many disasters, caused by the boyars during your minority."[17] On Tsar Ivan's insistence, the majority of the boyars finally swore allegiance to Tsarevich Dmitri. But, lying in his bedchamber where tapers flickered before the ikons and priests intoned prayers, he was tortured with anxieties for the future of his wife and son. He mistrusted the good faith of those who had taken the oath. For several weeks he lay ill and then, against all expectation, he recovered. The experience of these weeks left deep scars; it intensified his conviction that many at court were ready to betray him and his family at the first opportunity.

The policy of reform continued. The central administration as well as local government were reorganised, and the new system established beyond challenge the position of Moscow as the administrative centre and capital of the country. Two central offices were set up to protect the interests of the serving gentry whose duties and importance were expanding. The problem of finding land to give them a secure economic base became more acute. The Tsar and the Chosen Council were not yet prepared, however, to revive the proposals for the secularisation of church lands. Army reforms and in particular ukazi defining the duties of the landowning class to serve and provide troops were introduced in 1555–56. They led to an important increase in the strength of the army which had by 1560 come to number 150,000 troops and by 1580 as many as 309,000.

The emphasis on military affairs was inevitable. A series of punitive campaigns proved necessary to subdue the Kazan Khanate and to strengthen the Tsar's authority along the Volga. In 1555 the Crimean Khan invaded Muscovy with an army 60,000 strong. He hurriedly retreated on finding the Russian forces drawn up in defensive positions. But Moscow could never relax its guard against Tatar attack.

Following the victory over Kazan, Silvestr urged Ivan to march against the Crimean Khanate. He could think only of winning a further triumph for the Cross over the Crescent. Adashev also favoured concentrating all forces against the Crimean Khan whose constant invasions tied down Russian forces and laid waste vast areas to the south of Moscow.

Ivan was not blinded by crusading zeal and he was not convinced by Adashev's arguments. At this time the Crimean Tatars were divided amongst themselves. Adashev was confident that by using the services of Tsarevich Tokhtamysh and other Tatars who had sworn allegiance to the Tsar the Crimean Khanate could be conquered. Ivan recognised the difficulties. A major campaign against the Khanate would involve moving massive forces over more than 700 miles of steppelands with supply problems and the constant danger of attack. Moreover, the Crimean Khan was the vassal of the Turkish Sultan. A Russian attack on the Crimea would mean war with the Turkish Empire, then at the zenith of its power.

Ivan knew that Russia was in no position to face such a challenge. Indeed, the wise decision would have been to develop the country's military and economic might before embarking on any major campaign. But, rejecting the advice of Adashev and the heated pleas of Silvestr, he resolved to conquer Livonia. His decision was to lead to disaster. The Livonian War lasted for twenty-four years. The Crimean Tatars, always prompt to take advantage of the fact that the main Russian forces were committed in the west, launched massive raids in nearly every one of those years. Fighting on two fronts, the country was reduced to exhaustion.

Ivan's decision to turn westward and to embark on the Livonian War was perhaps inevitable at this time. The Russian drive westwards had gathered momentum. Secure access to the Baltic was essential to the political and economic growth of the nation. But Sweden, the Teutonic Knights, Lithuania, and Poland strenuously opposed Russia's westward expansion. They feared this new nation which had begun to stir in the east.

In 1553, as though in response to the growing need for trade and closer relations with the West, an important event took place. Richard Chancellor, an English sea-captain, anchored his ship, *Edward Bonaventure,* off the mouth of the North Dvina River. He had sailed in company with two other vessels, *Bona Speranza* and *Bona Confidentia,* in an expedition commanded by Sir Hugh Willoughby, which was to find the north-east passage to the fabled riches of Cathay. A storm off North Cape separated the ships. Willoughby, with two of the vessels, took shelter in a deserted fjord where he and the crews froze to death during the Arctic winter. Chancellor, a more skilful seaman, sailed his ship into the White Sea.

The English were then hardly aware of the existence of Russia. Chancellor was surprised to learn from a fisherman "that this country was called Russia or Moscovie, and that Ivan Vasilievich (which was at that time their King's name) ruled and governed far and wide in those places".[18] After some delay in Kholmogory, he was summoned to Moscow. He set out on 23 November, travelling in sledges by way of Vologda and Yaroslavl. He was observant and his account of the journey to Moscow is full of interest. He noted in particular that the country between Yaroslavl and Moscow "is very well replenished with small villages which are so well filled with people that it is wonder to see them: the ground is well stored with corn which they carry to the city of Moscow in such abundance that it is wonder to see it. You shall meet in a morning seven or eight hundred sleds coming or going thither, that carry corn and some carry fish".[19]

Chancellor was shown every courtesy in Moscow and he was impressed by the magnificence of the court. In the outer chamber where he awaited the summons "sat one hundred or more gentlemen, all in cloth of gold very sumptuous and from there I came into the Council Chamber where sat the Duke [Tsar] himself with his nobles which were a fair company: they sat around the chamber on high, yet so that he himself sat much higher than any of his nobles in a chair of gilt, and in a long garment of beaten gold with an imperial crown upon his head, and a staff of crystal and gold in his right hand and his other hand leaning on the chair".[20]

Chancellor withdrew after the exchange of courtesies. Two hours later he was recalled to dine in the Tsar's presence, which was a signal honour. Again he was struck by the richness of the court. The Tsar sat now in a silver gown and "there sat none near him by a great way . . . And for his service at meat it came in without order, yet it was very rich service . . . The number that dined there that day was two hundred persons and all were served in golden vessels".[21]

Rulers in fifteenth- and sixteenth-century Europe rivalled each other in the ostentatious display of gold and silver plate at their courts. It was a mark of wealth and power, and in times of crisis the plate could be melted down and converted into money. Ivan, like his father and grandfather, took pride in the magnificent collection of the Kremlin Palace, and was to welcome the gifts brought by English embassies.[22]

Tsar Ivan readily agreed to allow "free mart with all free liberties" to English merchants. Chancellor returned to England in 1554, where on 26 February in the following year the Russia or Muscovy Company was incorporated by charter, granted in the names of Philip and Mary. He sailed again to the White Sea, but on the return voyage in 1556 lost his life when saving the first Russian ambassador, Osip Nepea, from drowning off the coast of Aberdeenshire. Nepea was richly entertained in England and was able to engage a number of skilled men for service in Russia. He returned in the ship of Anthony Jenkinson, a gallant seaman like Chancellor, who won the respect and affection of Tsar Ivan and was to play an important role in the troubled relations which developed between Russia and England.

For thirteen years after Chancellor's discovery of the North Sea route, Tsar Ivan received all Englishmen with great favour. He granted to the Russia Company a virtual monopoly of European trade with Muscovy. Indeed, he conceded all that Anthony Jenkinson asked. He received little in return. Queen Elizabeth, who came to the throne in 1558, actively supported her rapacious merchants, but she could not accede to all of the Tsar's requests and she found to her surprise that England's relations with Russia aroused a storm of diplomatic protests.[23]

Ivan appears to have been genuinely attracted to the Englishmen who came to his court, and he was eager to develop trade with

England. But he wanted much more, and in particular the services
of skilled technicians and armaments. The West had developed
new military and other techniques which the Russians, isolated by
the Tatar occupation and then struggling towards nationhood
while beset by Tatar and other enemies, had failed to acquire.
Moreover, the western countries on Russia's frontier obstinately
thwarted all attempts by their neighbour to learn such new
methods and techniques. In 1547, for example, Tsar Ivan had
engaged a Saxon, named Schlitte, to enlist skilled Germans for
service in Russia. Schlitte managed to assemble 123 men in
Lubeck. The Livonians and others urgently complained to the
Emperor, Charles V. The outcry was so vehement that he finally
gave authority for preventing the departure of these specialists
for Russia. They were dispersed, but a certain Master Hans
persevered in his attempts to reach Moscow and, captured near
the frontier, he was executed. In fact, Russia's western neighbours
maintained a partial blockade.

Resenting their efforts to keep his country backward, Ivan
warmly welcomed the opening of the route to the White Sea and
the arrival of English seamen and merchants. The English, who
did not feel themselves to be threatened by Russia, were eager to
trade and to provide skilled men. Ivan looked to them to develop
Russia's western trade and to provide weapons and expertise
which would equip his country to subdue the Teutonic Knights
and to establish its right to direct access to the Baltic Sea.

Livonia was part of the dominions of the feudal Order of
Teutonic Knights. They elected their own Grand Master and
had grown rich in their campaigns of crusading and conquest. In
1242 Aleksandr Nevsky, Grand Prince of Novgorod, had defeated
the Knights on the ice of Lake Peipus, thus halting their eastward
drive. The Order had suffered a further severe setback in 1410
when Jagiello, the Lithuanian Grand Prince, had crushed its forces
in the battle of Tannenberg. Corrupted by wealth and power, the
Order had begun to decline, but it continued to rule the Baltic
coastlands from Esthonia and Livonia to East Pomerania.

Livonia had been at peace with Muscovy for some years. In
1554 an embassy arrived in Moscow to renew the peace and now
the Russians insisted on payment of tribute to the Tsar. The
Livonians agreed, but for three years made no payments. Meanwhile, Lithuania, which also sought direct access to the Baltic,
intervened. The Grand Master concluded in 1557 a military
alliance with Sigismund Augustus, King of Poland and Grand
Prince of Lithuania, against Muscovy. This was a violation of
Livonia's 1554 agreement with Moscow. In January 1558 Russian

troops invaded Livonia from Pskov. They captured Narva and Dorpat, and occupied northern Latvia as far as Riga. At this time Aleksei Adashev who was conducting foreign policy urged the Tsar to accept the offer of mediation, made by the King of Denmark. Ivan was eager to continue the campaign. He recognised, however, that in one swift operation he had gained the immediate objective of securing direct access to the Baltic. He therefore acted on Adashev's advice and agreed an armistice to last from May until September 1559.

The Order was on the point of dissolution and other countries were scrambling for its possessions. Before the armistice period had expired the Grand Master, Gothard Ketler, concluded (on 31 August, 1559) an agreement, placing the Order under the protection of the Lithuanian Grand Prince. Lithuanian troops moved at once in support of Livonia. At the same time King Frederick II of Denmark annexed the island of Oesel for his brother, Duke Magnus. In the summer of 1561 Sweden occupied Revel (Tallinn) and the west and central regions of Esthonia. On 28 November, 1561, by agreement between King Sigismund Augustus and Grand Master Ketler the Livonian Order was dissolved. Ketler became Grand Duke of Courland. By formal treaty, signed in the following year, Livonia became part of Poland-Lithuania.

Ivan now regretted the armistice, believing that it had proved contrary to Muscovite interests, and he blamed Adashev. Impatiently he launched a new campaign in which his troops overran Livonia during the spring and summer of 1560. But the other countries were now actively involved. Rivalries between them prevented the formation of a coalition against Russia, but they were eager competitors for the spoils of Livonia. Adashev now urged the Tsar to secure Russian possession of Eastern Latvia, including the key ports of Narva and Dorpat, by making minor concessions to Lithuania and negotiating a treaty with Sigismund Augustus who was anxious for peace. But Ivan was not interested in compromise; he was determined to capture the whole of Livonia.

Notes
1. R. Hakluyt, *The Principal Navigations, Voyages and Discoveries of the English Nation* (Dent Edition, London, 1927) I, pp. 429–30.
2. J. L. I. Fennell (Ed. and Trans.) *The Correspondence Between Prince A. M. Kurbsky and Tsar Ivan IV of Russia 1564–1579* (Cambridge, 1963) pp. 75–77.
3. Solovyev, III, VI, p. 430.

4. The main evidence of Ivan's delight in cruelty at this age comes from Prince A. M. Kurbsky's *History of Ivan IV*. Kurbsky related that about the age of twelve he would throw animals from the top of buildings and watch their death agonies on the ground. About the age of fifteen, "he began to harm people" by galloping with bands of companions through the crowded squares and market places, knocking people down, and further that he and his companions "beat and robbed the common people . . . And in truth he committed real acts of brigandage and performed other evil deeds which it is not only unbefitting to relate, but shameful too . . ." (J. Fennell [Ed. and Trans.] *Kurbsky's History of Ivan IV* [Cambridge, 1965] pp. 10–11).

   Kurbsky was an unreliable witness. His hatred of the Tsar to whom he was a traitor was so intense that he was prepared to say and do anything that would blacken the Tsar's name. His campaign of denigration was influential and no one contributed more than Kurbsky to the portrayal of Ivan as a depraved monster. This has to be borne in mind in all references to Kurbsky's *History* and correspondence.

   Ian Grey, *Ivan the Terrible* (London, 1964) pp. 151–9.

5. Solovyev, III, VI, pp. 431–2.

6. Ivan III, grandfather of Ivan IV, had used the title of Tsar of all Russia on occasions, but without the full significance that Ivan IV gave to the title.

   Ivan III's grandson, Dmitri, had been crowned Grand Prince of Vladimir, Moscow, and all Russia on 4 February, 1498, and on this occasion the Shapka Monomakha and the great collar *(barmy)* had been used and the Byzantine precedents followed. But Dmitri had never succeeded to the throne and he had not been crowned Tsar.

   J. Fennell, *Ivan the Great of Moscow* (London, 1961) p. 337.

7. The Muscovite practice was to assembly comely noble maidens from all parts of the country from among whom the Tsar chose his bride. Ian Grey, *Ivan the Terrible* (London, 1964) pp. 63–64, 69.

8. Vernadsky, *The Tsardom of Moscow 1547–1682* (New Haven, 1969) I, p. 31.

9. R. Hakluyt, *op. cit.*, I, p. 255.

10. Sigismund von Herberstein, *op. cit.*, II, p. 5.

11. Karamzin, writing three centuries later, believed that "for the correction of Ivan it was necessary that Moscow be consumed by fire" and then that a remarkable man, Sylvestr, should suddenly appear before him. Karamzin, II, VIII, Cols. 60–62.

Russia has a tradition of churchmen, some Patriarchs and Metropolitans, others simple priests, who have by their ability, piety, or by overpowering personality, exercised great influence over the Tsar of the time. They include Iosif of Volokolamsk, Metropolitan Makary, and Sylvestr in the sixteenth century, Patriarch Nikon and Archpriest Avvakum in the seventeenth century, and Rasputin, who was strictly not a priest, in the twentieth century.

12. The Chosen Council, its composition and function, has been a matter of controversy. See S. V. Bakhrushin, "The Chosen Council of Ivan the Terrible" in *Istoricheskie Zapiski* Vol. 15 (1945) and A. A. Zimin, *Reforms of Ivan the Terrible* (Moscow, 1960); Ian Grey, *Ivan the Terrible* (London, 1964) pp. 74–76, 77.

13. Karamzin, II, VIII, Cols. 64–65.

14. It is not certain that the thousand chosen men were settled on service estates near Moscow. A. A. Zimin has produced evidence to the effect that because of the land shortage no estates were in fact granted and that the Tsar's scheme was not implemented until 1565 when the Oprichnina was instituted.
   A. A. Zimin, *The Reforms of Ivan the Terrible* (Moscow, 1960) pp. 366–71; Ian Grey, *op. cit.,* pp. 85, 90; see below pp. 61.

15. A. A. Zimin and D. S. Likhachev (Editors) *The Works of I. Peresvetov* (Moscow-Leningrad, 1956) pp. 158–59.

16. *Ibid.* p. 189.

17. Solovyev, III, VI, p. 526.

18. R. Hakluyt, *op. cit.,* I. p. 275.

19. *Ibid.* p. 255.

20. *Ibid.* p. 256.

21. *Ibid.* pp. 256–57.

22. I. Zabelin, *The Domestic Life of the Russian Tsars* (Moscow, 1872) p. 5; C. Oman, *The English Silver in the Kremlin 1557–1663* (London, 1961) pp. 1–4.

23. T. S. Willan, *The Early History of the Russia Company 1553–1603* (Manchester, 1956) pp. 63–64.

CHAPTER V

Ivan the Terrible
The Time of Terror and Defeat,
1560–1584

THE CHANGE THAT TOOK PLACE IN IVAN IN 1547 WAS FOLLOWED by another equally dramatic change in 1560, when he discarded the tutelage of Silvestr, Adashev, and the Chosen Council and began to rule alone as autocrat. He struck out at princes and boyars whom he considered to be traitors. His repression was to cause unrest and instability in the army and throughout the country. In Livonia he suffered defeat and at the same time the Crimean Tatars devastated the southern regions and even burnt Moscow.

Volatile and extreme in conduct, Ivan appeared to undergo sudden transformation. His estrangement from his chosen advisers, however, was not sudden. He had never forgotten that many princes and boyars had been ready to betray him while he lay ill, seven years earlier. His mistrust of Silvestr, Adashev and others had then been aroused and had grown like a cancer.

It may be doubted, however, whether Ivan would have continued indefinitely under the tutelage of the fervent, stubborn priest or of Aleksei Adashev, who was young, sincere, and bold in pressing his counsel. Ivan was a natural autocrat, convinced that his power was from God and not to be shared, influenced, or overruled by counsellors, no matter how wise. He was to denounce them furiously not only for betraying him but also because "they began to hold counsel in secret and without our knowledge, deeming us to be incapable of judgement; and thus did they begin to give worldly counsel in the place of spiritual, and thus did they begin little by little to lead all the boyars into contumacy, taking the splendour of our power from us . . ."[1] But, although he was to condemn Silvestr and Adashev as "curs and traitors", he continued to hold them in some respect and did not persecute them. He was able to claim that:

We exercised our wrath with mercy; the death penalty we did

not inflict, but we banished them to various places. But the priest Silvestr, seeing his advisers set at naught, for this reason left of his own free will; but we, having given him our blessing, did not dismiss him, not because we were ashamed but because we did not wish to judge him here, but in the world to come, before the Lamb of God, for the evil he has done to me while ever serving me and in his cunning manner overlooking me. There will I accept judgement for as much as I have suffered, spiritually and bodily at his hands.[2]

The event which stunned Ivan and at the same time hardened him towards Silvestr and Adashev was the death on 7 August, 1560, of Tsaritsa Anastasia. He blamed them for withholding medical help by "cunning scheming".[3] He was nevertheless reticent concerning their hostility towards this devout, gentle, and self-effacing woman.[4] Kurbsky stated that enemies of Silvestr and Adashev had alleged that they had caused her death by sorcery, a most serious charge. Evidently Ivan himself did not believe it, for it was not one of the accusations that he made against his former advisers.[5]

Ivan himself probably contributed to the early death of his wife. He was driven by restless energy. He went frequently on pilgrimages to distant monasteries, on hunting expeditions and other travels, and he required his wife and family to be with him. She was a devoted but anxious wife and mother, who did not have the strength to keep up with him. In thirteen years of married life she had borne him six children and had seen four of them, tightly swaddled as was Muscovite practice, die in infancy. She was distressed by the savage antagonisms at court and she knew that, if anything happened to him, she would be torn from her children and sent to some distant monastery to die of cold and neglect. Such anxieties apparently preyed on her mind.

In October 1559 Ivan and Anastasia were in Mozhaisk, some sixty-five miles south-west of Moscow. Winter had set in early and was exceptionally severe. News came that the Livonians had broken the conditions of the armistice, agreed a few months earlier. At once Ivan decided that they must return to Moscow, although snow drifts blocked the roads and travel was almost impossible. His wife was exhausted by this journey. Ivan wrote later: "How shall I recall the hard journey to the ruling city from Mozhaisk with our ailing Tsaritsa Anastasia?"[6] She was ill for several months and on 7 August, 1560, she died. She had won the affection of the Muscovites and great crowds followed her coffin to the burial in the Novodevichy Monastery.

Ivan was always to cherish tender memories of Anastasia or "my young one", as he called her in a letter written seventeen years later.[7] Two sons of the marriage, Tsarevichi Ivan (1554–81) and Fedor (1557–98) were living, but he set about finding another wife to ensure the succession. In August 1561 he married Maria, the beautiful daughter of the Kabardan prince, Temryuk. She bore him a son, Vasily, who died when only five weeks old, and the marriage did not last. Contemporaries claimed that she merely fostered his cruel and dissolute tastes.[8] Drunken orgies became far more frequent at court after the death of Anastasia who had evidently had some calming influence on him. Moreover, in 1563 Makari, the venerable Metropolitan, died and his restraint was removed. During this period Ivan gathered around him new favourites who were men of lesser calibre than Silvestr, Adashev, and others of the Chosen Council. They included Boyar Aleksei Basmanov, Prince Afanasy Vyazemsky, Vasily Gryaznoi, and Malyuta Skuratov-Belsky, who was to be the father-in-law of Boris Godunov.

One man who had been close to Ivan for many years was Prince Andrei Kurbsky, who came of an illustrious princely family. He was two or three years older than Ivan and outstanding in intelligence and ability. As a military commander he had distinguished himself in the conquest of Kazan, in Livonia, and elsewhere. In 1556 Ivan advanced him to the rank of boyar in recognition of his services. But Kurbsky was unstable in temperament and incapable of loyalties. He had been close to Silvestr and Adashev and a member of the Chosen Council, but had remained in favour after their departure from Moscow. At some early stage, however, he had begun to harbour resentment towards his Tsar, which grew into a passionate hatred. King Sigismund Augustus learnt of his wavering loyalty and sent him letters, promising rich rewards if he transferred his allegiance to Lithuania. Kurbsky's renown as a general extended beyond Muscovy and his defection would be not only a moral and political victory over the Tsar but also a military gain for Lithuania. Early in 1564 Kurbsky suffered an ignominious defeat by a small Polish force and, fearing the Tsar's anger, he made his decision. He took leave of his wife and nine-year-old son, whom he abandoned in Dorpat, and at the end of April 1564 he fled across the Lithuanian frontier.

At once Kurbsky began a furious campaign against his former sovereign. He harassed the Lithuanians with plans to attack and also to incite the Crimean Khan to invade Muscovy. The Lithuanian attempt to take Polotsk in October 1564 was repelled. But the Khan at the head of an army of 60,000 invaded the Ryazan region in the same month. At this time Ivan was expecting to receive the Khan's envoy, bearing a treaty of alliance. The Muscovite forces were mainly deployed in Livonia. The Tatars, meeting no resistance, ranged over a vast area, carrying off an abundance of booty and thousands of prisoners to sell into slavery.

In his desperate efforts to assail and revile the Tsar, Kurbsky was little concerned that he was causing terrible suffering and loss of life among his former countrymen. He achieved his objective most effectively, however, not in the military field but in his writings. He wrote his first letter denouncing Ivan soon after his flight. He wrote further letters and also his *History of the Great Muscovite Prince*.[9] His writings provoked Ivan to write two lengthy letters in reply, which are among the most dramatic and illuminating documents in Russian history.

Kurbsky was prepared to lie and distort facts in order to calumniate the Tsar and to justify himself. His malevolence sprang from personal fear and hatred, but in his letters he was also reflecting the general discontent among the boyars. The Grand Princes had always ruled, so he maintained, in consultation with their boyars, and Ivan's determination to rule absolutely and alone as autocrat would cause disaster. He held that the evil influence of Sofia, wife of Ivan III and grandmother of the Tsar, had brought about the break with Muscovite tradition and the decline in the beneficent role played by the Boyar Duma. But he denied that he wanted to revive the old independent principalities, and expressed support for the new nation, united under the Tsar. He was at heart, however, the ruler of a petty principality. He resented the fact that in a united Muscovy he had lost all independence and was merely the subject of the Tsar.

Ivan was stung to fury by Kurbsky's temerity in writing publicly to him and charging him with all manner of crimes. His first reply, a document of some eighty-six pages compared with Kurbsky's letter of just over four pages, was a magnificent refutation. Written in the white heat of anger, it abounds in telling phrases and in allusions to the history of Muscovy, ancient Greece and Rome, and Byzantium and Persia, but the most pervasive and strong influence was the Bible.[10]

Kurbsky's treason made a profound impression on Ivan. He felt the intensity of Kurbsky's hatred and believed that he reflected the implacable hostility towards him of the whole boyar-princely class. He became convinced that in Moscow and throughout the country they were planning treason against him.

Early in the winter of 1564 rumours spread in Moscow that the Tsar was going away. Trusted boyars, serving officers, and servants were summoned to the city and told to make preparations to travel. Mystery surrounded the Tsar's plans.

By first light on the morning of 3 December the Kremlin was crowded with sledges. The Tsar's servants began loading them with his personal clothing, ikons, the court treasure, and articles which were not usually taken when he went on pilgrimages or other journeys. The people watched uneasily and the rumours among them became ominous. Ivan appeared and accompanied by the church hierarchy and boyars he went to pray in the Uspensky Cathedral. He then took his seat in the sledge with the Tsaritsa and his two sons. Servants wrapped them in furs against the savage winter cold. Then, escorted by his trusted favourites and mounted guards, he departed from Moscow, leaving the people mystified and disturbed.

In Moscow, churchmen, boyars, and people were more and more unsettled by the Tsar's absence. On 3 January 1565, however, couriers came from Aleksandrovsk, hidden in dense forests some seventy miles north of Moscow, where Ivan had finally halted. They brought a message for the Metropolitan and another addressed to the people of the city. In the message to the Metropolitan, Ivan complained of the misdeeds of the boyars who continued to betray his trust. But when in righteous anger he punished these traitorous subjects the Metropolitan and other churchmen spoke out on their behalf, and so thwarted his will and his justice. "Consequently," the message read, "not wishing to endure your treachery, we with great pity in our heart have quitted the Tsardom and have gone wherever God may lead us!"[11] The second message which was read out to the assembled merchants and people of the city stated that his anger was not directed against them and assured them of his love and goodwill.

This tactic of setting the merchants and people against the upper class of boyars and senior officials was effective. The commoners bewailed their fate. There was an outcry that "The Sovereign has deserted us! We will perish! Who will be our defender against the foreigners? What will happen to the sheep without the shepherd?"[12] The mood of the people became menacing. "Let the Tsar point out the traitors to us! We will destroy them ourselves!"[13]

On 5 January the Archbishop of Novgorod and the Archimandrite of the Chudov Monastery, both appointed by the Metropolitan, led a mission to Aleksandrovsk, followed by a straggling crowd. Ivan received them kindly. In response to their petition he agreed to return to Moscow, but on the conditions that he should be free to rule as absolute monarch without hindrance and that he should be able to punish traitors without interventions or reproaches. The churchmen and all with them readily accepted his conditions.

Early in February (1565) Ivan made his ceremonial entry into the city. He had been away for two months and many noticed the physical change in him. He had been tall and impressive with a thick head of hair, heavy beard and moustache, and great vitality had marked his movements. On his return from Aleksandrovsk he appeared to have aged strangely. He had become stooped, bald and stumbling as though he had been ravaged by a terrible mental and spiritual crisis.

At an assembly of boyars, churchmen, and officials convened on the day after his return, Ivan announced a further condition. For the safety of himself and the Tsardom he would set up a private establishment, to be known as the *Oprichnina*, which would be an independent state within the Tsardom, belonging to the Tsar personally, and with its own special guards, the *Oprichniki*. He was in effect creating an independent principality within which he could isolate himself from all whom he mistrusted. The Oprichnina also had the purpose of giving him full licence to massacre those whom he feared as threats to his power, his person, and his dynasty. His grotesque plan meant dividing Muscovy into his personal domain, and the rest of the nation, known as the *Zemshchina*, over which he remained absolute monarch.

The requisitioning of lands for the Oprichnina, which expanded gradually until it embraced nearly half of the Tsardom, involved drastic confiscations of estates and the uprooting of large sections of the population. Nothing was done to assist the resettlement of evicted families with the result that the internal administration and in particular military organisation were severely disrupted.

The selection of the life-guards or Oprichniki, which was limited initially to 1,000 men, was closely scrutinised by Ivan himself with the assistance of Aleksei Basmanov, Malyuta Skuratov-Belsky, and others among the new favourites. The Oprichniki owed complete loyalty to him personally and were outside the law of State and Church. They wore uniforms of black and carried on their saddles the emblems of a broomstick and a dog's head, signifying that they would sweep and hound treason from the land. The selection was unpredictable. Prince Vasily Shuisky, a member of the family which had terrorised Ivan in childhood and a representative of the class that he regarded with strongest suspicion, was chosen to serve in the Oprichnina. The Zakharin-Yuriev and the Godunovs were chosen. Boris Godunov, being only fifteen or sixteen at this time, may not have been enlisted until later, and he was to play little part in the Oprichnina. Prince Ivan Mstislavsky and others who were close to the throne by marriage or through long service were excluded. Evidently the sole criterion was whether Ivan trusted them. The institution of the Oprichnina was to spread instability and suffering throughout the country.

Within two days of his return to Moscow Ivan launched a period of terror, which lasted for nearly seven years. The first victims were Prince Alexander Gorbaty and his seventeen-year-old son, Peter. Accused of complicity with Kurbsky and of conspiring to kill Ivan and his family, they were executed together. Prince Dmitri Shevyrev was killed by the horrible method of being impaled upon a sharpened and greased stake which with the weight of his body slowly penetrated upwards through the intestines and towards the heart; he endured a full day of agony before he died.[14] Princes Ivan and Dmitri Kurakin were forced to become monks in distant monasteries. Many others, including officials and members of the gentry, were executed or banished to Kazan and more distant places.

The Oprichniki marauded and plundered not only the boyars and wealthy merchants but also the common people. Ivan did nothing to restrain them. Indeed, he took the Stroganov family and the agents of the English Russia Company into the Oprichnina in order to protect them and their property. He even abetted the Oprichniki in their evil exploits. On a night in July 1568, certain of his favourites, including Malyuta Skuratov-Belsky and Prince Afanasy Vyazemsky, led a band of Oprichniki who broke into the houses of certain officials and merchants who were known to have beautiful wives. They carried off the wives, and later presented them to Ivan who made his choice, leaving the other women to the pleasure of their captors. On the same evening he rode to the outskirts of the capital with Oprichniki who destroyed the houses of boyars and princes who were in disgrace. Returning to the Kremlin Palace he gave orders for the ravished wives to be returned to their husbands.

No one dared to attempt to restrain him. Afanasy, the elderly monk who had succeeded Makari as Metropolitan, was ineffective and in 1566 ill-health forced him to retire. The appointment of the head of the Russian Church was made by the Tsar on the recommendation of the church council. But Ivan took the matter into his own hands. Apparently he was determined to find a man who was able and devout, and who would not be a mere figurehead. His choice finally fell upon Filip, the son of a boyar, who had entered the Church and won renown as the Abbot of the Solovetsky

Monastery. Established on an island in the White Sea, this monastery, where the monks lived austerely and endured the rigours of Arctic winters, was of special sanctity because it contained the relics of Savvatyi and Zosima, revered saints of the Russian Church. Filip refused the appointment, but then yielded under the pressure of Ivan's insistence. He even signed a paper, containing undertakings that he would not interfere in the Oprichnina or resign office because the Tsar declined his advice or requests.

Metropolitan Filip was increasingly distressed by the executions and the oppression of the people by the Tsar. At the same time he lost the confidence of Ivan who came soon to believe that he was in league with the boyars who wished to destroy the Oprichnina. A clash between Ivan and Filip, both dominating personalities, was inevitable. It happened on a Sunday in July 1568. Filip was standing before the great golden ikonostasis which separated the body of the Uspensky Cathedral from the holy sanctuary. Ivan entered the cathedral, accompanied by a personal guard of Oprichniki. He went towards the Metropolitan and then stopped, awaiting his blessing. When Filip, staring at the holy ikons on the ikonostatis, ignored the Tsar, certain boyars said to him: "Holy Father, here is the Sovereign! Bless him!" Filip refused the blessing and began castigating him.

"In the most heathen and barbaric realms," he said, "there is law and justice, there is compassion towards the people—but not in Russia! The goods and the lives of our citizens go unprotected! Everywhere plundering and everywhere murder . . . and these deeds are carried out in the name of the Tsar!"

Filip continued his rebukes for some minutes. Suddenly Ivan struck the ground with his staff.

"Be quiet, for I will speak! Be quiet, Holy Father!" he thundered. "Be quiet and bless me!"

"Our silence," Filip replied, "lies as a sin upon your soul and will bring death!"

"Those close to me rose against me and they seek to harm me— but what business is it of yours to interfere in our tsarish counsels?"

"I am pastor of the Christian flock!"

"Filip! Do not thwart our power, for you will bring our wrath upon yourself!" Ivan shouted and he added, "Better that you leave the Metropolitanate."[15]

On the evidence of two priests brought from the Solovetsky Monastery, Filip was subsequently arraigned before an ecclesiastical court on vague charges. Ivan presided over the court. Filip brushed aside the charges with contempt and again rebuked him.

Ivan did not have him seized at once. He knew that Filip was widely respected and might become a martyr.

On 8 November (1568) in the Uspensky Cathedral Boyar Aleksei Basmanov entered with a detachment of black-clad Oprichniki, as Filip conducted the service. The vast congregation fell silent. Basmanov ordered that the sentence of the ecclesiastical court be read out. Filip was to be degraded and dismissed from the Metropolitanate. Oprichniki tore off his splendid vestments and clothed him in the plain white robe of the repenting sinner. For a time Filip was held in the Nikolaevsky Monastery on the banks of the Moskva River. People began gathering there in crowds, hoping to set eyes on the saintly monk. He was removed to another monastery near Tver. There a year later (December 1569) Malyuta Skuratov-Belsky strangled him in his cell.

Ivan had always regarded Novgorod with rancorous suspicion. Among the Novgorodtsi there were still, so he was convinced, many who continued to dream of restoring the city's greatness and independence. In the summer of 1569, a report reached Moscow that the people of Novgorod were conspiring to defect in a body to Lithuania. The evidence of this conspiracy was slight, but Ivan accepted it and vowed to destroy Novgorod and its people so that the city would never again threaten the security of Muscovy.

In December 1569 Ivan with his guards set out for Novgorod. An advance force cordoned the city to ensure that no one escaped. On 6 January, 1570, accompanied by Tsarevich Ivan, he entered the city with his personal escort of 1,500 guards. The massacre began on the following day. Priests and monks were beaten to death with staffs. A special court was set up at the Tsar's headquarters on the eastern side of the city. Here Novgorodtsi were brought for interrogation and the most horrifying tortures were applied in extracting confessions. After interrogation the victims were trussed and cast into the Volkhov River, which did not freeze in this region. Women and children were tied together and suffered the same fate. For five weeks the massacre continued. The snow and ice on the banks of the river were stained with blood and the river itself was choked with corpses. Some 60,000 men, women, and children were said to have perished. It took six months to clear the Volkhov of bodies and severed limbs. Food supplies were exhausted and by the summer the few survivors were facing starvation as well as plague.

Ivan was still not convinced that all who had been involved in the conspiracy in Novgorod had been judged. Archbishop Pimen, who had been most deeply compromised, was taken to Moscow. Under interrogation he and other witnesses divulged information, directly implicating certain of Ivan's closest and most trusted men, including Aleksei Basmanov, Ivan Viskovaty, and Prince Afanasy Vyazemsky.

On 27 July 1570, eighteen gallows were erected in the Red Square in Moscow. Fires and instruments of torture were prepared around them. Ivan pardoned 180 of the accused, but nearly 400 men were executed in four hours on that day. Ivan Viskovaty was stripped naked, tied up by his feet, and slowly hacked to pieces. The former Treasurer to the Tsar, Funikov, was dipped in cold and then in boiling water repeatedly until he died in agony. Vyazemsky had died under torture during his interrogation. Adding to the horrors of these weeks, plague and famine afflicted Moscow and the surrounding country.

In May 1565 Lithuanian ambassadors arrived in Moscow with proposals for an armistice. The conditions were that Sigismund Augustus would concede Polotsk and parts of Livonia, occupied by Muscovite troops, in return for Muscovite recognition of Lithuanian possession of the regions held by the king's troops. The proposal attracted Ivan, especially as it acknowledged his acquisition of Dorpat and Polotsk. The Livonian war was a serious drain on the economic and military resources of Muscovy. Another factor was that the Turkish Sultan was preparing to mount an expedition to recapture Astrakhan. This would probably start rebellions among Tatars along the Volga River, and the Crimean Khan would certainly take advantage of Muscovite commitment on other fronts.

Ivan hesitated nevertheless to accept the Lithuanian proposal. Possession of the whole of Livonia had become the chief objective of his foreign policy. He decided to put the matter to the Assembly of the Land *(Zemsky Sobor)*.

Meeting in Moscow in the summer of 1566, this Assembly, attended by 374 delegates, was larger and more representative than the first Assembly of the Land, which had met sixteen years earlier. The delegates were members of the church and boyar councils; many were serving gentry and officials from government offices, as well as leading merchants and certain landowners with estates near the Lithuanian frontier. They did not represent the people in any democratic sense, but they were the men upon whom the Tsar and the government depended.

Ivan addressed the Assembly and put the question clearly. Should he accept the peace proposals of the Lithuanian king or should he wage war until the whole of Livonia was in Muscovite possession? In an impressive demonstration of patriotic fervour and of loyalty to the Tsar, the Assembly expressed overwhelming support for continuing the war. The delegates were then presented with a resolution, setting out what had been agreed, and each delegate kissed the cross, thus solemnly swearing to carry out the terms of the resolution.

Months passed in negotiations. Sigismund Augustus remained anxious to agree a permanent peace or at least an armistice. Lithuania was exhausted and he was concerned also about the projected union of Lithuania with Poland. The two countries had been linked in the person of their ruler, who was both King of Poland and Grand Prince of Lithuania. The Lithuanians had always resisted Polish pressure for a closer union, fearing that they would be taken over and absorbed. Ivan's refusals to come to terms, in spite of Sigismund Augustus's persistent attempts, left them no alternative. For their part the Poles recognised that Lithuania could not stand against the might of Muscovy and that, if the Russians defeated them and consolidated their hold on Livonia, Poland too would be threatened. The Poles therefore pressed more strenuously for the union and now the Lithuanians reluctantly agreed. Meeting in Lublin in June 1569 the Polish and Lithuanian *Seyms* (Assemblies of the Nobility) agreed to the organic union of the two countries which would have king and Seym in common. The immediate effect of the Union of Lublin was that the military strength of Lithuania was doubled.

Early in 1570 Lithuanian ambassadors arrived in Moscow to make yet another attempt to negotiate peace. When their proposals were rejected, they asked to speak to the Tsar directly. To him they reported that the Seym had considered the succession to the Polish-Lithuanian throne and had agreed to offer it to the Tsar and his dynasty. Among both Poles and Lithuanians there was, in fact, a strong body of opinion which favoured the election of the Tsar. He was a Slav, renowned as an outstanding monarch and the conqueror of Kazan, and known for his religious tolerance. The savageries of his reign, publicised by Kurbsky, evidently had not diminished this support. But Ivan treated the invitation coolly. He was concerned not about the throne of Poland-Lithuania, but the conquest of Livonia. The war was draining his resources and to gain a respite he concluded a three-year armistice on the basis of maintaining the existing position in Livonia.

During these years Ivan's goodwill towards the English seemed unbounded. In 1567 he granted further concessions to the Muscovy Company, amounting to a monopoly of all trade through the White Sea and the right to travel freely through Russia to trade with Persia and Cathay. In making new concessions, however, he was preparing the way for his own demands. On the departure of Anthony Jenkinson from Moscow, he was entrusted with special messages to Queen Elizabeth.

Ivan's proposals took Elizabeth and her ministers by surprise. He asked her to "license masters to come unto him which can make ships and sail them" and to give authority for him "to have out of England all kinds of artillery and things necessary for war". Then came the astonishing request which revealed the depth of his suspicion of his boyars and of his fears for the safety of himself and his dynasty. This request was that Elizabeth should grant him asylum in England if he had to flee from Muscovy. Finally, he proposed an offensive and defensive alliance in which they would be "joined as one" and she would be "friend to his friends and enemy to his enemies and so per contra". He ended his message with the urgent request that her answer should reach him by 29 June, 1568, an impossibly short time.[16]

In June, Elizabeth appointed a professional diplomat, Thomas Randolph, to carry her reply to Moscow. He was to assure the Tsar that he could always count on finding a welcome and safe refuge in England. On other proposals he was to express general agreement and goodwill, but in respect of the proposed alliance, he was to "pass those matters in silence".[17] Angry at not receiving the reply by the date he had set, Ivan had begun putting pressure on the Muscovy Company. Narva was then in his possession and he granted trading privileges there to other merchants, including an independent group of Englishmen who were in competition with the Company. Learning of this, Elizabeth at once sent envoys to the Tsar with the demand that he send "those naughty Englishmen" engaged in private trade back to England. Ivan was reluctant to arrest them, however, for he had apparently conceived an affection for them.[18] Moreover, he was still angry, believing that she had been dilatory in responding to his proposals.

Thomas Randolph reached Moscow in October 1568 and had to wait four months before he was received in audience. But when in July of the following year he sailed for England, he was in a position to report that the Tsar's goodwill had been renewed and that the Company's privileges had been restored in full. On this voyage he was accompanied by the Tsar's ambassador, Andrei Savin, who carried messages and a draft treaty which Elizabeth was evidently expected to sign and ratify forthwith.

Ivan was more impatient now to conclude an alliance with England. Denmark, Poland and Sweden had resolved their differences and he feared that they would join forces against Muscovy. Elizabeth appreciated that the alliance was of special importance to him. She was not prepared, however, to accept the Tsar's enemies as her own. Finally she agreed to an alliance with provisos that, if the Tsar suffered damage caused by another monarch and she was satisfied as to the justice of the Tsar's cause, she would call on the aggressor to desist and, if he refused, then, but only then, would she consider going to the Tsar's aid. She confirmed that she readily conceded all other requests. In particular, she assured him that in the event of him and his family seeking refuge in England, she would appoint a residence for them, but on the niggardly condition that he would pay for it.[19]

On receiving the queen's reply, Ivan exploded in anger. He at once revoked all of the Company's privileges and sequestered its goods. To Elizabeth he wrote bluntly that she had set aside his "great affairs" and had shown herself to be ruler only in name for "now we perceive that there be other men that do rule, and not men but boors and merchants, the which seek not the wealth and honour of our Majesties, but they do seek their own profit of merchandise".[20]

Elizabeth made haste to recover the Tsar's goodwill and in particular to have the Company's privileges revived. She appointed Anthony Jenkinson to carry out this difficult mission. Learning that he was returning to Moscow, Ivan was mollified. Closing his letters to Elizabeth he expressed his pleasure: "And even now have we had tidings that Anthony [Jenkinson] is here arrived and when Anthony cometh unto us we will gladly hear him . . ."[21]

When in July (1571) Anthony Jenkinson made the journey from the White Sea to Moscow he was struck by "the miserable state of the country". In a letter to Lord Burghley he wrote that famine was critical. The people were eating bread made from tree-bark and "in some places they have eaten one another". Plague had carried off some 300,000 people. The Tsar had "by sundry torments put to death a great number of his people".[22] But a greater catastrophe was about to befall.

Ivan had secured his grip on Kazan and the upper Volga region and on Astrakhan. He could never relax his guard, however, against attacks from the south. The Sultan was insisting that the Crimean Khan, Devlet Girei, join in campaigns to recover Astrakhan and Kazan. Sigismund Augustus was offering the Khan enormous payments of treasure if he would renew hostilities against Muscovy. The Khan was unwilling, however, to bear the brunt of such campaigns and anxious to avoid coming under the closer control of the Sultan. At this stage he was even prepared to make peace with the Tsar if gifts of sufficient value were offered.

During the summer of 1570, however, frequent reports of large-scale movements of Tatar troops reached Moscow. Ivan himself hastened twice to join his army on the Oka River to repel Tatar invasions. The reports were evidently false. But in the spring of 1571 the Khan massed an army of 120,000 troops. Russian forces 50,000 strong took up defensive positions on the Oka River. But Muscovite traitors, demoralised by the Tsar's persecution or by the hardships afflicting the country, fled to the Khan. They advised him of the desperate state of the people and the low morale of the army, and promised further to guide the Tatars across the Oka so as to avoid engaging the Muscovite defence forces.

Following their guidance, the Khan led his army over the river. Ivan suddenly found himself cut off from his main forces and retreated to Aleksandrovsk and thence to Rostov. Learning what had happened, the Muscovite commanders hurriedly moved from their positions and reached the outskirts of Moscow on 23 May. The Tatars arrived on the following day and, without engaging the Muscovite forces, they began setting fire to the outer suburbs. A great wind began to blow, whipping up and spreading the fires until they enveloped the whole city. Thousands of Muscovites were trapped and burnt to death. In the intense heat the Tatars could not plunder and the Khan finally ordered them to withdraw. They carried away with them some 150,000 prisoners. In the summer of the following year the Khan again invaded but this time a strong army, commanded by Prince Mikhail Vorotynsky, routed his forces.

By this time Ivan was showing signs of weariness. He had occupied the throne for nearly forty years. The isolation of supreme office and his obsessive suspicion that members of the boyar-princely class were plotting treason had taken their toll. On 1 September, 1569, his second wife, Tsarita Maria, had died suddenly. It was rumoured that she had been poisoned or killed by sorcery. The court had gone into mourning, but there had been none of the popular demonstration of grief that had followed the death of Anastasia.

Ivan declared his intention of taking another wife. Couriers galloped through the country, calling on the fathers of beautiful and virtuous daughters to present them for preliminary examination by the Tsar's officials. More than 2,000 virgins were assembled for this purpose in Aleksandrovsk. Twelve were selected and were inspected by the Tsar's doctor and then passed to chosen women of the court for more intimate examination.[23] The maiden who would be the Tsaritsa had to be beautiful, gentle, and devout, and without blemish.

Ivan chose as his bride Marfa, daughter of Vasily Sobakin, a Novgorod merchant. At the same time Evdokiya Saburova was selected from the twelve to be the wife of Tsarevich Ivan. As was customary the families of the two brides were elevated at court and granted estates. Marfa had no sooner been chosen than she went into a decline. Witchcraft and slow poison were suspected. The family of the Tsar's second wife, who had been displaced by the newcomers, were found guilty, and several people were executed. On 28 October, 1571, Ivan married Marfa, but after sixteen days of unconsummated marriage she died.

Disturbed by the death of his young wife, Ivan took it to be a mark of God's anger. He turned for companionship to his favourites, chief among whom were Malyuta Skuratov-Belsky and Boris Godunov, who had married Malyuta's daughter, Maria, only a few months earlier. Malyuta and Boris had each acted as *Druzhka*, or best man, at the Tsar's marriage with Marfa and they remained close to him. In 1572, however, Malyuta was killed in the siege of a Livonian town.

Little is known of these early years in the life of Boris. He may have been taken into the Oprichnina at the age of sixteen or seventeen. It would seem probable that before gaining prominence at court when he married at the age of about twenty, Boris had been the regular companion of the Tsarevichi Ivan, who was some four years younger, and Fedor, who was some seven years younger than he was. It was customary for the Tsarevichi to have a band of chosen companions, and Boris would have stood out among them. Then and increasingly in later years the Tsar welcomed his company. Apparently he did not involve Boris in the debaucheries or in the executions which overclouded his reign. But this is not certain. He took Tsarevich Ivan, then aged sixteen, to Novgorod in 1570 and the boy was at his side during the massacres. Ivan would not have hesitated to require the presence of the young favourite if he saw fit. But if Boris witnessed any of the horrors of Ivan's reign the effect upon him was to confirm his distaste for cruelty. Throughout his life and especially in wielding power, he was never guilty of savageries and even avoided imposing the death sentence. It may be that his natural dislike of cruelty and bloodshed was intensified by all that he witnessed during Ivan's reign. But he must have exercised great tact in avoiding all expression of criticism or disapproval, which his Tsar would never have tolerated.

In 1571, within two months of Marfa's death, Ivan took as his fourth wife Anna Alekseevna Koltovskaya, a beautiful girl of humble origin. This marriage was sudden and furtive. Ivan knew that a fourth marriage was not allowed by canon law and he hastened to obtain the blessing of the Church. The hierarchy was summoned to the Uspensky Cathedral where he addressed them. He spoke of the death of his first wife by witchcraft and of his second wife by poison. "I waited for some time," he went on, "and I decided on a third marriage, partly for my bodily need . . . for to live in the world without a wife is full of temptations." He referred to the death of Marfa and then said, "In despair and grief I wanted to dedicate myself to the monkish life, but seeing again the tender youth of my sons and seeing the Tsardom in the midst of disasters, I dared to take a fourth wife."[24] Certain penances were imposed and the marriage was blessed, but anxious that the Tsar's action should not serve as a precedent the church council proclaimed that any man who took a fourth wife would be anathematised.

In the summer of 1572 Ivan made his final testament. He was no more than forty-two years old, but felt that death was at hand. "My body grows weak," he wrote. "My soul is sick. Sores of the flesh and the spirit multiply and there is no doctor who can heal me. I waited for someone who would grieve with me—but no one have I found to console me. All have returned me evil for good, hatred for love . . ."[25] He bequeathed the throne and the Tsardom to his elder son, Tsarevich Ivan, making only a small bequest of fourteen towns to the younger son. He enjoined upon both sons that they must stand together in everything, while sweeping treason from the land and binding the people to them in love.

Ivan had made this testament in Novgorod. While there he received the news of the crushing defeat of Devlet Girei's Tatars by the Muscovite army, commanded by Prince Vorotynsky. Soon afterwards the news came that Sigismund Augustus had died in July (1572). Ivan hastened back to Moscow where the people welcomed him. For the first time in many years they were in high spirits. The plague had passed and food was plentiful. The defeat of the Crimean Khan had erased the disgrace of the burning of Moscow in the previous year. In 1572, too, Ivan disbanded the Oprichnina. He had become increasingly dissatisfied with the system. He no longer trusted the Oprichniki, some of whom had been found guilty of sedition. They had failed to defend Moscow against the Tatars. Moreover, Vorotynsky and his army were from the Zemshchina. He was alarmed, too, by the hatred of the Oprichniki shown by the people, who had always demonstrated strong loyalty for him and his dynasty. The abolition of the Oprichnina could not happen suddenly and completely. The situation was complex and the reallocation of land required time. The sinister division of Muscovy into two separate states was only gradually healed.[26]

Ivan's fears for the security of himself, the dynasty, and the Tsardom were more than chimera, as was shown by several cases of treason during the 1570s. Prince Ivan Mstislavsky, who stood high above all princes and boyars in rank and nobility, confessed that he had aided Devlet Girei and his army in their crossing of the Oka in 1571. Ivan pardoned him after the Metropolitan had interceded on his behalf. But several priests and others, implicated in Mstislavsky's treachery, were beheaded in 1574, and their heads thrown into the forecourt of his palace. A series of executions were reported in the following two years, but during the last eight years of Ivan's reign no further executions were recorded.[27]

The election of a successor to Sigismund Augustus had divided Poles and Lithuanians into several regional and class factions. Ivan had wide support. Orthodox Lithuanians regarded him as their natural sovereign. Protestants believed that he would enforce religious toleration. Many others supported him because he would curb the great magnates among them and also defend the country against the Emperor, the Sultan, and the Crimean Khan.

Ivan displayed no real interest in the throne of Poland-Lithuania. It evidently attracted him only as a means of advancing his plans for Muscovy. Perhaps in this last decade of his reign he was reluctant to take on such vast new responsibilities. Whatever the reason, he was half-hearted in his response to the approaches made to him. Finally he himself recommended the election of Archduke Ernst, son of the Austrian Emperor. But the pro-French faction, supported generally by the Catholics and also by the Sultan, procured the election of Henry of Valois, son of Catherine of Medici. He was crowned in Cracow in February 1574, but soon afterwards deserted the throne to return to France. In the confused elections that followed Stefan Batory became king and was crowned on 29 April, 1576.

Hungarian by birth, Stefan Batory had become a national hero in Hungary and Transylvania as the leader of the struggle against the Habsburg Emperor. The Polish gentry welcomed him as a champion against the great magnates and the Habsburgs. He was to prove a bold and able ruler, showing none of the caution of Sigismund Augustus, and he was to thwart Ivan's efforts to secure Livonia and Muscovy's access to the Baltic.

Ivan received the news of Stefan Batory's election with indifference. The Polish ambassadors, who arrived in Moscow in 1576, bearing the new king's proposals for a permanent peace, merely angered him, for they did not address him by his proper title of Tsar and they referred to Batory as King of Livonia. At this time Batory was fully engaged in subduing the powerful city of

Danzig which refused to acknowledge his election or to swear allegiance to him. Not until the end of 1577 was he able to conquer the city and to compel its citizens to accept him as king.

Ivan had decided in the meantime to pursue his conquest of Livonia. In January, 1577 the Muscovite army, 50,000 strong laid siege to Reval, but met with stout resistance and after six weeks was forced by the winter cold and sickness to raise the siege. In the spring Ivan and his two sons travelled to Novgorod and Pskov, where troops from all parts of the country were assembled. Although the armistice with Poland was in force, he sent his army into southern Livonia, occupied by the Poles. The invasion was unexpected and the Muscovites captured six major towns. The conquest of southern Livonia continued until only Riga and Reval remained to be taken.

Gratified by these successes, Ivan sought to strengthen his position by alliances. But negotiations with Emperor Rudolph who had succeeded to the imperial throne on the death of Maximillian in 1576, came to nothing. The Danish king, Frederick, who was hostile to Sweden and to Poland-Lithuania, sent his envoys to Moscow to propose an eternal peace, but this initiative yielded no results.

Ivan grasped any opportunity to establish peaceful relations with the Crimean Khan. Devlet Girei died in June 1577 and was succeeded by his son, Mahomet Girei. Without delay Ivan sent an embassy bearing presents and greetings to the new Khan and proposals for a permanent alliance. Mahomet refused to consider such proposals unless Astrakhan was evacuated and the Cossacks of the Don and Dniepr were removed. Ivan replied that Astrakhan was part of his realm and that the Don Cossacks were vagrants and brigands whom his commanders had orders to suppress, while the Cossacks of the Dniepr were the responsibility of the King of Poland. Ivan's initiative met with no further response and Mahomat Girei was to prove an implacable enemy.

In January 1578 Stefan Batory sent his ambassadors to Moscow to propose a new peace treaty. He had settled the problem of Danzig and was impatient to deal with Muscovy. He displayed caution at this stage, because he knew that the Poles and Lithuanians were intimidated by Muscovite power. But when his embassy returned from Moscow with agreement for a three-year armistice, he refused to accept it. He had already requested the Seym to vote subsidies to enable him to mobilise an army to invade Muscovy. The Seym would sanction subsidies only for a defensive war, but this was enough to allow him to start his campaign.

In June 1579 Batory declared war. His army of 60,000 troops advanced over the frontier and laid siege to Polotsk. Ivan moved his main forces to Novgorod and Pskov, and from there detached 20,000 troops to defend Karelia and Izborsk against the Swedes. During the siege of Polotsk, however, Ivan did not attempt to engage Batory's army in a decisive battle. Polotsk, although considered almost impregnable, finally surrendered. Mistrust of his boyars as well as natural caution were probably the main reasons for Ivan's inaction. On the surrender of Polotsk, Batory offered generous terms to all Russian officers and men who would enter the Polish service. It was notable that to a man the Russians rejected his blandishments.

Batory returned in triumph to Vilno and at once began preparations for a new campaign. His objective was to capture Velikie Luki. From this stronghold he would be able to mount a campaign to capture Novgorod, Pskov, and Smolensk, and then he would be able to plan the conquest of Moscow.

Batory took Velikie Luki and continued the campaign during the winter of 1580–81 in Livonia and in Muscovy. In November (1580) the Swedes invaded Karelia and also moved into Livonia, taking Wesenberg. At this time Ivan was also concerned that the Turks and Crimean Tatars were about to attack. He made strenuous efforts to negotiate an armistice with Batory. In 1580 he had sent ambassadors with peace proposals. Arrogant in victory, the Poles were at pains to humiliate the Tsar's representatives. Ivan and the Muscovites were always sensitive about their dignity, but he now instructed his envoys not to insist on protocol. The concessions which they were to offer amounted to the surrender of all Russian gains in Livonia, except only four towns. Batory demanded higher terms, however, including the payment of 400,000 gold crowns.

In February 1581 Batory persuaded the Seym to vote further subsidies. He believed that he was invincible and that he could conquer Muscovy in the next campaign. The Poles were reluctant, however, to continue the war and would have preferred to negotiate from their position of strength. By force of personality and leadership Batory persuaded them to support a third campaign.

The Polish objective this time was Pskov. Batory's army had declined, however, in equipment and morale and he underestimated the strength of the Russian garrison, commanded by V. F. Skopin-Shuisky and Ivan P. Shuisky. The Polish attempts to take Pskov were repelled. Polish troops were near to mutiny. At this time an attack by the main Russian forces would have crushed the Poles. Ivan held back. Sweden had captured Narva, Ivangorod, Yam, and Koporie. He was reluctant to commit his main forces in a single battle when enemies were attacking or poised to attack on other fronts.

Desperately seeking an armistice with Batory, Ivan appealed first to the Emperor and then to the Pope to intercede. Rome saw in this appeal the chance to draw Muscovy into a crusade against the Turks and at the same time to promote the union of the eastern and western Churches. Pope Gregory responded promptly by sending a Jesuit priest, Antonio Possevino, whose mediation led to a new round of negotiations. Batory himself now needed peace urgently. His army had suffered heavy losses in sorties by the Russian garrison in Pskov and was exhausted. Ivan's envoys might have gained a peace on advantageous terms, but they were bound by the Tsar's strict instructions. On 6 January, 1582, they concluded a ten-year armistice on humiliating terms. Muscovy ceded the whole of Livonia, together with Polotsk. The Baltic was again closed to Muscovy. Nearly 150 years passed before Peter the Great recovered these vital lands and established Russia as a Baltic power.

It was at this time of great stress, when awaiting the results of the peace negotiations, that Ivan killed his elder son in an outburst of anger. This tragic event and then the failure of his Livonian policy, sealed by the treaty with the Polish king, reduced Ivan to despair. He talked of retiring to a monastery to end his days in solitude and prayer. The boyar and church councils expressed alarm over this suggestion. "We do not want a Tsar other than him given to us by God—you and your son!" they declared.[28] He bowed to the general will and talked no more of vacating the throne.

Indeed, Ivan began to rule actively. His vitality and his lively interest in all matters drew him out of his grief and solitude. At this time, moreover, he was receiving reports of exciting conquests beyond the Urals.

The Stroganovs were a family of frontiersmen and colonisers whose bold commercial enterprise had brought them tremendous wealth and influence. They had always shown full loyalty to Moscow and had been rewarded and protected. Ivan had taken them into the Oprichnina so that their industries and estates would not be molested. Indeed, he looked upon the Stroganovs as general contractors and bankers to the throne.

The capture of Kazan and Astrakhan had opened the way for the colonisation of Siberia. In January 1555 the Siberian Khan had sworn loyalty as the Tsar's vassal. There appeared to be no obstacles to the peaceful annexation of this vast area. But soon the Tatars and other peoples of Siberia were struggling among themselves and against Moscow's authority.

Ivan could not spare troops at this time to restore order in

Siberia. In 1558, however, Grigori Stroganov petitioned for concessions to settle the virgin lands along the banks of the Kama River and its tributaries. Ivan granted a charter for twenty years, conferring rights on the Stroganovs to settle and develop these lands, which in effect became an independent principality. The Stroganovs—Anika, an impressive patriarchal figure, and his sons, Grigori, Yakov, and Semeon—were granted further charters. Their vast territories were fertile, rich in fur-bearing animals, fish and minerals, and the family flourished.

At first relations with the Ostyak, Cheremis, Mordva, Tatar, and other peoples of the Kama and Ural regions were peaceful. In 1572 reports began reaching Moscow of attacks on Russian settlements. More serious trouble was threatened by the new Siberian Khan, Kuchum, who was hostile to Moscow and was seeking to unite the Siberian tribes under his rule. The Stroganovs now petitioned the Tsar to extend their authority beyond the Ural Mountains. This would enable them to maintain effective defences against the Khan. Ivan readily granted their request, giving them the right to develop the lands and establish industries on the banks of the Irtysh, Ob, and Tobol Rivers.

The Stroganovs had some troops in their service, but to deal with the Khan and with rebellious groups in such an expanse of territory far from Moscow they recruited a small private army. They were forbidden to enlist runaway peasants, criminals, and deserters from the Tsar's armies. In the main they depended on Cossacks, the freebooters, raiders, and robbers of the riverlands who harried the Turks and Tatars, and served the Tsar when it suited them. In the 1570s Ivan sent a punitive force against bands of Cossacks whose raids were disrupting trade along the Volga. One band of 540 Cossacks, led by Ataman Ermak Timofeev, fled to the north-east and in the spring of 1579 entered the service of the Stroganovs.

In the summer of 1581 the Stroganovs added to Ermak's force some 300 foreign mercenaries, mainly Germans, Lithuanians, and Tatars, and fitted out this small army for a campaign against the Siberian Khan. Ermak's expedition set out on 1 September, 1581 and in a series of heroic exploits in which the Cossacks were usually greatly outnumbered, they finally took Isker, the capital of the Siberian Khan, and put him to flight.

Ivan had taken a close interest in Siberia since the capture of Kazan and the grant of the first charter to the Stroganovs. He established a special Siberian Ministry to watch over this eastward expansion. Boris Godunov was said to have encouraged him in this interest. At the time of Ermak's expedition, however, Ivan was angry with the Stroganovs because they had engaged a band of fugitive Cossacks and also because they were, he suspected, putting their own interests above those of the Tsardom. But on learning of Ermak's conquest of Siberia he forgot his anger. Ataman Ivan Koltso, who brought the news, approached Moscow in trepidation. He was one of the fugitive Cossacks and he feared the Tsar's anger and punishments. But Ivan, having listened intently to his report, pardoned him and his comrades and rewarded them richly. Bells rang out in Moscow and there were services of thanksgiving in the churches as the Muscovites celebrated, saying to each other: "God has bestowed a new Tsardom on Russia."[29]

Ivan also renewed his efforts to form an alliance with England. His westward policy had failed and his plans to develop Russia's Baltic trade had been thwarted. England thus became even more important than before as a source of armaments and experts. Moreover, he retained a strong personal predilection for England and Englishmen, and especially for Anthony Jenkinson.

Ten years earlier (in 1571) Jenkinson had had the difficult task of regaining the goodwill of the Tsar who was furious over Elizabeth's virtual rejection of his proffered alliance. He had found Ivan in a benign mood and ready to restore all privileges. Apparently he had decided not to press for the alliance at this juncture. In 1582, however, he renewed his proposals to Elizabeth in almost the exact same form as previously. But he added now the curious request that she should provide him with an English bride and indeed he asked for the hand of Lady Mary Hastings, a cousin of the queen.

The request was curious because he had only recently taken a seventh wife. She was Maria Fedorovna, daughter of Fedor Nagoi, whom he married without the ceremony and blessing of the Church. The marriage was, in fact, illegal according to canon law. In 1582 she bore him a son, christened Dmitri; his name was to cast a malevolent spell upon the last years of Boris Godunov's life.

Elizabeth replied to Ivan's requests in the same terms as before and she hedged over the proposed marriage. At the same time she pressed boldly for greater privileges for the Russia Company. Fedor Pisemsky, the Tsar's ambassador, carried her replies back to Moscow. He was accompanied by her new ambassador, Sir Jeremy Bowes, who was brave but high-tempered and arrogant. Again Ivan was infuriated by Elizabeth's response to his proposals. In several stormy meetings he expressed himself bluntly to Bowes who returned equally heated replies. In fact, the effrontery of Bowes was such that he was fortunate not to be cast into prison or expelled from the country. But once again Ivan displayed a friendly restraint.

Bowes quickly made himself hated by all at court. Anxious that his mission should not fail, he became more persuasive, even suggesting that the queen might reconsider her replies. He reported to London that Ivan had decided to send a new embassy to the queen. On 18 March, 1584, however, Bowes received a message from the Muscovite chancellor, reflecting Muscovite resentment of Ivan's Anglophile sentiments. The message was that "the English Emperor was dead".[30]

Portents appeared to forecast the death, as they had heralded the birth, of Ivan. Early in 1584, looking across the golden domes and crosses of the Uspensky and Arkhangelsky Cathedrals, Ivan observed a comet with a long tail that formed a cross. He went out on to the Red Staircase, the grand entrance to the palace, and watched the comet intently. Then turning to members of his suite, he said: "That is the sign of my death."[31]

Ivan had begun to show symptoms of illness early in the winter. His health declined and at the same time he became obsessed with the omen of the comet. He spent hours in prayer and sent couriers to monasteries, ordering special prayers that his sins might be forgiven and his health restored. In Moscow the cathedrals and churches were crowded as his subjects prayed for his recovery. He summoned astrologers and soothsayers from all parts of Russia and even from Lapland. Some sixty of them were accommodated in one building in the city. He sent daily to learn their predictions. Their message was that death was at hand, and some even predicted that it would happen on 18 March.[32] Distressed by their messages he abruptly sent orders that they were to cease their predictions. At one stage, feeling some improvement in his health, he ordered the execution of the "lying astrologers".[33] But on 18 March, when about to play a game of chess with Bogdan Belsky, he suddenly collapsed and soon afterwards died.

Notes

1. J. L. I. Fennell (Ed. and Trans.) *The Correspondence between Prince A. M. Kurbsky and Tsar Ivan IV of Russia 1564–1579* (Cambridge, 1963) pp. 86–89.
2. *Ibid.* pp. 98–99. Aleksei Adashev was sent to Livonia in summer 1560 and in August was appointed as one of the governors of the newly captured town of Fellin. Later he was transferred to Dorpat. Here, so Kurbsky alleged, he was held in prison by order of the Tsar and died of fever after two months. Adashev's enemies suggested that he committed suicide by taking poison because he thought that he might be tried afresh and sentenced to more severe punishments. G. Vernadsky considers it more likely that he was poisoned on

orders from Moscow. See *The Tsardom of Moscow 1547–1682* (New Haven, 1969) I, p. 102.
Silvestr took refuge in the Solovetsky Monastery in the White Sea.

3. J. L. I. Fennell, *op. cit.*, pp. 98–99.

4. Ivan wrote only that "Owing to one little word did she rank as worthless (in their eyes)."
J. L. I. Fennell, *loc. cit.* The reasons for their antagonism remain unknown.

5. Kurbsky alleged that Silvestr and Adashev were banished from court because of accusations that they had caused the death of the Tsaritsa by using poison or witchcraft. But both men departed from court apparently by their own wish and they were not expelled. Moreover, their departure preceded the death of the Tsaritsa. In listing in his letter to Kurbsky the crimes of Silvestr and Adashev, Ivan made no mention of the witchcraft or the poisoning of Anastasia. If he had entertained any suspicion of their guilt on this score, he would have condemned them outright and would hardly have permitted them to live undisturbed in exile from Moscow.
J. L. I. Fennell (Ed. and Trans.) *Prince A. M. Kurbsky's History of Tsar Ivan IV* (Cambridge, 1965) p. 153; J. L. I. Fennell (Ed. and Trans.) *Correspondence*, pp. 94–99; N. Ustryalov (Ed.) *Statements of Prince Kurbsky* (St. Petersburg, 1833) pp. 78–79, 391.

6. J. L. I. Fennell (Ed. and Trans.) *Correspondence*, p. 97.

7. *Ibid.* pp. 190–1.

8. Karamzin, II, IX, Col. 26.

9. J. L. I. Fennell (Ed. and Trans.) *Kurbsky's History of Ivan IV* (Cambridge, 1965) contains a valuable translation and commentary.

10. When in 1577 Ivan came to write his second letter to Kurbsky, he was comparatively subdued. He appeared then to think of himself as being in the position of Job, plagued by misfortunes. His arrogance was muted by a greater awareness of human frailty, especially his own frailty.
J. L. I. Fennell (Ed. and Trans.) *Correspondence* (Cambridge, 1963) pp. 186–97.

11. Karamzin, II, IX, Col. 43.

12. *Ibid.* Cols. 43–4; Solovyev, III, VI, pp. 551–2.

13. Karamzin, *loc. cit.*

14. *Ibid.*, III, IX, Cols. 47–48.

15. *Ibid.* Col. 62; Solovyev, III, VI, p. 556.

16. E. D. Morgan and C. H. Coote (Eds.) *Early Voyages and*

Travels in Russia and Persia (Hakluyt Society, London, 1886) II, pp. 236–8; G. Tolstoy, *The First Forty Years of Intercourse between England and Russia 1553–93* (St. Petersburg, 1875) pp. 44–46.

17. G. Tolstoy, *loc. cit.*
18. When in response to Elizabeth's pressure Ivan finally withdrew trading rights from these private Englishmen and agreed to send them home, he added in his letter to the queen the special plea "for our sake to show favour unto them and to take away thy displeasure from them".
E. D. Morgan and C. H. Coote, *op. cit.*, II, p. 283.
19. *Ibid.* pp. 290–2.
20. *Ibid.*
21. *Ibid.*
22. *Ibid.* pp. 336–7.
23. Karamzin, III, IX, Col. 110.
24. *Ibid.*
Tsaritsa Anna was shorn as a nun three years later either because she failed to bear a child or simply because Ivan had tired of her. He took a fifth, sixth, and finally a seventh wife but without the ceremonial or blessing of the church.
25. Solovyev, *op. cit.*, p. 561.
26. Karamzin, Solovyev, and Klyuchevsky considered that the Oprichnina was abolished only in name, but that the separate establishment continued. S. V. Veselovsky in "The Institution of the Oprichny Establishment in 1565 and its Abolition in 1572" (*Voprosy Istorii* [1946] No. I, pp. 86–104) argued strongly, however, that the Oprichnina was in fact abolished.
27. There are reports of further executions. Indeed, one such source alleged that 2,300 of the troops who surrendered at Polotsk were executed in Moscow in 1582. Executions on such a scale would have been reported in detail by the Chroniclers. In fact, it is beyond reasonable doubt that no executions of troops or boyars took place during these last years of Ivan's life.
Karamzin, III, IX, Col. 210 and note 617; Solovyev, *op. cit.*, p. 565.
28. Karamzin, III, IX, Col. 208.
29. *Ibid.*, Col. 235.
30. R. Hakluyt, *op. cit.*, II, p. 262.
31. Karamzin, III, IX, Col. 256.
32. Solovyev, III, VI, p. 704.
33. Karamzin, III, IX, Col. 257.

CHAPTER VI

Boris Emerges, 1584–1588

THE MUSCOVITES WERE DISTRESSED BY THE DEATH OF IVAN. They did not blame him for the Oprichnina and the many misfortunes which had befallen the country during the later years of his reign. They had venerated him as their crowned and anointed Tsar, the autocrat and head of their patriarchal society.

At the same time all Muscovites were desperately uneasy about the succession. Of Ivan's two surviving sons, Fedor, although twenty-seven years of age, was said to be unfit to rule; Dmitri, then two years old, was still in swaddling clothes and as the child of Ivan's seventh marriage he was hardly considered as a possible successor. All dreaded the anarchy of rival boyar factions struggling for power. Moreover, any sign of weakness in the government would bring Poles, Lithuanians, Germans, Swedes and Tatars invading and plundering. This was a real danger, when the security of the country depended on the ability and leadership of the sovereign. The succession of a strong Tsar was of direct personal concern to every Russian, and for this reason popular grief was overlaid by anxiety for the future.

Fedor, who was unquestionably the legal heir to the throne, was regarded with affection. He was the son of Tsaritsa Anastasia, Ivan's first wife who had been loved by the people and memory of whom was still cherished. Fedor was, however, gentle, exceedingly devout and unworldly, and he displayed none of the qualities of an autocrat. His father had dismissed him as a *Postnik* or keeper of fasts, and as a *Molchalnik,* a monk belonging to an order which maintained the rule of silence.

In physique Fedor was small and weakly. He was strikingly unlike his father who had been tall with a strong aquiline face and a majestic presence as well as a powerful intellect. His complexion was pallid and he seemed to be continually smiling. Foreigners wrote that he was half-witted and a *Durak* or idiot. To

81

most Muscovites he appeared saintly and even a "fool of God" whom the Orthodox regarded with affection and even veneration. Although he was noted for his piety, his inadequacies were clear to all and his succession could only aggravate popular anxiety.

Struggles for power were ready to erupt even during Ivan's last hours. On the night of his death a conspiracy by the Nagoi, the family of Maria, Ivan's seventh wife, was uncovered. The Nagoi hoped to place the child, Dmitri, on the throne so that following Muscovite practice they would dominate the regency. Their conspiracy miscarried. Boyars, supporting Fedor, had the whole family arrested and held under close guard.

In Moscow the general alarm mounted. The people wandered the log-paved streets, crowded the churches, and gathered in the Kremlin, exchanging and inflating rumours of coming disaster. The boyars ordered detachments of guards to patrol the city and had cannon mounted in the Red Square and at other points to put down any attempts to seize the throne. As a further precaution they sent Tsarevich Dmitri with his family under guard to Uglich, the small apanage principality bequeathed to him by Ivan. Fedor, tender-hearted and unwilling to hurt anyone, least of all a child, kissed Dmitri and wept at their parting as though reluctant to banish him and his ambitious family from the capital. It was probably on his insistence that Dmitri and the Nagoi were maintained in Uglich with a full court in accordance with their rank, although under close supervision. Many others who were close to the Nagoi and involved in their plotting were banished to more distant places where they languished in prisons and died of privation.

At this early stage it was not clear who was wielding power on behalf of Fedor. Ivan himself was said to have appointed certain boyars to guide his son. Jerome Horsey, the English agent, reported that he had set up a pentarchy for this purpose, comprising Princes Ivan Mstislavsky and Ivan Shuisky, Boyars Nikita Romanovich Yuriev and Boris F. Godunov, and Oruzhnichy (Arms-bearer) Bogdan Belsky. But Horsey was reporting rumours, for there is no evidence of such appointments. In fact, Fedor probably turned to those who were closest to him by family relationship and whom he felt he could trust. They were his uncle, Boyar Nikita Romanovich Yuriev and his brother-in-law, Boris Godunov, and possibly Ivan Mstislavsky, who was a second cousin.[1]

Ivan Shuisky was the leader among the princes of the Rurik line. He was energetic and able, and renowned for his defence of Pskov against Batory's army. Ivan Mstislavsky was the senior boyar, but neither he nor his family, descendants of the ancient princely line of Gedimin, were noteworthy in any way. Bogdan Belsky had been a close favourite of Ivan's in the closing years of his reign, but had not been raised to boyar rank. He was clever and greedy for power. Indeed, he had been implicated in the Nagoi's plot to place Dmitri on the throne. When they and their supporters were banished, however, he managed to remain in Moscow.

On 2 April Belsky's activities gave rise to an explosive situation in the capital. The boyars had left the Kremlin to return to their homes after the audience of the Lithuanian envoy, Lev Sapega. Belsky had gained the support of the Streltsi guards, and on his orders they had shut the Kremlin gates. He then sought to persuade Tsar Fedor to maintain the "court and Oprichnina", as they had been in the reign of his father. Presumably he expected that under such a regime he would be able to dispose of Mstislavsky, Romanovich Yuriev, and others and to secure for himself the leading position at court.

As soon as they learnt that Belsky had closed the Kremlin gates, the boyars hurried there, demanding to be admitted. The Streltsi, guarding the gates, refused. Somehow Mstislavsky and Romano-vich Yuriev gained entry, but without the numerous suite of servants that usually accompanied senior boyars. These servants and followers now raised an outcry that Belsky was about to kill their masters. Crowds quickly gathered in the Red Square which with its many market stalls was always one of the busiest parts of the city. Shut out of the Kremlin, the crowds were readily inflamed by rumours. A mob tried to break into the Kremlin. Streltsi opened fire, killing twenty and wounding over a hundred. Men from Ryazan and other towns, led by serving gentry, brought up a large cannon and prepared to blow down the Spasskie Vorota, the tallest and most imposing of the entrance gates. A vast crowd was ready to storm the Kremlin.

Mstislavsky and Romanovich Yuriev had managed, however, to make their way into the Tsar's palace and to seize Belsky. They found the Tsar unharmed. He promptly sent them to calm the mob in the Red Square. They explained to the people that they had been falsely aroused to anger and asked what it was they wanted. The crowd listened attentively and then began shouting: "Give us Bogdan Belsky! He is going to destroy the Tsar's dynasty and the boyar families!"[2] The two boyars went to consult with the Tsar and returned with his message that he had banished Belsky to Nizhny Novgorod. This apparently satisfied the people, for they quietly dispersed. Belsky passed from the scene for several years.

During these uneasy days Boris remained in the background and

he apparently had little power or influence. Nikita Romanovich
Yuriev was generally accepted as the boyar to act as regent for Tsar
Fedor. Boris nevertheless stood high in the affection and respect of
the new Tsar. Fedor had no desire for power and indeed feared it
as leading inevitably to sin. He accepted the throne as a heritage
which he could not reject, but he recognised that he must delegate
his authority. It cannot be known whether he decided to delegate to
Boris or whether his wife, Irina, guided him towards this decision.
She enjoyed wide respect and popularity for her piety and virtue.
She loved her brother, but her devotion to her husband was
complete. She was undoubtedly a woman of great strength of
character, who wielded influence over her husband and was her
brother's close ally. Nevertheless Fedor turned increasingly to
Boris not because of Irina's influence, but more probably because
he trusted him and recognised his outstanding ability.[3]

On the death of Ivan couriers were sent to all parts of the
country to administer new oaths of allegiance. Evidently the
couriers also carried the summons to all leading men, especially
among the serving gentry, to proceed at once to Moscow. Detachments of troops were sent to the key frontier-towns of Kazan,
Astrakhan, Smolensk, Pskov, and Novgorod to relieve or reinforce
the existing garrisons. The leading boyars in Moscow considered
that this was an essential precaution. They actively feared that
the country's enemies, taking the accession of Fedor to mean that
the government was weak and divided, would invade.

On 4 May the assembly of leading men met in Moscow. Jerome
Horsey, who was in the city at this time, called it "a Parliament".[4]
The Metropolitan, archbishops and bishops, abbots and boyars
and all senior serving men took part, in the presence of Fedor.
This assembly was in essence a revival of the Zemsky Sobor which
Ivan had summoned on two momentous occasions in his reign.
Many urgent matters demanded consideration, but foremost
amongst them was the need to ensure that Fedor was formally
crowned without delay. With one voice the assembly begged him
to confirm his acceptance of the throne and to agree to his
coronation at the earliest possible date. Humbly Fedor bowed to
the general will. Muscovite custom required that the deceased Tsar
should be mourned for forty days. The coronation could not take
place until this period had expired. The date agreed was 31 May.

The Uspensky Sobor, the Cathedral of the Assumption of
the Blessed Virgin, was the most sacred in Russia. Around the
walls have been buried all the Metropolitans and Patriarchs of the
Russian Church and in it have been crowned all the Tsars of Russia.
It was not a large cathedral, but the magnificence of the golden

ikonostasis, the richness of the ikons and paintings on the columns, reaching up to the high vaulted ceiling, were renowned.[5]

In preparation for the coronation, Persian carpets and red English cloth were laid along the path to be walked by the Tsar. Velvet canopies were draped over the places to be occupied by dignitaries. From the cathedral entrance, bridges were erected three feet above the ground so that the Tsar could pass in procession unjostled by the crowds, to the adjoining Blagoveshchensky and then to the Arkhangelsky Cathedral where his father, brother, and earlier Muscovite rulers lay in their tombs.

At dawn on 31 May a terrible storm burst upon Moscow. Thunder, lightning, and torrential rains alarmed the crowds already gathering to witness the coronation procession. They were always ready to regard such phenomena as portents of catastrophe. The storm passed, however, and the sun shone on the gilded domes and crosses of the numerous churches of the city. By this time the crowds had grown more dense and as they pressed forward, seeking positions from which to see better, a number of people were crushed to death. It was only with difficulty that armed guards cleared the way to the cathedral for the Tsar's confessor, bearing the coronation regalia, followed by Boris Godunov with the golden orb. It was significant that Boris was already appearing before the people with this sceptre-globe, the symbol of absolute power. At this time the bells of Moscow were tolling, but they were silent as the Tsar moved in procession from the palace to the cathedral.

Fedor wore robes of pale blue and his suite wore robes of gold. Preceded by the Metropolitan and the rest of the church hierarchy, he made his way with slow almost faltering steps. The crowds within the Kremlin watched in prayerful silence as this procession moved slightly above them along the bridges. The only sound at this stage was the resonant singing of the priests and monks who carried the sacred banners and ikons.

Within the Uspensky Cathedral a platform had been erected near the centre of the nave. Here Fedor was crowned with the *Shapka Monomakha* and with the full Byzantine regalia and ceremonial. He held the sceptre-globe in his right hand and the sword of justice in his left, while six crowns, representing his six Tsardoms, were set before him. Boris was prominent throughout the long ceremony, standing close by Fedor's right hand. Nikita Romanovich Yuriev stood near Boris. The other boyars were at a distance.

Jerome Horsey was present at the coronation and was amazed by its magnificence. He wrote that in the cathedral the Tsar wore

an upper robe adorned with precious stones of all sorts, orient
pearls of great quantity . . . it was in weight 200 pounds, the
train and parts thereof were borne by six dukes, his chief
imperial crown upon his head very precious . . . at last the
Emperor came to the great church door and the people cried
"God save our Emperor Fedor Ivanovich of all Russia!" His
horse was there ready most richly adorned with a covering of
embroidered pearls and precious stones, saddle and all furniture
agreeable to it . . .[6]

Horsey noted that Boris again carried the sceptre-globe before
the Tsar as the procession returned to the palace. Almost out-
shining the Tsar himself, "the Lord Boris Fedorovich was sump-
tuously and richly attired with his garments decked with great
orient pearls, beset with all sorts of precious stones . . . In like rich
manner were apparelled all the family of the Godunovs."[7] Other
boyars and their families appeared in all the splendour that they
could command.

The day closed with banquets and the bestowal of gifts and
honours. Boyars, churchmen, leading merchants and the English
and Dutch representatives in Moscow brought rich presents. The
Tsar himself announced measures to celebrate his coronation.
Many who had incurred Ivan's displeasure and were languishing
in prisons or in distant places were freed. As required by his
father's testament, Fedor also ordered the release of prisoners of
war. Taxes which had become an intolerable burden were reduced.

Then came the announcement of honours. Eleven men were
raised to the rank of boyar. They included Princes Andrei and
Vasily Shuisky, and three Godunovs, Stepan, Grigori, and Ivan
Vasilievich Godunov, who were all second cousins of Boris and
Tsaritsa Irina. Prince Ivan Petrovich Shuisky was granted the title
of "Hero" for his defence of Pskov and also an annual income from
the city.

Far exceeding these honours, however, were the rewards which
Fedor showered on Boris. He was made *Konyushy* or Master of
the Horse, an ancient honour which was rarely bestowed. He
received the special title of *Blizhny Veliky Boyarin* or Privy Grand
Boyar, and the governorships of the Tsardoms of Kazan and
Astrakhan. At the same time he was given extensive estates, including some of the best lands in the country. His income from
high offices and from his estates brought him enormous wealth and
great power. Horsey observed that he could mobilise from his own
estates an army of 100,000 men within forty days.[8]

Nikita Romanovich, the Tsar's uncle, who was still his main

guardian, was elderly. In August 1584 he fell seriously ill, probably from a stroke, and he could not take any active part in the government of the country. A close bond existed between him and Boris, both related to the ruling family and representatives of the old untitled Muscovite boyar lines. About this time Nikita entrusted the supervision and protection of his children to Boris, who swore to treat them as his brothers and assistants in government. Boris also had the support of the brothers, Andrei and Vasily Shchelkalovy, who were state counsellors of great ability and prominence. He had in fact already taken over the dominant role of guardian and regent, but he was not yet secure in this position.

Opposed to Boris were the princely boyars who resented the rise of this untitled boyar. Prince Ivan Mstislavsky was nominally leader of this group in which he was supported by the Shuisky, Vorotynsky, and Golovin as well as sections of the gentry and the people of Moscow. There was some plot to dispose of Boris, either by inviting him to a banquet in Mstislavsky's palace and killing him there or in some other way. The plot was discovered. Ivan Mstislavsky was forced to become a monk in the Kirillov monastery. The Vorotynsky, Golovin, and many others were imprisoned or banished to distant places. Prince Mikhail Golovin was in the country at this time and, learning of the fate of his family, he fled to Lithuania and took service with Stefan Batory.

At this time the Shuisky were the real leaders of the conspiracy and of the opposition to the Godunovs generally. More astute than the others, they were not implicated in Mstislavsky's plot and remained free. They enjoyed considerable support among the people of Moscow and had turned many of them against Boris. The tension between the two rival parties of the Godunovs and the Shuisky was evidently felt throughout the country and particularly in the capital. It was reported that a mob in Moscow wanted to stone Boris in the belief that this would force him to come to terms with the Shuisky.[9]

The Metropolitan, Dionysii, tried to mediate. He called Boris and the Shuisky together and implored them to make peace. They bowed to his entreaties. When, however, Prince Ivan Shuisky told a crowd of merchants and traders about the peace, they were sceptical. Two merchants came forward and exclaimed that Boris would now dispose of them all. During the evening these two merchants were seized, presumably on the orders of Boris, and they disappeared.

The Shuisky now prepared a new plan, designed to appeal to the anxiety of the people of Moscow over the future of the dynasty. The plan depended on the removal of Tsaritsa Irina. She was, so the Shuisky and others believed, the real source of Boris's influence over the Tsar. If she could be relegated to a nunnery, the removal of her brother would present no problem. Irina had been pregnant several times, but had either miscarried or her children had been stillborn. The Shuisky now alleged that she was barren. Prince Ivan Shuisky supported by a number of boyars and merchants agreed to petition the Tsar to put away his wife and to marry again in order to have children and to continue the dynasty. Metropolitan Dionysii was persuaded to endorse the petition with all the authority of his high office. The conspirators were evidently confident that the Tsar would feel duty-bound to heed their petition.

The plan miscarried. It involved a presumptuous interference in the family life of the Tsar. The suggestion that the Tsaritsa was barren was insulting. She had conceived many times. Both she and the Tsar were young. She might, and in fact did, have children subsequently. Moreover, the petition assumed that no bonds of affection existed between Fedor and Irina and that he would readily discard her. Nothing is known about Fedor's reaction nor about the manner in which Boris handled the matter. It is clear, however, that he had the Tsar's full support and that he acted as the defender of the autocrat's family life and the dignity of the throne. He could maintain that the Shuisky and their supporters were guilty of treason in inflaming the common people in this way.

Early in 1587 Boris struck against his enemies. Servants of the Shuisky had informed against them. It had come to be recognised that the petition was malicious. Metropolitan Dionysii found himself in a false position in relation to the Tsar and to popular opinion. He was obliged to resign from the Metropolitanate and to retire to a monastery. The Shuisky were arrested together with all their associates. Ample evidence against them was amassed. According to the chronicles of the time, which have to be read with caution, Prince Ivan was banished to Beloozero and Prince Andrei Shuisky was sent to Kargopol, and it was reported that both were strangled soon after reaching their destinations. Fedor Nagoi and six of his comrades who were involved in the conspiracy were beheaded. Others were banished to distant places or were held in prison.[10]

Throughout these troubles Boris behaved with calm dignity as the defender of the Tsar and law and order. He had not acted arbitrarily, ordering public tortures and executions as Tsar Ivan had done on many occasions. He had not appeared as the aggressor, striking down his enemies. In fact, he had been obliged to act defensively for he was not Tsar or even heir to the throne. But it was also Boris's character to act quietly, leaving it to his enemies to put themselves in the wrong.

By the summer of 1587 it was clear that Boris had triumphed over all of his opponents and that there was no one to challenge him. Nikita Romanovich Yuriev had died and his children, known by the surnames of Nikitich and Romanov, were under his protection. The boyars accepted his primacy and the people of Moscow, volatile in their quick-changing moods, had apparently begun to recognise him as the defender of the throne. At the same time, being a devout people of simple faith, they did not dismiss their Tsar as a pious simpleton, but believed that his piety brought upon the Tsardom the special benevolence of God. It was proper that the Tsar wishing to dedicate himself to God should delegate matters of government to Boris, his chosen counsellor. This popular attitude counteracted any suggestion that he was taking advantage of Fedor's unworldliness to usurp the autocratic power.

Boris was anxious, however, not only to entrench his position but also to invest it with an aura of legality and permanence. With the Tsar's approval he began using new and impressive titles. He was "Brother-in-law of the great autocrat, Ruler, Servitor, Master of the Horse". In fact, from about 1588 he was normally referred to as *Pravitel* or Ruler and "His Majesty", and was recognised as the co-ruler of the Tsardom. Further, he was granted the right to conduct relations with foreign governments and to combine his name with that of the Tsar in all state documents. He corresponded directly with the monarchs of other countries. Ambassadors to Moscow were made aware that Boris was the real power and that all affairs were carried on "by the will of the great autocrat but on the orders of his Tsarish Majesty's brother-in-law". His unique position was impressed upon them by the new protocol of the Kremlin. Boris had his own court no less magnificent than that of the Tsar. Ambassadors were received in audience by the Tsar and then independently by Boris at his own court. They brought him gifts and addressed him as "Most Excellent Majesty" and "Most Serene Highness".

With such power, position, and wealth, Boris might have been tempted to displace his Tsar. Fedor was often absent from the capital on pilgrimages to the Troitsa Monastery and other places of special sanctity. He had shed most of the burdens of ruling and devoted himself increasingly to prayer and meditation. For a man as resourceful as Boris it would not have been difficult to dispose of him by poison or some other method. No such thought appears, however, to have entered his mind. He had served Tsar Ivan loyally even at times when he must have felt strongly opposed to his policies or conduct. He now devoted himself to the service of Tsar Fedor and of his country.

Boris attained his great office by virtue of his outstanding abilities, his high standards of conduct and his honesty. His contemporaries recognised his qualities. Ivan Timofeev, a *Dyak* or state secretary, wrote that there were none in Moscow to compare with him in intelligence and ability.[11] A Dutchman, Massa, who was generally hostile towards Boris, nevertheless acknowledged his remarkable competence and amazing memory.[12] It was widely believed, and historians have repeated, that he was illiterate. He was, in fact, well educated by the standards of the time and documents bearing his signature have been preserved.[13] But he was not in any sense a scholar. He was a practical statesman with great knowledge and a broad outlook. He thought deeply and, although imbued with the spirit of old Muscovy, he was interested in cultural and other developments in the West. Indeed, in certain ventures he was to be a forerunner of Peter the Great.

Ivan Timofeev and other contemporaries also paid tribute to his humanity and goodness. He was gentle and courteous to all who approached him, and especially to the poor and rejected. He was the "prompt protector" of all who suffered injustice at the hands of the powerful boyar or landowner. He had grown to manhood during the years of terror in Ivan's reign. Far from having become debauched or his standards debased by this experience, it seemed to have made him resolve to live differently. His court was maintained with full dignity. His own moral standards were high and in later years his bitterest enemies could cast no slur upon his private life. He hated corruption and lawlessness and made strenuous efforts to stamp them out. He struggled to establish order and justice and during the reign of Fedor he achieved some success.

While dealing with the massive problems which were the aftermath of Tsar Ivan's reign, however, Boris could never relax his guard. He had disposed of Mstislavsky and the Shuisky for a time, but a revival of active opposition among the boyars was a continuing threat. He believed evidently that his best defence against such challenges when they came was to provide the country with humane and effective government.

Notes
1. Solovyev, IV, VII, pp. 190–3; Karamzin, IX, VII, Col. 256; S. F. Platonov, *Boris Godunov* (Petrograd, 1921) pp. 23–24.
2. Solovyev, IV, VII, p. 193.
3. Karamzin, X, I, Cols. 9–10.

4. R. Hakluyt, *op. cit.*, II, p. 276.
5. The Uspensky Cathedral has been superbly restored to its former glory. It is maintained, however, as a museum of history and art and inevitably has lost the warmth and vitality of a serving church. The Uspensky Cathedral and the Troitsky Cathedral in the Troitse-Sergiev Monastery in Zagorsk, which are both serving churches and have been restored, and also the Smolensk Cathedral in Novodevichy Monastery, all of which are thronged with worshippers, enable the visitor to envisage the majesty of the services as they were conducted in the Uspensky Cathedral in the Kremlin in the sixteenth century.
6. R. Hakluyt, *op. cit.*, II, pp. 271–2.
7. *Ibid.*
8. *Ibid.* p. 273.
9. Solovyev, IV, VII, p. 195.
10. The chroniclers were without exception hostile to the Godunovs and their accounts, written in the following century and after the new Romanov dynasty had been installed, were often untrustworthy. In this instance it is possible that the Shuisky and their fellows suffered nothing more than being restricted to their country estates and that only their servants were executed. It was a general practice that princes and boyars were punished by banishment, while traders and peasants were punished by death, but Tsar Ivan IV had shown no hesitation in departing from this practice. Solovyev, IV, VII, pp. 196–7. S. F. Platonov *op. cit.*, pp. 28-9.
11. S. F. Platonov, *op. cit.*, p. 34.
12. *Ibid.*
13. *Ibid.* p. 35.

CHAPTER VII

Foreign Affairs in the Reign
of Tsar Fedor

BY THE END OF TSAR IVAN'S REIGN, THE PRESTIGE OF MUSCOVY beyond its frontiers had fallen and the morale of the people was low. The successes of the first part of his reign had been followed by defeats and disasters, for which he himself was largely responsible. The terror and the Oprichnina had dislocated traditional social relationships. Peasants had fled to the south and increasingly to the east leaving towns and villages deserted and depopulating the important central region. Agriculture declined and the army was weakened. The country was near to exhaustion.

Muscovy needed now a period of peace and stability. It could then recover its strength for the renewal of the struggle to gain direct access to the Baltic and the right to trade freely with the West. This was the traditional Muscovite policy, enunciated by Grand Prince Ivan III and followed by Tsar Ivan. It reflected the country's strong, instinctive striving after full membership of the Western comity of nations, which reached a triumphant climax in the reign of Peter the Great early in the eighteenth century. While pursuing this objective, Muscovy had to be on guard against Tatar attacks from the south and to maintain its advance beyond the Ural Mountains which had been gathering momentum since the conquest of Kazan.

Boris recognised these basic purposes, but, unlike Tsar Ivan, he was flexible in pursuing them. He maintained peace and by astute diplomacy he restored Muscovite prestige. He established effective defences against Tatar invasions. He ensured the final conquest of the Siberian Khanate and laid the foundations for the defence and colonisation of Siberia. In effect, he was carrying on the policy that Aleksei Adashev had advocated and Tsar Ivan had overruled. This policy was to give priority to the problem of the Tatars and to the eastward expansion and to avoid for the time being the renewal of the struggle for access to the Baltic and the consequent danger of further war against Poland. Boris consulted regularly with the Boyar Council and he had two able advisers in Dyak Andrei Shchelkalov and, after 1594, in his brother, Vasily, who served as heads of the Foreign Office. But he himself was the directing intelligence and, bearing in mind the short period of his rule, his achievements were remarkable.

At the time of Fedor's coronation two ambassadors were present in Moscow. They were Sir Jeremy Bowes and Lev Sapega. Bowes was in a mood of blustering indignation. He had been restricted to his house since the death of Tsar Ivan and considered his treatment to be a form of persecution. In fact, it was the custom to restrict ambassadors in this way during an interregnum for their own safety. Other foreign representatives received the same treatment. But Bowes complained loudly, blaming everything on the "self-appointed Tsars", as he called Nikita Romanov and Andrei Shchelkalov. Their patience with him was exhausted and, when he was released to return to England, it was without any of the customary respects and ceremonial extended to ambassadors.

In his condemnation of everyone and everything Russian Bowes made an exception of Boris, who was his sole protector. He wrote that "a noble and honourable courtier, a certain Boris Fedorovich ... zealously showed him every favour, but he still does not hold power."[1] Boris also sent Bowes a gift of brocade and sables with the message that he desired close friendship between his country and England. This was the policy which he pursued actively when he obtained power and directed Moscow's foreign policy.

Lev Sapega, the other ambassador in Moscow at this time, represented King Stefan Batory who was still the main threat to Moscow. On learning of Tsar Ivan's death, Sapega at once informed the boyars that he could not present his respects to the new Tsar or discuss relations between their countries until he had received his king's instructions. He was not received in audience until 22 June and then with cold formality, for Moscow was expecting Batory to renew hostilities.

Stefan Batory considered that Tsar Ivan's death had put an end to the ten-year armistice, agreed in January 1582. This suited him well, for he was already carried away by a grandiose plan. This plan involved the conquest of the whole of Muscovy, the Caucasus, and Persia and, launched from Asia Minor, the capture of Constantinople and conquest of the Turkish Empire. In this plan Batory had the support of Antonio Possevino and other Jesuits, who in turn had enlisted the keen interest of Pope Sixtus V.

Batory was convinced that the conquest of Muscovy would present no difficulties. The new Tsar was ailing, and he expected that the boyars would be struggling among themselves for power, thus weakening the country further. Mikhail Golovin, who had defected and joined his service, encouraged him in the belief that Muscovy was ready to collapse.

Batory was impatient to march and to capture at least Smolensk as the first step in his plan of conquest. He was held back, however, because he could not gain the support of his nobility. The Polish magnates were more powerful and independent of the throne than the Muscovite nobility who had been subordinated to the rule of the Tsar. Batory could not impose his policies on the Polish-Lithuanian magnates, but had to win their approval in the Seym. They were united only in their determination not to concede more power and money to the king than was unavoidable. Moreover, wearied by the long campaigns against Muscovy, they were in no mood to embark on a new war and Batory's ambitious policy made little appeal to them.

From Moscow, Mikhail Izmailov had been sent as envoy to inform the king of the coronation of Tsar Fedor. The Poles were arrogant and deliberately humiliated him, but he behaved with restraint. On his return Izmailov reported that Batory had wanted to declare war immediately on receiving the news of the Tsar's death. The Seym had withheld its support, for the further reason that Poland was suffering from a failure of the harvest and from famine. While seeking to inspire the magnates to embark on a new campaign, Batory resumed negotiations with the Muscovite embassy which arrived in Poland in January 1585. Its leader, Boyar Prince Troekurov, had instructions to be courteous and flexible, especially exploiting every difference between Batory and his nobles. Muscovy still needed peace desperately. He was therefore to avoid a breakdown in the negotiations, but when ever occasion offered he should stress that, while Tsar Fedor was prepared to be conciliatory, he was also ready to attack as well as to defend his tsardom.

After the exchange of formalities, Batory made demands for the surrender of Smolensk, Severiya, Novgorod, and Pskov, and threatened to break off negotiations if these cities were not conceded. He agreed in the end to an armistice for two years, expiring on 3 June, 1587. Further exchanges of envoys and of demands and counter-demands, led in August 1586 to an agreement to extend the armistice for two months. On 2 December, 1586, however, Batory died, and Poland-Lithuania entered upon a confused period.

In Moscow the immediate reaction to this event was to do all possible to have Tsar Fedor elected to his throne. The lesson of the previous election had not been forgotten. Tsar Ivan had been offhand towards efforts to advance him or his son towards the throne. Then he had been contemptuous about the election of the little-known Hungarian. But Stefan Batory had inflicted disastrous defeats upon his armies and had wrested from him the important Baltic lands.

Tsar Fedor's boyars were eager now that he himself should be elected to the throne or that, failing him, Archduke Maximilian, brother of the Habsburg Emperor, Rudolph II, should be king of Poland-Lithuania. They were determined to prevent the election of Crown Prince Sigismund, son of King John of Sweden. The danger, as seen in Moscow, was that he would unite Sweden and Poland-Lithuania, the two chief enemies of Muscovy in the west.

Two powerful factions, one supporting Maximilian, and the other Sigismund, divided Poland-Lithuania. As 30 June, 1587, the day of the meeting of the election Seym, approached, the two parties threatened to plunge the country into a bloody civil war. Support for the election of Tsar Fedor nevertheless mounted. Apart from the Orthodox Lithuanians and other sections of the population which had special reasons for wanting the Tsar elected king, there was increasing support among Poles who were unwilling to see their country dominated by one or other of the powerful factions.

In the event the Muscovites mishandled the election. Envoys from Moscow did not come with ample money and gifts to buy votes among the Polish magnates, as was expected of them, nor was the Tsar prepared to travel to Poland as requested. In negotiations with members of the Seym, the Muscovites were merely obstinate. They stated bluntly that if elected the Tsar would not live in Poland or in Lithuania, would not change his faith, and would be unlikely to make concessions to the nobility or to any other section of the nation. Moreover, they laid down conditions which were patently unacceptable to the Poles.

The election procedures were complex. At one stage both Sigismund and Maximilian were declared elected by their factions. But Sigismund's party gained increasing support until he was declared king and on 16 December (1587) crowned in Cracow. This was a setback for Moscow, but the disappointment was lessened by the fact that in August 1587 an armistice for fifteen years had been concluded with the Polish Seym. Moreover, at the beginning of 1591 an embassy from Sigismund confirmed the armistice. This was especially important because it relieved Moscow of the threat of Polish attack at a time when war against Sweden appeared inevitable.

Muscovite policy after the death of Tsar Ivan was to avoid hostilities with Sweden while there was danger of attack by Poland-Lithuania. For this reason Moscow was eager to negotiate a new peace, notwithstanding grave Swedish discourtesies, such as deliberate failure in state documents to address Fedor as Tsar and to use his full titles. In October 1585 Boyar Prince Fedor Shestunov and Dumny Dvoryanin (Counsellor) Ignatii Tatishchev met Swedish representatives at the mouth of the Plyussa River not far from Narva. The discussions were heated and nearly broke down several times over the excessive demands made by both sides. Finally an armistice for four years was agreed.

In the summer of 1589 negotiations between Moscow and Stockholm began afresh. But at this time the Muscovite envoys acted more boldly. Batory was dead and Poland-Lithuania was bound by a fifteen-year armistice. Another important factor was that Sweden was torn by internal strife. The exchanges became threatening. The Muscovites insisted on the return of Narva, Ivangorod, Yam, Koporie, and Korela as the price of peace. Finally the Muscovite plenipotentiary declared bluntly: "If our sovereign has not recovered his patrimony namely the towns of Livonia and of the Novgorod land, why should he make peace with your sovereign?"[2] The Swedes again rejected these demands.

In January 1590, immediately on expiry of the armistice, a large Muscovite army crossed the Swedish frontier. Tsar Fedor was at the head of his troops, accompanied by Boris Godunov and Fedor Romanov. Yam, Ivangorod and Koporie were captured, but strenuous efforts to take Narva failed. The Swedes were, however, in no condition to continue the war. They were troubled by famine and plague and John, who had proved a disastrous king, was in direct conflict with his nobles. The Muscovites, having failed to take Narva, were prepared to sign an armistice for one year. But their campaigning had impressed both the Swedes and also the Poles and Lithuanians. Tsar Fedor whom all had dismissed as a pious weakling had personally led his army. The Muscovites had not hesitated to attack and defeat an enemy who had been victorious against Ivan the Terrible.

In 1592 King John died and Sigismund, King of Poland-Lithuania, succeeded him as King of Sweden. His reign was brief. He antagonised the Swedish people by his hostility towards Protestantism and in other ways until he was soon as unpopular there as he was in Poland. His uncle, Karl, became regent on the return of Sigismund to Poland, and he was soon gaining the support of the Swedish people.

In these circumstances the Swedes were eager for peace with

Ivan the Terrible, from a portrait on wood, painted in the late
sixteenth or early seventeenth century (The Copenhagen Museum)

ц҃рь велиѡкїи кн҃зь   борⷭ҇ феодорокичь

Boris Godunov (The State Historical Museum, Moscow)

Boris Godunov (The Museum of the History and
Reconstruction of Moscow)

Tsarevich Dmitri.
From the *Grand State Book*
1672 (The State Historical
Museum, Moscow)

The False Dmitri
(The State Historical
Museum, Moscow)

The two sides of the
Seal of Boris Godunov
(The Ashmolean Museum,
Oxford)

Chain armour of Boris Godunov
(The Armoury, Moscow)

The throne of
Boris Godunov
(The Armoury, Moscow)

The carriage presented
as a gift from Queen
Elizabeth I of England
to Boris Godunov
(The Armoury, Moscow)

Burial place of
Tsarevich Dmitri,
Arkhangelsky Cathedral,
The Kremlin

Tomb of Ivan IV,
Arkhangelsky Cathedral,
The Kremlin

Muscovy. There had been inconclusive fighting in 1591 and 1592, but in January 1593 a two-year armistice was agreed and later in the same year negotiations for a permanent peace began. The Muscovites surrendered their claims to Narva, while the Swedes conceded the ancient Novgorod lands from the Narova River to Korela. Although only a partial victory, Moscow was pleased with the peace and the territorial gains which it confirmed, and particularly the districts of Ingria and Karelia, providing an outlet to the Gulf of Finland. It meant that Muscovite trade in the Baltic still had to pass through Swedish territory and in particular through Narva. But Boris was concerned to advance cautiously and to avoid Tsar Ivan's mistake of demanding all at once.

Relations between Moscow and Vienna, and also Prague where the Emperor lived at this time, were friendly and conducted with great dignity and exact observation of protocol. This gave the Muscovites satisfaction, especially as the Habsburg court was regarded as the most senior in Europe and accepted as the arbiter in such matters. Always exceptionally sensitive about protocol, they felt that the prestige of the Tsar was enhanced by the punctilious respect shown him by the imperial court.

Diplomatic exchanges between the two courts were complex and their purposes were sometimes obscure. They were in close contact after the death of Batory, because both Tsar Fedor and Archduke Maximilian were candidates for the throne of Poland-Lithuania. But Emperor Rudolf had a further purpose. He was convinced that Tsar Ivan had made provision in his last testament that in the event of Tsar Fedor dying without heir, the house of Habsburg was to be considered first as the source of a new Tsar. This prospect of a dynastic union appealed strongly to the Emperor who saw in it a means of conquering the Ottoman Empire. No such testamentary provision has been found. At the time, however, it gave rise to many rumours. The fact that in the elections to the Polish-Lithuanian throne, Moscow undertook to support the candidacy of Maximilian was taken by many to signify that Moscow favoured union with the Habsburg dynasty.

Boris himself valued the diplomatic relations with the imperial court in which he was always shown respect, similar to that shown to the Tsar. But he was more concerned about the Emperor's support against Poland-Lithuania and especially against the Crimean Khan and the Turkish Sultan. The Empire also suffered from Tatar attacks. It was clearly in the interest of both countries that they should act jointly against these common enemies. To this end Moscow sent material aid to the Emperor in the form of valuable furs, but he could never be brought to action. Boris was not impressed when in 1597 the Emperor asked that the Tsar should send him money rather than furs. The Muscovite ambassador, Bestuzhev-Ryumin, expressed the view of his court when he wrote that "in general they were dissatisfied that the Emperor talked much of his allies, but no action of any kind resulted."[3]

Moscow remained on guard against the Crimean Tatars. Tsar Ivan's conquest of Kazan and Astrakhan had intensified Tatar hostility towards the Russians. It had also involved the Turkish Sultan who was feared throughout Europe. In 1569 he had mobilised a large army on the Don with the object of seizing the portage stretch on the Volga at Tsaritsyn (Stalingrad, now Volgograd) and advancing from there to capture Astrakhan. This operation had failed, but further action by the Turks to recover Astrakhan was expected.

The Crimean Tatars had usually struck towards the centre of Muscovy. Their greatest success had been in 1571 when they had reached the walls of Moscow and had burnt the city to the ground, leaving only the Kremlin standing. This invasion and the resulting devastation had stunned the Muscovites. It led, however, to extensive defence measures, including the creation of a *dikoe pole* or wild steppeland region, a kind of protective no-man's-land on Muscovy's southern frontiers, which were further strengthened by the erection of fortresses and fortified towns.

The main responsibility for carrying out these defence works fell to Boris who was an enthusiastic builder. He directed the erection of the towns of Kursk, Kromy, and the occupation of the banks of the Bystraya Sosna River as well as the building of the towns of Livny, Elets, and Chernavsky. Also the line of the Oskol River was secured by the erection of the towns of Oskol and Valuiki. He was responsible for building the important towns of Voronezh on the Don and Voronezh Rivers and Belgorod on the Donets River. This network of fortified towns dominated the lines of communication in the upper steppe region and at the same time secured a vast area of land as part of Muscovy. Moreover, the network closed the Tatar invasion route. The Khan could advance on Moscow in future only if he had an overwhelming superiority of arms.

During the years 1584–88 the Crimean Tatars were taken up with internal rivalries and were frequently under attack by Cossacks. The Khan, Mahomet Girei, was murdered by his brother, Islam Girei, who had the support of a detachment of Janissaries, provided by the Sultan. The sons of Mahomet Girei, Saidet and Murat, were expelled by their uncle. They returned in the following year, however, with a force of 15,000 Nogai Tatars and ejected Islam Girei, seizing his wives and treasure. Two months later with Turkish troops Islam Girei defeated his nephews and again became Khan. Saidet and Murat sought asylum in Muscovy which was readily granted. Saidet was permitted to live with the Nogai Horde near Astrakhan. Murat was summoned to Moscow where he was treated generously by Tsar Fedor and Boris. He then settled in Astrakhan, where he called himself *Vladyka* or Lord of the four rivers—Don, Volga, Yaik, and Terek.

It was a bold act of policy to allow the two Tatar princes to settle in this region where the Nogai were restive and unreliable. They might have seized Astrakhan and have established a separate Khanate. But this decision by Boris, who was usually cautious, was amply justified. Murat and Saidet both served Moscow zealously. Murat put an end to unruliness among the Nogai who became obedient subjects of the Tsar. He persuaded them to accept also that the Tsar had built the towns of Samara and Ufa for their security and to keep the Cossacks under control.

Islam Girei knew that his nephews were determined to overthrow him. He was unpopular with his people and had to rely on Turkish support. He wrote to the Tsar, demanding the surrender of Saidet and Murat, which was refused. The Khan also complained about the Cossacks, equally without result. The Zaporozhsky Cossacks from their *Sech* or headquarters at the rapids on the Dniepr River had carried out daring and successful raids into the Khanate. The Cossacks of the Don and the Terek Rivers preyed on the Tatars and also on the Turks. The Khan wrote in hurt tones to Boris that

Your Don Cossacks harry the town of Azov; your same Cossacks from the Don and from Samara have come by stealth to the Ovechii waters to our *ulus* [camp] and they steal cattle. The Sultan has written to me that he has lost money, that he took the town of Derbent but now his people have no route from Azov to Derbent: Russian Cossacks who live on the Terek at the portages and narrow places, attack them; the Sultan cannot suffer this to happen and with his great army he wants to take the town and to make war on Moscow.[4]

In 1588 Islam Girei died. His successor, Kazy Girei, protested friendship and asked the Tsar for money on the ground that he was about to march against Moscow's enemy, Lithuania. Exchanges dragged on until June 1591 when it was learnt in Moscow that the Khan was advancing with a vast army not into Lithuania but against Moscow itself. Bypassing the new fortress towns, the

Tatars moved fast on their sturdy horses. By the evening of 1 July Muscovite troops which had been hurriedly recalled from Novgorod and Pskov, where they were standing in readiness for a Swedish invasion, were drawn up before Kolomenskoe to the south of Moscow. On the following day the Tsar joined his army. Boris shared the supreme command with Prince Fedor Mstislavsky, who held office by virtue of family seniority. Boris was determined that the Tatars should be halted before they reached Moscow. Hurriedly fortifications were erected and monasteries were converted into strongholds. Between the Kaluga and Tula routes a small fortified town on wheels was built.

On 3 July news came that the Khan and his army had crossed the Oka River and were moving rapidly towards Moscow. Inconclusive skirmishing took place, but as he approached the city on the following day the Khan was astonished to find that the main Russian army, which he thought was far away to the west, was drawn up in strong defensive positions. The Tatar forces came under fire from Russian cannon which, on the orders of Boris, maintained their fire steadily into the night. The Tatars were demoralised and, without waiting until the dawn, the Khan ordered the retreat, abandoning all supplies. Russian detachments, sent to overtake the retreating Tatars, could not catch up with the main force, but destroyed the rear guard near Tula.

The Russian army then moved from its entrenched positions as far south as Serpukhov. Here on 10 July Prince Kozlovsky came from Moscow, bearing a severe reprimand to Mstislavsky, because in his despatches to the Tsar he had written in his own name, making no mention of Boris. Later on the same day *Stolnik* (Court Official) Ivan Nikitich Romanov arrived bringing the Tsar's congratulations to the army on its victory over the Tatars and rewards of gold for Boris and Mstislavsky and other commanders. On his return to Moscow, Boris was rewarded further with a fur coat from the Tsar's shoulders, with a gold chain and plate, three towns, and the title of *Sluga,* or Servitor, an unusual rank which stood above that of boyar. Other commanders received gifts, but it was clear from the scale of awards that Fedor considered Boris to have been the main author of the victory over the Tatars.

In May 1592 the Crimean Tatars devastated vast areas of the Ukraine as far north as Ryazan and Tula, as though seeking vengeance for their ignominious repulse from the capital. The Muscovites no longer feared the Tatars, however, as they had in the past. As they advanced into the Caucasus they were more concerned with the danger of military conflict with the mighty Ottoman Porte.

Russian penetration of the Caucasus region, where Turkey and Persia guarded their spheres of interest, began after the capture of Astrakhan in 1554. Until the eighteenth century, however, this penetration was limited to the northern region along the line of the Terek River. The southward advance brought Muscovy into conflict with the Turks who made use of the Crimean Tatars and the fierce tribes of Daghestan against them.

The Turks showed special concern over Moscow's efforts to establish a stronghold on the Terek River. The first attempt was in 1563, soon after Tsar Ivan's marriage with Maria, daughter of Prince Temryuk Aydorovich of Kabarda, who had placed himself under Moscow's protection. Two or three further attempts were made to build this stronghold. The Sultan and the Khan regarded this as an encroachment and a hostile act directed against them. They were not mollified by the Tsar's explanation that it was intended to protect Temryuk against his enemies. Boris evidently took a special interest in the erection of this fortified town which was firmly established in 1587–88.

The second complaint made by the Sultan and the Khan concerned the unbridled activities of the Cossacks of the Terek. The free Cossacks, composed mainly of fugitives from Muscovy who had intermarried to some extent with women from Turkic tribes, were constantly raiding and disrupting trade on the Terek and Don Rivers. The Sultan inveighed against them, especially when they ventured into the Sea of Azov and even the Black Sea in their small boats, known as *Chaykas,* and attacked Turkish shipping.[5]

In July 1584, the Tsar's ambassador, Blagov, had travelled to Constantinople to notify the Sultan of Tsar Fedor's coronation and of his desire for peace and friendly relations. He was assailed by Turkish complaints about the Cossacks. He replied boldly: "You yourselves know that on the Terek and the Don live vagabonds, fugitives beyond my sovereign's control who obey no one, and what can I do about the Cossacks?"[6] Muscovite officials consistently disclaimed responsibility. In fact, they quietly encouraged the Cossacks to harry the Turks and Tatars. The danger was that the Sultan, rejecting the Russian plea that the Cossacks were outside the Tsar's control, might declare war. Thus on Boris's instructions Blagov gave promises that the stronghold on the Terek would be razed to the ground and that the Cossacks would be swept from the region. Boris had no intention of implementing either promise, but was anxious to restrain the Cossacks for a time while he prepared new plans to expand Moscow's influence in the Caucasus.

In April 1592, Boris sent Nashchokin at the head of an embassy to Constantinople. He was instructed to call on the Cossacks en route and to request them in the Tsar's name to live in peace with the peoples of the Azov region and to release their Turkish prisoners, while the embassy was in Constantinople. The Cossacks rejected both proposals.[7]

The Sultan received the embassy and was apparently prepared to continue peace talks. He was proposing to send his own ambassador to Moscow for this purpose, when reports reached him that the Don Cossacks had attacked Azov, taking 150 prisoners, and that the Tsar had built four new towns on the Don and Terek Rivers. The Grand Vizir angrily exclaimed to Nashchokin: "Is this the love that your sovereign has for ours? This is a reason to draw sabres rather than to make friends!"[8] Anger cooled, however, and talks continued.

Moscow's intervention into the Caucasus was formally justified by the fact that the Orthodox Georgians had asked for the Tsar's protection. Georgia had been a united and flourishing kingdom. The Mongol onslaught in the thirteenth century and the invasion of Tamburlaine in the fourteenth century had destroyed its unity. The country became divided into the rival kingdoms of Kakheti, Kartli, and Imereti and several small independent principalities. The Turks and Tatars were prompt to take advantage of Georgia's weakness. In 1555 the Sultan and the Shah formally agreed on their respective zones of interest.

In his efforts to maintain his kingdom, Alexander, King of Kakheti, sent his ambassador to Moscow in 1586 to declare his allegiance to the Tsar. He was readily taken under Moscow's protection. Boris made every effort to strengthen communications between Astrakhan and Georgia and for this purpose erected a new town at the mouth of the Terek River. The *Shevkal* or Lord of Daghestan, lying to the north of Georgia, dominated the route from Astrakhan into Georgia. On two occasions Boris sent expeditions against him. In 1593 Prince Andrei Khvorostinin was instructed to erect two strongholds in the region, but his forces were defeated and Boris's plans were thwarted.

At this time when the Kakhian king was seeking Moscow's protection, the Persian Shah was proposing alliance with Muscovy against the Sultan. In 1586 the Shah's army suffered a major defeat by the Turks. Desperate for the Tsar's support, the Shah offered to cede not only Baku and Derbent but also to recognise his sovereignty over Kakheti. But nothing came of the Persian proposals.

In Siberia, Boris was faced with the task of re-establishing the Tsar's authority. Ermak and his Cossacks had been weakened by famine during the winter of 1583–84. Kuchum, the Siberian Khan, who had been defeated, had mustered troops and had taken the Cossacks by surprise in their camp on the bank of the Irtysh River. Ermak himself was drowned in the river. In August 1584 the remnants of the small Cossack force abandoned the town of Sibir and began to make their way back to Moscow. Kuchum and then Seidyak, who displaced him, set about uniting the peoples of the vast region under the rule of the Khan.

Boris had no intention of allowing Siberia to pass out of Moscow's control. At the beginning of 1586 he sent a detachment of troops there with the purpose of building fortified towns at strategic points. This was the usual Muscovite method of establishing the Tsar's rule over new territories and it proved effective in Siberia. Tyumen was built on the bank of the Tura River in the summer of 1586 and in the following year Tobolsk on the Irtysh, which was soon known as the chief city or regional capital. Tatars made several vain attempts to capture Tobolsk and to compel the Russians to withdraw. But under Boris's direction Moscow's hold on the Siberian lands was rapidly strengthened. New towns began to spring up, ensuring control over the main lines of communication. In 1593 Pelym, Berezov, and Obdorsk were built, in 1596 Narymsky Ostrog (Stronghold) and Ketsky Ostrog, in 1598 Verkhoture, in 1600 Turinsky Ostrog, in 1601 Mangazeye, and in 1604 Tomsk. Moreover, Boris guarded this new land jealously as was demonstrated in his rejection of an English request to be allowed to travel and trade as far to the east as the Pechora and Ob Rivers.

With England, relations were constantly disturbed by bickering to which both sides contributed. Relations would have declined seriously but for the patience and frequent intercession of Boris. He showed favour to the English whereas Tsar Fedor came near to breaking off talks on several occasions. From the start he was unwilling to renew the generous privileges granted by his father. These privileges, which Thomas Randolph had obtained in 1569, had given the Russia Company the monopoly of the trade with Russia without payment of duty and also the right to travel through Russia in order to trade with Persia and countries farther afield. During Fedor's reign, Queen Elizabeth made frequent but unavailing efforts to recover this favourable position for the Company. She was relieved, however, that Moscow made no attempt to renew the embarrassing demands which Tsar Ivan had pressed so obstinately.

In May 1584, soon after the death of Tsar Ivan, Fedor granted new privileges to the Company. Sir Jeremy Bowes apparently knew nothing of them and, since he had made himself hated in Moscow, negotiations were presumably carried on directly with the Company's agents. The new privileges were but a shadow of the old. The Company lost its monopoly and duty-free trade and other rights. It was favoured only in being able to trade on payment of half-duty. In December 1584 Fedor sent his interpreter, Reynold Beckman, to London with a letter to the queen, informing her of this privilege. At the same time he complained strongly of Bowe's "uncomely dealing".[9] In reply to Elizabeth's letter carried back to Moscow by Beckman, he renewed his complaints and made numerous charges against the Company's servants.

In March 1586 Elizabeth sent a letter with Jerome Horsey, who spoke Russian and was experienced in dealing with the Russian court. He was laden with presents for the Tsar and for Boris, including dogs, lions, bulls, pistols, armour, wines, drugs, organs, virginals, "perrell chaines", plate, and "other costly things of great value".[10] Horsey also carried a letter from Elizabeth to Tsaritsa Irina, in which she wrote that she was sending "an expert and tried midwife" as well as Dr Robert Jacob, "a trustworthy man already known to you".[11] This led to misunderstanding and was greatly resented by the Tsar. Anxious about his sister's failure to bear a son and heir to the throne, Boris had asked Horsey to procure "soom doctoritza that had skill in women's matters, to make them conceive". Horsey evidently misunderstood the request. The midwife was sent home. The Tsar was to hold this incident against Horsey. At the time of this visit, however, Horsey was received with all courtesies and in 1587 he obtained new privileges for the Company. The monopoly was not restored, but full exemption from customs duties was granted. Numerous minor matters, mainly concerning the remission of debts charged to the Company, were also settled. Horsey made other claims, which cannot be substantiated, and it has to be borne in mind that he was always prone to exaggerate his achievements.

The Company was dissatisfied. It stubbornly pursued the two former privileges, namely the monopoly of the White Sea trade and also the monopoly of English trade with Russia. Indeed, the Company seemed most disturbed by the fact that English merchants, not among its members, were allowed to trade in Russia. In June 1588 Giles Fletcher was sent as ambassador, bearing letters from Elizabeth to the Tsar and to Boris, pressing for the Company's monopoly of English trade and asking that English merchants who did not belong to the Company should be returned to England.

Giles Fletcher was received with scant courtesy and Elizabeth was to complain later that he was treated "so basely as the lyke hath not ben shewed and used to our princely highness by any Prince in Europe".[12] In the summer of 1589, however, Fletcher returned to England with a new grant of privileges, but it did not revive the old monopolies or add to the privileges conceded in 1587. The Company was stated to have exemption from half customs duties only, but, due to Boris's intervention, it paid no duty. In their letters of reply, however, both the Tsar and Boris urged Elizabeth to open the Russian trade to all of her merchants.

Fletcher had difficulty in recovering the expenses of his mission from the Company and had to appeal to the Privy Council. But he also disturbed the Company by publishing in 1591 a graphic and highly critical book on Russia, entitled *Of the Russe Commonwealth, or Maner of Government of the Russe Emperor,* which he dedicated to the queen.[13] The Company complained at once to Lord Burghley that the book would incur the Tsar's anger and damage relations with Russia. The book was suppressed, but by good fortune a few copies survived.

Elizabeth was greatly displeased by the treatment of Fletcher in Moscow and by the outcome of his mission. She wrote an angry letter, filled with bitter complaints, and chose as her envoy Jerome Horsey, knowing well that the Tsar detested him and had stated on his departure from Moscow in 1589 that he deserved death for his misconduct. The Company, too, was disturbed by the choice of Horsey. It had described him as "a principall mover of all the disturbances which have fallen amongst our people in Russia". Indeed for reasons which are not known, Horsey seemed to have been discredited among all who knew him except the queen, Burghley, and Boris himself.[14]

Horsey's mission was, not unexpectedly, a failure. The Tsar refused to receive him, and in a letter written in July 1591 he protested strongly about Elizabeth's continued employment of such a man. Elizabeth's next letter was conciliatory, although still containing complaints. In May 1596, thanks to the good offices of Boris, however, new privileges were granted to the Company. This time the immunity from customs duties was confirmed, but the Company failed to regain its monopoly of the northern route and the right to trade with Persia through Russia.

By this time Elizabeth and the Company were more or less resigned to the restricted privileges and accepted that the old monopolies of Tsar Ivan's reign would never be recovered. Elizabeth wrote now to Fedor, expressing her appreciation that he had granted to "our merchants more privileges than the foreigners of all other countries".[15] To Boris she wrote in warmest terms of gratitude for his "love and goodwill" and for the fact that Fedor "our most dear and beloved brother" had been "blessed that God has given him such a counsellor" whose "great understanding and zeal" had "increased the love between us".[16] Although expressed in fulsome terms, this tribute was just. Boris had guarded the interests of his country. He recognised that in the expanding trade by the northern route the English monopolies had to be restricted, but by personal diplomacy he had retained the goodwill of the queen and maintained the basic good relations between the two countries.

Notes

1. T. S. Willan, *The Early History of the Russia Company 1553–1603* (Manchester, 1956).
2. Solovyev, IV, VII, p. 232.
3. S. F. Platonov, *Boris Godunov* (Petrograd, 1921) p. 49.
4. Solovyev, IV, VII, p. 262.
5. W. E. D. Allen, *Russian Embassies to the Georgian Kings 1589–1605* (Hakluyt Society, Cambridge, 1970) I, p. 3.
6. Solovyev, IV, VII, p. 272.
7. *Ibid.* pp. 274–77.
8. *Ibid.* p. 276.
9. T. S. Willan, *op. cit.*, p. 167.
10. E. A. Bond (Ed.) *Russia at the close of the 16th Century* (Hakluyt Society, London, 1856) p. 217.
11. *Ibid.* p. lxviii.
12. G. Tolstoy, *The First Forty Years of Intercourse between England and Russia 1553–93* (St. Petersburg, 1875) p. 364.
13. Giles Fletcher's book has been edited and published in *Russia at the Close of the 16th Century* edited by E. A. Bond (Hakluyt Society, London, 1856).
14. In a historical novel, *The Muscovite,* written by Alison Macleod (London and Boston, 1971), Jerome Horsey is portrayed as the hero. The novel gives a convincing description of the period, but failed to convince this author that Horsey was anything but a rogue.
15. T. S. Willan, *op. cit.*, p. 225.
16. *Ibid.* p. 226.

CHAPTER VIII

The Patriarchate, 1589

THE CREATION OF THE RUSSIAN PATRIARCHATE WAS THE FIRST MAJOR political achievement which gained for Boris the acclaim of his contemporaries. It won for him also the abiding gratitude of Tsar Fedor. To a people so devout and committed to their Church, it was an event of tremendous significance.

On conversion to Orthodox Christianity towards the end of the tenth century, Russia became a metropolitanate under the rule of the Patriarch of Constantinople. He consecrated the Metropolitans who were almost invariably Greeks. When at a later period Russians came to be appointed to this high office, it was not questioned that the Patriarch of Constantinople alone had the power of consecration. In 1300 the Metropolitans had moved their see from Kiev to Vladimir and later to Moscow. The laws and conventions of the Russian Church remained unchanged during the Mongol-Tatar occupation, and the role of the Patriarch continued.

For some years, however, Constantinople had been negotiating with Rome on the possibility of the reunion of the Eastern and Western Churches. The Russians, who regarded Rome and the papacy with hostility, were troubled and suspicious about these negotiations. In 1436 the Patriarch of Constantinople consecrated Isidor, a Bulgarian or a Greek, as Metropolitan, having rejected Jonah, the candidate of the Muscovite Grand Prince. Isidor arrived in Moscow to take up his office and five months later he set out for the Council of Florence as the representative of the Russian Church. There he championed the reunion of the Churches and with the title of Cardinal and Papal Legate he returned triumphantly to Moscow in March 1441. One of his first acts was to conduct mass in the Uspensky Cathedral after which he proclaimed the reunion of the Eastern and Western Churches. The Muscovites were horrified. Isidor was arrested and imprisoned in a monastery. Early in 1442 he fled from Muscovy, fortunate to escape with his life.

In effect the Russian Church declared its independence when in 1448 a council of Russian bishops and senior clergy elected Jonah, one of its number, to be Metropolitan in succession to Isidor. Normally this would have brought denunciations from Constantinople, but in 1453 the Turks captured the city. All Russians saw this as an act of divine justice and the punishment of Byzantium for its betrayal of the Christian faith at the Council of Florence. But since its foundation Muscovy had drawn on the inspiration of Byzantium and it could not break suddenly from these traditions. It was recognised that the Tsar and the Patriarch must be the two pillars of the nation, and the absence of a Russian patriarch had been regretted by all at the coronations of Tsars Ivan and Fedor. Indeed, in expressing approval of Ivan's formal adoption of the title of Tsar, the Patriarch of Constantinople had emphasised that he alone had the power to crown the Tsar. The Turkish conquest of Byzantium had left Muscovy, however, as the sole independent Orthodox country. It had inherited the mission of preserving true Christianity. Moscow was the third Rome and the logical seat of the Russian Patriarch. On national as well as on religious grounds there was an urgent desire among all classes of the people that the country should have its own patriarchate.

The problem was how to attain this objective. The fact that a council of Russian bishops and clergy had elected Jonah as Metropolitan in 1448 evidently could not serve as a precedent for creating a patriarchate. In 1586 the Patriarch of Antioch, Ioakim, arrived in Moscow. This was an important event. Greek priests came regularly for alms and subsidies on which the Eastern patriarchates were largely dependent, but never before had a patriarch visited Moscow. Ioakim was treated with profound respect. The Tsar received him with great ceremony. No full record of his discussions in Moscow has survived. It is clear, however, that Tsar Fedor talked with his wife and close boyars about the creation of a patriarchate in Moscow. He then entrusted to Boris the task of conveying the Tsar's wishes to the Patriarch. Evidently as a result of these approaches Ioakim promised to raise the matter with his brother patriarchs and the archbishops and bishops of the sacred council. The Tsar and the boyars were satisfied that this important matter would be advanced rapidly. On his departure a special envoy set out with Ioakim with instructions to approach the other patriarchs and to hasten their approval. But Moscow's hopes were premature. The Eastern patriarchs jealously guarded their position. They wanted subsidies from Moscow, but had no wish to strengthen the Russian Church in this way.

In 1588, the Patriarch of Constantinople, Ieremiya, arrived in

Russia. The Tsar and Boris had been expecting ambassadors and documents, creating the new patriarchate. The arrival of the supreme prelate of the Orthodox Church was extraordinary. Tsar Fedor was not sure whether to believe it. He ordered discreet enquiries to establish the purpose of his journey and whether he was indeed the Patriarch of Constantinople. In particular he wanted to know what had happened to Ieremiya's predecessor, who had in fact been deposed by the Sultan. Having established that this was truly the Constantinople Patriarch, the Tsar and all Moscow waited expectantly for his proposals for consecrating a Russian patriarch. Ieremiya was received with adulation and the most magnificent ceremonial. Never before had Moscow welcomed such a guest. The Muscovites were astonished, however, to learn that he had come only for alms and that he brought no word concerning their own patriarchate.

His presence nevertheless provided the opportunity to press the matter further. A plan was devised, probably by Boris himself and certainly carried through by him, whereby Ieremiya would be held in Moscow until he agreed to establish the Russian patriarchate or at least solemnly promised to summon the supreme council of the Orthodox Church to approve it immediately on his return to Constantinople.

Ieremiya was magnificently housed and treated with deepest respect. Boris, whom the Tsar had entrusted with all dealings with him, visited him frequently for confidential talks. The Patriarch was moved by his treatment in Moscow. He talked to Boris about his hardships under Turkish rule. The Sultan had arrested him, removed him from the patriarchal throne and then had restored him. The Orthodox Church had been impoverished by Turkish depredations. He and his fellow Christians lived in misery. Gradually he was brought to discussion of the Tsar's request. He told Boris that he alone could not create the Russian patriarchate. He was indebted to the Tsar, however, for great kindness and for support for his Church. He suggested that this difficult problem might be resolved if he himself remained in Moscow as Patriarch.

This proposal was discussed by the Tsar and his boyars. The Tsar's reply was that "if the Constantinople Patriarch, Ieremiya, wishes to be in our Tsardom, then he may be Patriarch in the original see of Vladimir, while in Moscow the Metropolitan will continue as before; if the Constantinople Patriarch does not wish to be in Vladimir, then in Moscow a patriarch is to be appointed from the Moscow hierarchy".[1]

Boris reported the Tsar's ruling to Ieremiya who objected strenuously. Vladimir, long neglected and crumbling in ruins, seemed more fitting as a place of exile than as the residence of the Patriarch. He asserted that the Patriarch must be at the side of the autocrat. But he confirmed his readiness to remain in Moscow where the magnificence of the Tsar's court attracted him. He was in no hurry to return to the penury and persecution of Constantinople. For their part the Tsar and Boris well knew that the Patriarch must be in Moscow and at the side of the autocrat. But they would not accept as their first patriarch a Greek who knew no Russian and had to communicate through an interpreter.

Six months passed. During this time Boris carried on countless discussions with Ieremiya, going over church history and precedents, and moving slowly towards the decision that the Tsar and all Russians wanted. Finally Boris brought him to agree in principle that he could establish the new patriarchate in Moscow. Once this principle was conceded, the matter moved forward rapidly. Metropolitan Iov was nominated for the patriarchal throne. Ieremiya objected that according to church law the Patriarch must be chosen by the church council. In January 1589 the Russian hierarchy held a solemn meeting and nominated three candidates from whom the Tsar chose Metropolitan Iov. On 26 January with full ceremony in the Uspensky Cathedral Ieremiya consecrated Iov as the first Russian Patriarch.

Obstacles still remained to the departure of Ieremiya and his suite from Moscow. It was necessary to prepare the formal document, confirming that the creation of the new patriarchate had been carried out in accordance with the laws of the Church. Ieremiya signed it, as did the Greek Metropolitan, the archbishop, and the archimandrite who were members of his suite, and also the Russian hierarchy.

In May 1589 Ieremiya and his companions were finally granted leave to depart. They were laden with gifts and alms, but their departure was conditional on his solemn promise that he would convene an assembly of the leaders of the Eastern Church to give final approval to this new creation. Ieremiya took nearly a year to reach Constantinople. He duly summoned the church leaders who disputed whether he had acted within the canon law. Finally they acknowledged, albeit grudgingly, the existence of the Russian patriarchate, allocating to it fifth place in the order of precedence of patriarchs of the Eastern Church.

In June 1591 the Ternov Metropolitan arrived in Moscow, bringing the document of confirmation. All in Moscow were indignant over the order of precedence. It had been expected that the Russian Patriarch would occupy at least third place, since Moscow was the third Rome and the Russian Church was in the position of sole protector of the Christian faith. Moscow's objections were considered by a second assembly of the Eastern Patriarchs at the beginning of 1593. An ambassador from Moscow, Grigori Afanasiev, attended, but the Eastern Patriarchs merely confirmed their decision. Moscow continued to insist that the Russian patriarchate should be placed after the patriarchates of Constantinople and Alexandria, but before those of Antioch and Jerusalem. Such issues were considered to be of crucial importance and the negotiations continued.

Although apparently achieved by a mixture of chicanery and duress, the creation of the patriarchate in Moscow was a major development. The Russian Church had long been autocephalous in practice, but it was now wholly independent and self-sufficient in accordance with canon law. The prestige of the Tsar and of Moscow was greatly enhanced. The patriarchate was also an essential element in establishing the new nation. At this time strong national feeling and xenophobic prejudices gripped the people. It had become increasingly unacceptable that their Church should have to look to a Greek in Constantinople as their supreme religious authority. Now the position had changed and all looked on Boris as the author of their final independence.[2]

Notes
1. Solovyev, IV, VII, p. 305.
2. Karamzin, X, II, Col. 73.

CHAPTER IX

Death of Tsarevich Dmitri

IN MAY 1591, TSAREVICH DMITRI DIED SUDDENLY IN UGLICH. IT was to prove an event of tragic significance for Boris and for Russia.

To the north of Moscow the country was covered with dense forest. The people lived in scattered towns and villages, which were linked by the river network. Uglich on the bank of the Volga in this region was one of the more important towns. It was on the main winter route from Moscow to the north, the summer route lying through Yaroslavl. Uglich had a population of between twenty and thirty thousand people, including many small traders and craftsmen, and it contained some hundred and fifty churches.[1] The town was centred on the small Kremlin, standing on the river bank, and fortified by a rampart and surrounding stone wall. The Kremlin Palace was occupied by the widowed Tsaritsa Maria, her son, Tsarevich Dmitri, her two brothers, Mikhail and Grigori Nagoi, and two cousins, Afanasy and Andrei Nagoi, as well as numerous servants and retainers.

The Tsarevich and his family had been sent to Uglich under guard soon after the death of Tsar Ivan. The Nagoi were greedy for power and hated at court. Even before the Tsar's death they had begun plotting to seize the throne for Dmitri and to displace Fedor, the legal heir. They had held a privileged position at court as part of the family of the Tsar and they knew that they would lose this position on his death. If Dmitri became Tsar, however, Tsaritsa Maria would be regent and the Nagoi would enjoy not only privilege but power. Their motives had been obvious to all. It had been essential to send them away from Moscow to preserve order.

The Nagoi were not, however, in disgrace. The Tsaritsa and her son maintained their own court, and were able to live in the style befitting their rank. Friendly relations were maintained between the courts of Uglich and Moscow. On anniversaries, for instance, Tsar Fedor sent gifts of furs, jewellery, and damask to the Tsaritsa and the Tsarevich. The Nagoi were nevertheless under surveillance which they resented as bitterly as their banishment. A *Dyak* or senior official, Mikhail Bityagovsky, an honest and conscientious servant of the Tsar, had been appointed in Moscow in 1590 to act as supervisor of the administration of Uglich and controller of the palace. In particular he was responsible for paying to members of the Nagoi family the allowances which the Tsar granted them. This was a source of petty disputes. Mikhail Nagoi became increasingly truculent in his demands for more money. Bityagovsky refused to pay any additions without the Tsar's approval. Relations became bitter and there were frequent quarrels. Bityagovsky had to reprimand him for engaging soothsayers and necromancers to foretell how long the Tsar and Tsaritsa would live and whether they would have children. In preparation for war against Sweden in 1590 there was a levy of men for military service. Mikhail Nagoi was notably reluctant to deliver the quota of men for Uglich. Bityagovsky reprimanded him severely for failing to honour his obligations to the Tsar, and Mikhail Nagoi deeply resented the reprimand.

The hostility of the Nagoi towards Bityagovsky was intensified by their fears for the safety of Dmitri. Their return to Moscow and all that it meant depended entirely on the boy. The Nagoi were convinced that certain boyars, and Boris Godunov in particular, were planning to dispose of him and that Bityagovsky had been especially appointed as their agent for this sinister purpose. They circulated rumours through friends and agents in Moscow to the effect that Dmitri was in danger.

Giles Fletcher, the English ambassador who was in Moscow in 1588 reported that the Tsarevich

is kept in a remote place from Moscow . . . yet not safe (as I have heard) from attempts of making away by practice of some that aspire to the succession, if this Emperor (Tsar Fedor) die without any issue. The nurse that tasted before him of certain meat (as I have heard) died presently.[2]

Fletcher probably obtained this information from Jerome Horsey who was the friend of Mikhail Nagoi.

Fletcher wrote further that

The Russians confirm that he is truly the son of Tsar Ivan Vasilievich because at a young age all the qualities of the Tsar began to show in him . . . He is delighted, they say, to see sheep and other cattle killed and to look on their throats while they are bleeding (which commonly children are afraid to behold) and to beat geese and hens with a staff till he see them lie dead.³

Such sadistic traits were probably fostered by the behaviour of those close to him. His mother and uncles expressed openly their hatred of Bityagovsky and of Boris and other boyars in Moscow. They talked constantly and impatiently about the death of Tsar Fedor. The boy was evidently quick to reflect their ruthless attitude. It is related that on one occasion he ordered his young companions to build several figures in the snow. He gave these snowmen the names of prominent boyars and then hacked each of them down, saying, "So it will be done to them in my reign."⁴

The health of Tsarevich Dmitri was also a matter of constant concern to the Nagoi. He was not a robust boy and he suffered severely from epilepsy, known to Russians as *nemoch paduchaya* or *bolezn chernaya*. His governess and others testified to the violence of his attacks. During Lent in 1591 he had a fit in which he cut his mother severely with his *svaya,* a metal bolt with a sharp end, weighing a pound or more, used in a popular game. At the beginning of April he had another fit. He bit the fingers of the daughter of Andrei Nagoi "and kept on biting them" until she was pulled away from him. Eye-witnesses declared that "when the illness overcomes him and the people around are holding him, he bites anything he can reach, being in a state of delirium". Andrei Nagoi, the playmates of the Tsarevich, and even chambermaids had been bitten.⁵

On Wednesday, 12 May, Dmitri had an epileptic seizure. He recovered fairly quickly and on Friday his mother took him to church. On the following day, Saturday, 15 May, she took him to church again and then allowed him to go into the palace courtyard to play with four young friends. His governess, Vasilisa Volokhova, his nurse, Irina Tuchkova, and his chambermaid, Maria Samoylova, were the only other people in the courtyard at this time. Evidently the boys were playing a game, known as *tuchka,* in which an open knife is thrown at a target.

Suddenly about midday there were screams. Irina Tuchkova, the nurse, rushed to Dmitri who had had a fit. He was holding a knife and had cut himself in the throat, severing an artery. The screams brought Vasilisa Volokhova to her side and others rushed from the palace. Grigori Nagoi was the first to reach the group, followed closely by Tsaritsa Maria and her brother, Mikhail Nagoi. The Tsaritsa became hysterical on seeing what had happened and began beating Vasilisa Volokhova with a piece of wood. Both she and Mikhail Nagoi were shouting that the Tsarevich had been murdered by the sons of Vasilisa and of Bityagovsky.

The bells of the Uglich Kremlin began tolling and churches in the town took up the tocsin. People began running through the Spaasky and Nikolsky gates into the Kremlin. Workmen, carrying axes and stakes, came from the boats in the river. The cry that the Tsarevich had been murdered spread rapidly through the town. The crowd, growing as more people pushed into the courtyard, was soon in an angry mood.

The pealing of the bells, the prompt gathering of the crowds, and the spread of the rumour that the Tsarevich had been done to death happened with remarkable speed and spontaneity. It was the time of day when most people broke off from their work for dinner. But there was evidence that the Nagoi had laid plans for a general uprising, taking advantage of the Swedish invasion, co-ordinated with an attack by the Crimean Tatars, expected about this time. The conspiracy had small chance of succeeding. It was in any case overtaken now by the death of the Tsarevich, which aroused the people of Uglich.

Mikhail Bityagovsky was dining at home. His son, Daniil, was with him. His guest was the priest Bogdan, the confessor of Grigori Nagoi. Hearing the tocsin, Bityagovsky sent a servant to find out what had happened. On the return of the servant he hurried to the Kremlin. In the courtyard he found himself facing an armed and hostile mob. He tried to speak and to deny that he or his son had killed the Tsarevich or had been involved in his death. The crowd, inflamed by rumours, would not listen. He tried to run away and took refuge in one of the palace buildings. There the mob cornered him and beat him to death.

Iosif Volokhov, the son of the governess, was next to be run down. The mob beat and tortured the boy who was barely alive when they carried him into the Kremlin church where the Tsaritsa had been led. There in her presence he was done to death. The mob now ran wild. They broke into Bitaygovsky's house where they murdered his son. They carried the mother and daughter off to the Kremlin and would have killed them in the courtyard but for the intervention of priests. Both women were, however, held under close guard with Vasilisa Volokhova. The mob plundered and then completely destroyed the house and property of Bityagovsky. Members of his staff and his servants fled from the town and were afraid to return. Inflamed by alcohol, the mob raged through the town, breaking into houses and looting. In all twelve people lost their lives.

News of the death of Tsarevich Dmitri reached Moscow on the evening of the following day. Boris acted promptly. With the approval of the Tsar he appointed a Commission of Inquiry. Prince Vasily Shuisky, Okolnichii Andrei Kleshnin, and Dyak Elizar Vyluzgin were the members. The Patriarch nominated as his personal representative the Krutitsky Metropolitan, Gelasii. The Commission was instructed to interrogate witnesses and assemble all evidence on two questions: first, what was the cause of the death of the Tsarevich and, second, what was the cause of the mob violence which resulted in the death of Mikhail Bityagovsky and others.

In the meantime certain of the Nagoi were active in trying to obtain evidence for their claim that Dmitri had been murdered. They intimidated and even tortured witnesses to ensure their support. Jerome Horsey recounted that he received a visit at midnight from Afanasy Nagoi who was highly excited. He told Horsey that "The Tsarevich Dmitri was dead, his throat cut by Dyaki, meaning the officials from Moscow." He added that one of the pages had confessed "upon the rack" that Boris had organised the assassination. His immediate purpose was to beg from Horsey some medicine for Tsaritsa Maria. He claimed that she had been poisoned and "upon point of death, her hair and nails and skin fall off". Horsey added that he "ran up, fetched a little bottle of pure salad oil (that little vial of balsam that the Queen gave me) and a box of Venice treacle". He gave them to Afanasy Nagoi, who rode back to Uglich.[6]

Rusin Rakov, the town commissioner, submitted two petitions. He wrote his first petition, addressed to the Tsar, shortly before the Commission's arrival in Uglich. He addressed his second petition to Metropolitan Gelasii. In the first, Rakov stated that on Sunday 16 May Mikhail Nagoi sent him a warning that he would be killed "like Bityagovsky", if he remained in Uglich.

In the second petition Rakov described how Mikhail Nagoi had ordered him to collect a few weapons, such as daggers, a sabre, and a club. He was to smear them with chicken's blood and then put them on the bodies of Bityagovsky and others, who had been killed by the mob. The purpose was evidently to make it appear that they had attacked the townspeople who had killed them in self-defence. Rakov carried out the instructions but with reluctance. He decided finally to denounce the Nagoi to the Commission.

On the evening of Wednesday 19 May the Commissioners arrived in Uglich. The investigation began at once. Mikhail Nagoi was the first to be interrogated. He asserted that the Tsarevich had been stabbed to death by Iosif Volokhov, Nikita Kachalov, and Daniil Bityagovsky. Tsaritsa Maria made the same charges. She was not interrogated, probably because she was so overwrought.

Indeed, she was so close to a nervous collapse that Afanasy Nagoi thought that she had been poisoned, as he informed Horsey. Also, as Dowager Tsaritsa, she was treated with special respect and the Commission would not have presumed to summon her as it summoned other witnesses. Metropolitan Gelasii questioned her, however, and made a special report to the Patriarch. From the evidence of others, too, it was clear that she believed that her son had been stabbed to death.

Faced with Mikhail Nagoi's statement, the Commission next interrogated those who had been in the courtyard at the time and had been eye-witnesses of the tragedy. Irina Tuchkova described the accident as follows: "On Saturday, Dmitri played with the knife with the boys and she had not been careful enough to notice when the epileptic fit occurred; and he had a knife in his hands, and he cut himself with that knife, and she took him in her arms, and he passed away in her arms."[7] All confirmed her testimony.

Grigori Nagoi, who had rushed from the palace on hearing the screams and was first on the scene, testified that the Tsarevich had fallen on a knife and had died in his presence. Andrei Nagoi stated that the Tsarevich was already dead in the arms of the nurse when he reached them. He added: "And they say that the Tsarevich was murdered, but he did not see who murdered him."[8] The four companions described the accident in exactly the same terms as the governess and the nurse. They confirmed also that the three boys, accused by Mikhail Nagoi of committing the murder, were not in the courtyard at the time. Other witnesses corroborated this evidence.

One further eye-witness was discovered unexpectedly. He was Simeon Yudin who told his master, Grigori Tulubeev, the steward of the buttery, that he had seen the accident. Summoned before the Commission, he stated that the Tsarevich "was playing with the children and the epilepsy overcame him; and he was thrown to the ground in convulsions and the convulsions lasted long; and he cut himself with the knife". Yudin added that he "was at that time on duty at the cupboard and saw it all".[9]

There was no doubt in the minds of the members of the Commission that the death of the Tsarevich had been an accident. The Tsaritsa may well have been so shocked by the death of her only son that she believed the story that she told. But the fact that she tried to suborn Vasilisa Volokhova and other witnesses to give false evidence in support of her story suggests that, like Mikhail Nagoi, she was driven by malice and hatred to destroy Bityagovsky and the others whom she accused. The evidence taken by the Commission also showed conclusively that the Tsaritsa and Mikhail

Nagoi had incited the mob against Bityagovsky and other officials. She admitted her guilt to Metropolitan Gelasii.

The Commission made its report on 2 June and the Tsar referred it to the Patriarch and the church council. Their judgment was that the Tsarevich had died by an act of God and that Mikhail Nagoi and the people of Uglich were responsible for the deaths of innocent people and deserved punishment. This was a matter for the civil authorities and the Tsar directed the Council of Boyars to decide on appropriate action.

The punishments were severe. Tsaritsa Maria was shorn as a nun and banished "to the deserted place beyond Beloozero".[10] The Nagoi were sent to distant towns and held in prisons. Certain of the people of Uglich were executed and others were held in dungeons, which often meant death by starvation. Most of the townspeople were sent to Siberia and settled in the region where the town of Pelym was soon to be founded. Legend relates that even the town bell which had started tolling the alarm on 15 May was banished to Siberia. Uglich was left almost deserted.

On the completion of the Commission's interrogations in Uglich, the body of the Tsarevich was buried in the Church of the Transfiguration of the Saviour. There was apparently no suggestion that he should be buried in the Arkhangelsky Cathedral. It was the practice to inter princes of the blood there and, when necessary, their bodies were brought to Moscow for the purpose. Evidently Tsarevich Dmitri was not considered entitled to this honour.

Tsar Fedor did not attend the burial service, which again was a departure from convention. About this time he was visiting the Troitsa Monastery which was on the way to Uglich. It may have been that he was reluctant to visit this apanage principality which was an independent enclave within the Tsardom. It is more probable that he thought little of this half-brother whose legitimacy was questionable and whose family, the Nagoi, commanded no respect. Among the people of Uglich the burial aroused little interest. The child was rapidly forgotten. When fifteen years later there was suddenly a move to canonise him, no one knew where his tomb was, and only after several days of feverish searching was it found.

Boris made no direct appearance in the events of May 1591. There was certainly no evidence involving him in the death of the Tsarevich. By this time he had become ruler in fact and wielded the full powers delegated by the Tsar. He was probably responsible for the appointment of the Commission and for the action taken on the basis of its report. In no other way was he involved. But the death of Tsarevich Dmitri was to be used as a political weapon to destroy him and his family and it has distorted the history of his reign.

1. Karamzin, X, II, Col. 82; M. N. Tikhomirov, *Russia in the 16th Century* (Moscow, 1962) pp. 214–15; G. Vernadsky, "The Death of the Tsarevich Dimitry" in *Oxford Slavonic Papers*, V (Oxford, 1954). Historians have questioned whether Uglich was so populous as Karamzin stated.
2. E. A. Bond (Ed.) *Russia at the close of the 16th Century* (Hakluyt Society, London, 1856) pp. 21–22.
3. E. A. Bond (Ed.) *loc. cit.*
4. S. F. Platonov, *Boris Godunov* (Petrograd, 1921) p. 97.
5. G. Vernadsky, *op. cit.*, pp. 16–17.
6. E. A. Bond (Ed.) *op. cit.*, p. 254.
   Venice treacle was a medicinal concoction of many ingredients, made into a paste and believed to be especially effective against poisoning.
7. G. Vernadsky, *op. cit.*, p. 16.
8. *Loc. cit.*
9. *Ibid.* p. 8.
10. S. F. Platonov, *op. cit.*, p. 102.

CHAPTER X

Muscovy in the Reign of Tsar Fedor

THE THIRTEEN YEARS OF FEDOR'S REIGN WERE A TIME OF PEACE AND recovery. Tsar Ivan had directed his policy of repression and terror mainly against the great princely families, but all classes had suffered. The savageries and excesses of the Oprichniki and the burdens of continual war had added to their hardships. They now welcomed the dramatic change in the policies and the temper of the government under the rule of Tsar Fedor and Boris Godunov, and in particular, the new concern for the welfare of the people and for just and efficient administration.

Jerome Horsey observed that "the state and government . . . so much altered as it was termed new, having put on, as it were, a new face, so contrary to the old, every man living in peace, enjoying and knowing his own, good officers placed, justice ministered everywhere . . ."[1]

With the passing years Tsar Fedor became even more devout and withdrawn from earthly affairs. His pilgrimages to monasteries near and far were more frequent. When in the Kremlin palace he would rise at four in the morning. As soon as he had dressed, he received his spiritual adviser who brought him the cross to kiss. Next the holy ikon of the saint who was to be celebrated that day was presented to him and he prayed before it. The priest then sprinkled him and the ikon with holy water.

After this ceremony, Fedor sent to enquire if the Tsaritsa had slept well. He himself went soon afterwards to greet her in an adjoining chamber from which they went together to church for an hour's prayers. On returning he took his place in the audience chamber where his boyars came to pay their respects. About 9 a.m. he went to a service which lasted some two hours. He rested before dining and after dinner he slept for two or three hours. He then attended yet another church service after which he usually spent the time with the Tsaritsa until supper. Jesters and dwarfs entertained them and on occasions he relaxed watching fights between men or between men and bears.

The Muscovite court was noted for its splendour. A force of 250 chosen Streltsi mounted guard duty with arquebuses loaded and slow-burning matches lit. The church hierarchy and the boyars, wearing rich robes, attended the Tsar in church and on pilgrimages. The reception of foreign ambassadors was always an occasion of great ceremonial. Furthermore the Boyar Council met formally from 7 a.m. until about 10 a.m. on Fridays and sometimes also on Mondays and Wednesdays. If the Tsar presided, he had to miss morning mass and prayers. He had discontinued, however, the great banquets, attended by all at court, which had been a daily feature of Kremlin life during the reigns of his father and grandfather. He preferred to dine quietly with two or three chosen boyars. Within the Kremlin palace, 200 *zhiltsi,* who were senior serving gentry, mounted a personal guard, occupying the third room from the Tsar's bedchamber. The two adjoining rooms were occupied by the Chamberlain and the senior courtiers of the bedchamber.

Enveloped like a chrysalis in religious and court ceremonies, Fedor was Tsar only in name. A strong Tsar, like Ivan IV, asserted his authority and his presence was felt throughout the city and the country. But Fedor had no will to exert his power or to be involved in state affairs. His one earthly desire was that Tsaritsa Irina, to whom he was devoted, might bear a child. To his delight a daughter, named Feodosia, was born in May 1592, but she died eighteen months later. In all other matters, he was relieved to be able to delegate his powers to Boris. He recognised the ability and integrity of his brother-in-law. He knew also that Boris possessed the qualities of generosity and concern for humble people which he felt. The two men appeared to be at one in their determination that there should be no repetition of the terror and the debasement of public and court life that had characterised Tsar Ivan's reign. Such factors and a genuine personal affection were the bases of Fedor's trust in Boris which appeared to be unbounded, and there is nothing to suggest that this trust was ever betrayed.

Boris nevertheless wielded power in the name of the Tsar. Although he elevated his position so that he was "Ruler" to whom fullest respects had to be paid, he was careful always to acknowledge his Tsar and his supreme office. In exercising power, moreover, he observed Muscovite practice in consulting with the leading men of the land. He discussed all questions of major importance, such as terms for peace with Poland and the reduction of taxes, at extraordinary assemblies, attended by members of the Boyar

Council, senior state officials, the Patriarch and senior churchmen. The Tsar himself sometimes presided at these assemblies. Giles Fletcher described them as the "Parliament", and the meetings were apparently dignified and businesslike.[2]

The easing of tension under the rule of Boris was achieved not only by maintaining peace and reducing taxation, but also by greater efficiency in government, and by promotion of trade, especially with foreigners. Lands which had lain uncultivated were ploughed anew and peasants began to return to the villages from which they had fled. During the 1590s agriculture recovered to the extent that many granaries had surpluses. These improvements led in turn to steady increases in the national income. The revenue from the Tsar's estates mounted. Giles Fletcher noted that Tsar Ivan had "kept a more princely and bountiful house than the Emperor now doth", but Fedor's treasury "riseth now by good husbanding of the steward, Grigori Vasilievich Godunov, to 230 thousand rubles a year" from some sixty thousand rubles in the reign of Tsar Ivan.[3] Grigori, the cousin of Boris, was head of the *Bolshoi Prikaz* or Great Office, responsible for the national revenues, and he was a careful and honest treasurer. Taxes levied on estates and their produce and customs duties, fixed as yearly contributions from towns and provinces began to yield more as a result of the improved administration and also of the vigorous campaign against corruption.

Boris was concerned about the low standards of conduct. He hated drunkenness and introduced special measures to ban the illegal distilling of spirits. He made strenuous efforts to halt the corruption which undermined every branch of the administration. A judge, found guilty of taking bribes, had to return the bribe and pay a fine of 500 to 2,000 rubles, and his property was confiscated by the treasury. A *dyak* who took a bribe was publicly whipped, with the bribe, whether in the form of money, furs or salt fish, tied around his neck. After the ordeal of whipping, he was imprisoned. Such measures deterred many officials, but corruption, like drunkenness and other vices, was deeply ingrained in Muscovite life and only stern enforcement of the law over several decades would have achieved Boris's purpose.

The general improvement in conditions suffered other setbacks. In the spring of 1591 a terrible fire swept through Moscow, burning most of the city to the ground. The Kremlin and Kitaigorod alone escaped damage. The majority of the people were homeless. The Tsar was away on one of his pilgrimages and the people turned to Boris. In such calamities he responded immediately. He was generous in making grants and organising the rebuilding of whole districts. This was a further reason for his wide popularity.[4]

The work of rebuilding the city after the fire had to be set aside in June–July when the Crimean Khan with a mighty army threatened Moscow. The Tatars were forced, however, to beat an ignominious retreat. Building began again in Moscow. Streets were widened and repaved with logs.

A special Department of Stone Works had been set up by Tsar Ivan shortly before his death, presumably on Boris's instigation. Boris had greatly expanded the office. He made it responsible for extensive building operations. New churches were erected within the Kremlin which soon had a total of thirty-five stone churches, while the whole city, embracing the Kremlin, Kitaigorod, and Belygorod, contained more than 400 churches by the end of Fedor's reign. He entrusted to a Russian building master, Fedor Savelev Kon or Konev, the erection of a stone wall around Belygorod and of timbered walls around the outer city, as well as the stone buildings for government offices adjoining the Arkhangelsky Cathedral.

In 1595 fire destroyed the whole of Kitaigorod in which the merchants and traders were concentrated. New houses and stalls, made of stone, arose within a few months. Arsonists attempted to start fires in the rebuilt suburb. Their motive was apparently to plunder the warehouses and even the nearby Cathedral of St Vasily during the confusion that was caused. The malefactors were caught before they could carry out their plan. Three were executed at the *Lobnoe Mesto* on the Red Square. Others were hanged or imprisoned for life. It was said that these punishments made a deep impression on the Muscovites who were "already unaccustomed to the spectacle of bloodshed".[5]

Boris had plans for further buildings, including a magnificent cathedral within the Kremlin which would replace the Uspensky Cathedral. Materials were assembled for the purpose, but events overtook him before the work could be started. The lasting monument to his tireless efforts to improve and beautify Moscow remains the tall belfry, known as Ivan the Great, which was completed in 1600. It reached upwards in three tapering octagonal tiers, until it towered high above all the buildings of the city, and it stands now as the centre piece of the Kremlin. For many years it served Moscow as the chief watch tower, for it commands a view of the whole city and the surrounding lands for a distance of twenty miles. It might fairly be called the Tower or Belfry of Boris Godunov, for it is the outstanding example of his passion for erecting buildings which were both beautiful and useful. But it has always been known as the Belfry of Ivan the Great, commemorating Ivan I, III, or IV, or even St John Climactus to whom a chapel had been dedicated earlier on this site.

The easing of tensions and revival of a degree of order and stability during Tsar Fedor's reign were, however, temporary. Jerome Horsey, in noting the general improvement in conditions since Tsar Ivan's reign, added, "Yet God hath a great plague in store for this people!"[6] Giles Fletcher without benefit of hindsight, writing about the Oprichnina, pronounced more ominously that, "This wicked policy and tyrannous practice (though now it be ceased) hath so troubled that country and filled it so full of grudge and mortal hatred ever since that it will not be quenched (as it seemeth now) till it burn again in civil flame."[7]

The Oprichnina was the worst of a number of calamities that had oppressed the people during Tsar Ivan's reign. But there had also been epidemics of plague, famine, the devastation of Novgorod by the Tsar in 1570 and of Moscow by the Crimean Khan in 1571, and the twenty-five years of the Livonian War which had led to heavier taxation and a severe drain on manpower. The experiences of these years had impoverished and embittered the Russians and were largely responsible for the mass flight of all classes from the central and north-western regions of Muscovy. The departure of peasants from these important regions had led to a sharp decline in agricultural output which had aggravated the economic crisis.

The mass migration was an extraordinary spontaneous movement. It began on a small scale about the middle of the sixteenth century. It developed rapidly until by the 1580s vast regions lay deserted; fields were uncultivated and the forest was reclaiming the cleared lands. Giles Fletcher in 1588 observed that "many villages and towns of half a mile and a mile long stand all un-inhabited, the people being fled all into other places by reason of the extreme usage and exactions done upon them".[8] Only thirty-five years earlier Richard Chancellor had noted how these lands were "very well replenished with small villages which are so well filled with people that it is a wonder to see them".[9]

According to the land registers of the time, between eighty-three and ninety-seven per cent of the peasant homesteads or families in the north-west were deserted. The country surrounding Moscow suffered most severely. Cadastral records for 1584–86 showed that only seventeen per cent of the arable land was still under cultivation, the remaining lands being covered with grass grown to a man's height. In cities and towns, too, population had dropped sharply. The population of Novgorod was reckoned to be eighty per cent lower than it had been thirty years earlier. In the important river-port of Kolomna ninety-five per cent of the houses stood empty in 1578. The decline was most acute in the region of Moscow, Novgorod, and Pskov, but other parts of the centre and the north-west suffered similarly.

The migration was to the east and south. Tsar Ivan's conquest of Kazan and Astrakhan and the pioneering of the Stroganovs had opened the way for expansion and settlement in Siberia. Others moved across the Oka River. The *dikoe pole,* the wild steppeland, lying between Moscow's southern frontier and the Crimean Khanate, offered the freedom for which so many peasants, oppressed by their landlords, yearned. Here the Cossacks were their own masters, and fugitives joined them in large numbers. There was also the lure of expanses of land where the soil was fertile and the forests teemed with fur-bearing animals and the rivers with fish. Many fugitives also made their way northwards to the basin of the Northern Dvina. The climate in this region was harsh and the land infertile, but there, too, the migrant could find freedom.

The malaise among the peasants and the mass flights were closely connected, however, with the growth of *pomestie* landholding, which gave rise to unbearable exploitation. The pomestie was an estate, granted on the condition that the holder rendered military service. This system of landholding was applied more widely in the sixteenth century and was a direct cause of the flight of many peasants.

The formation of the Muscovite state, centralised on Moscow, had brought about a revolution in landholding. At one time the right to own land had been open to all men, but gradually it was restricted to those who could render service to the Tsar. The Church was a wealthy landowner, enjoying exemptions which placed it in a special category. Private landowners held land in the form of *votchiny* which were inherited estates, originally held independent of service to the Tsar or the State. By an *ukaz* of 1556 Tsar Ivan required that all members of the landowning class should give service. Gradually the holder of a votchina was regarded as being in the same position as the holder of a pomestie, or an estate granted and held on the condition of service.

Grand Prince Ivan III was the first to show strong preference for the granting of pomestie. The owners of votchiny were mainly the princes and their boyars whose loyalty was often suspect in Moscow, and who were in any case too few in numbers to be able to meet the demands of the developing nation. The new class of serving gentry were more reliable and their services were urgently needed by the Muscovite Grand Princes as they absorbed other principalities, asserted their authority and defended their frontiers. The gentry increased in number and importance, and more land

was required to provide them with estates. Conquests and confiscations of votchiny did not meet the demand. Secularisation of
church lands would have solved the problem. The Church was,
however, a strong pillar of Muscovite power and in these formative
years the sovereign was not prepared to anatgonise the Church.

Tsar Ivan's Oprichnina was the most extreme method used to
settle trusted serving gentry on pomestie. The men, enlisted as
Oprichniki, were drawn mainly from the lesser nobility or gentry
class. They were settled on pomestie near Moscow, formed from
confiscated estates which had been held over the years by noble
families. The lands taken into the Oprichnina eventually amounted
to about half of the Tsardom. In the course of this expansion many
of the old votchiny with the traditional loyalties, that had been built
up over decades, were destroyed. The princely landowner was up-
rooted and all who served him and worked his lands found their
way of life suddenly disrupted. If they could accompany their lord,
they usually did so and perished with him, or if freed from his
service, they were driven into vagabondage. By Muscovite custom
a noble who incurred the Tsar's disgrace had his property confiscated and his title deeds destroyed. The effect of this was that
his serfs and peasants received their freedom, but they were usually
forbidden to enter the service of another landowner. They were
thus doomed to starve, unless they could make their way to the
south or to the virgin lands to the east. Thousands of Muscovites
suffered from such sudden and complete disruption of their lives
as a result of the confiscation of the great princely estates. They
suffered, too, from the pillaging and persecution of the Oprichniki,
who were under the Tsar's protection and did not limit their
attentions to the princely class.

Conditions of the peasants working on the pomestie of the
serving gentry were harsh. Such estates were usually small and the
landlord was hard pressed, even with occasional cash payments
from the State, to support his family and to maintain his military
equipment and horses to serve the Tsar when required. He could
not borrow against his pomestie, since he was not the owner. The
result was that the serving gentry were concerned only to squeeze
all that they could from their estates and their peasants. The old
patrimonial estates provided the peasant with a better way of life.
The large-scale landowner was less tempted to bleed his peasants,
who could benefit also from the formation of free peasant-
communes to manage their affairs, which was not possible on the
small pomestie.

The whole trend of development in the sixteenth century was,
however, to meet the needs of the State by expanding the serving

gentry class. The peasantry responded by migrating in increasing numbers. A migratory fever spread through the country so that peasants fled also from the estates of the great nobles and of the monasteries. Agriculture and the whole economy was faced with a severe crisis. In seeking to ensure that there was a stable labour force, successive governments imposed restrictions on the peasantry until by the seventeenth century they were completely enmeshed in the evil system of serfdom.

Peasants had the right to move from the estate of their landlord and to work elsewhere. The *Sudebnik* or legal code of 1497 had restricted this freedom. The peasant could leave his landlord only in the week before and the week after St George's Day, 25 November, when the crops had been harvested. Moreover, he had to pay exit dues as well as settling all debts to the landlord before departure. A complex web of obligations and payments grew around this right of the peasants, until flight was often the only escape.

Peasant labour was in such demand, however, that often the wealthier landlords would pay the exit fees and debts in order to secure the peasant for his own estate. This method of pirating labour, known as *vyvoz*, became more and more common as competition for labour grew. Violence often broke out when the agents of the powerful landlords vied with each other to abduct peasants. The serving gentry were inevitably the losers in such competition. Deprived of their peasants they faced ruin and were, of course, unable to render the services on which the State depended.

In 1580 Tsar Ivan took the action of banning all free movement of peasants in what were called *zapovednie gody* or forbidden years. Before long the forbidden years had become continuous and the peasants lost completely their freedom to move, although with the limitations of exit dues, payment of debts, and other obligations this freedom had become more or less nominal. But in a country so vast, such laws were difficult to enforce. Landowners continued to poach the peasants on other estates, and peasants ran away, lured by promises of better conditions or seeking new freedom farther afield.

With the purpose of making the law more effective and of protecting the serving gentry, Tsar Ivan ordered a cadastral survey in 1581, and it was completed in 1592. It recorded the names of male peasants on every estate. This was followed by an ukaz, issued in November 1597, which required that all peasants, who had moved or fled within the preceding five years, should be returned to the estates to which, according to the registers, they belonged. This decree, binding the peasant to the lord to whose estate he belonged in 1592, was a major step towards the full enserfment of the peasantry.

Boris had inherited social and economic problems of extra-ordinary complexity. The flight of peasants and others had aggravated the shortage of labour. Powerful landlords acquired peasants by paying their debts and exit fees and, especially after the cadastral survey and the ukaz of 1597, by violent methods. Landlords also gained labour through the system of bondage. A peasant could pledge himself to give lifelong service instead of paying the interest on a loan of money received from a landlord. As a *kholop kabalny* or bonded peasant, he was not considered to be a person, but the movable property of his lord. Unlike the ordinary peasant, he ceased to be liable to pay taxes and was thus lost to the state as a source of revenue.

In handling these problems, Boris gave priority to the interests of the country as a whole rather than to any specific class. The princely clans believed that he was simply enforcing the policies of Tsar Ivan, their arch-enemy. Giles Fletcher was convinced that the government of Boris was committed to those policies, especially in the "endeavour by all means to cut off or keep down all of the best and ancientest nobility".[10]

Boris recognised, however, the need to support the serving gentry. It was on this class, which the old nobility resented so bitterly, that the State depended for military service and for the general administration of the country. Indeed, his own class of Muscovite landed boyars was critical of his measures to strengthen the gentry and to ensure that they had the labour and the economic base to enable them to render the services that the State needed. In pursuing this policy he was upholding the development, launched in the previous century by Ivan III, and clearly necessary for the survival of Muscovy as a nation.

In his relations with the Church, too, Boris demonstrated that state, not personal or class, interests, were paramount. He had had always the support of the Orthodox hierarchy, which exercised an even greater authority after the creation of the Russian patri-archate. The Church was, however, an immensely powerful land-owner, and active in attracting peasant labour to its estates. Boris nevertheless subjected the estates of the Patriarch, Metropolitans, and the monasteries to the same prohibitions as the estates of other great landowners. Indeed, since church lands were free of the liability of providing services and paying taxes, special measures were introduced to protect the national interest. Several practices, such as the leasing of civil estates to monasteries, which were de-signed to evade payment of taxes or services, were forbidden by ukaz in 1590. Further, in 1593–94 Boris initiated a general investigation of all monastery lands, including those of the most revered monasteries such as the Troitsa. This was a further enforcement of Tsar Ivan's ukaz of 1582, which had been confirmed in July 1584, when an assembly of churchmen and boyars had declared that the Church and monasteries must return all ancient princely estates and leasehold lands in their possession. The formal record of the assembly stated, in particular, that, "Lands and villages, relinquished to monasteries for the repose of souls, are to be bought back by descendants, or, if there are none, by the Sovereign for distribution among military men (serving gentry)".[11] As a result of this investigation, many estates to which adequate evidence of title could not be produced were confiscated by the Tsar.

The policy of improving conditions of the serving gentry and in particular protecting them against encroachments by the powerful landowners led inevitably to harsher restraints and burdens on the peasantry. Their right to free departure from their lord's estate in the week before and after St George's Day almost ceased to exist. The cadastral registers, completed in 1592, tied peasants effectively to their lords. Boris's law of 1597, allowing the recovery of any peasant who had run away during the previous five years, led many historians to indict him as the creator of serfdom. But the charge was patently false. Under Boris's administration conditions improved and the mass flights from central Muscovy slowed down. Deserted lands were repopulated and agriculture revived. He introduced special measures, designed to protect the peasantry from the excessive demands and rapacity of their masters. The peasantry clearly benefited, but the process of enserfment continued, and far from being the work of Boris or any other ruler, the system developed inexorably over several centuries in response to the special needs of the growing Russian nation.

Notes

1. E. A. Bond (Ed.) *Russia at the Close of the 16th Century* (Hakluyt Society, London, 1856) pp. 205–6.
2. *Ibid.* pp. 29–32.
3. *Ibid.* pp. 48–49.
4. Karamzin missed no opportunity to report rumours attributing sinister motives to Boris. Writing of the fire, for example, he added, "And the disaster in the capital served him well in enabling him to gain the love of the people. But there were rumours, believed by many, that he had secretly started or instigated the fires . . ." Karamzin, X, II, Cols. 83–84.

5. *Ibid.* X, III, Col. 122.

The *Lobnoe Mesto* is a stone platform with a balustrade on the Red Square near the Cathedral of St Vasily or Pokrovsky Cathedral. It bears (May 1972) a notice explaining that it was the place from which proclamations were made and where the Tsar or his officials addressed the people of Moscow on special occasions. The notice also states incorrectly that it was not used for executions. There is ample evidence in Russian history to the contrary and in Russian folklore, as many *Byliny* or popular verse legends bear witness, it was a dreaded place—

> Where terrible executions are carried out,
> Where eyes are put out from their sockets
> And tongues are torn from their roots.

N. Kershaw Chadwick, *Russian Heroic Poetry* (Cambridge, 1932) p. 195.

6. E. A. Bond, *op. cit.,* p. 206.
7. *Ibid.* p. 34.
8. *Ibid.* p. 61.
9. R. Hakluyt (Ed.) *The Principal Navigations, Voyages* . . . (Dent Edition, London, 1927) I, p. 255. See also Jerome Blum *Lord and Peasant in Russia* (New York, 1964) p. 122.
10. E. A. Bond (Ed.) *op. cit.* p. 35.
11. Karamzin, X, III, Col. 140.

CHAPTER XI

The Election of Tsar Boris, 1598

TOWARDS THE END OF 1597 TSAR FEDOR FELL ILL. IT WAS SOON seen that this time his illness was mortal. The Muscovites had loved him for his piety and goodness and believed that through him God had blessed the Tsardom with peace and the revival of prosperity. But, as at the time of the death of his father, there was general anxiety over the succession. The anxiety was all the greater now because Fedor was the last monarch of the Rurikid dynasty.

As Fedor lay dying, the Patriarch asked him: "To whom do you entrust the tsardom, us orphans, and your Tsaritsa?"[1] Fedor's reply, according to the official church *Zhitie* or biography, was that he bequeathed the sceptre to his wife. Other records state that he made no direct bequest, but merely said that she would remain on the throne after him. Death was at hand and the Patriarch forebore to press the question. Dr Mark Ridley, the Englishman who had been the Tsar's physician since 1594 and was a man of great learning and ability, could do no more. Fedor was anointed and received the last rites. At 1 a.m. on 7 January 1598 he died peacefully.

Tsaritsa Irina remained alone on the throne. Indeed, as though anticipating that this would happen, Fedor had begun earlier to involve her directly in state affairs. Now the Patriarch, Boris, and leading boyars, desperately seeking to avoid an interregnum, hastened to swear the oath of loyalty to her. But Irina was hardly aware of what was happening. She was overwhelmed by grief for her husband and by intense feelings of guilt that through her failure to bear a son she herself had brought the ancient dynasty to an end. She was also suffering from a breakdown in health and possibly had tuberculosis, which led to her death five years later.

Soon after the death of her husband, Irina declared that she would not occupy the throne, but would take holy orders, spending the rest of her life enclosed as a nun. The Patriarch and boyars repeatedly petitioned her to remain as Tsaritsa, leaving the exercise of power to her brother, Boris, as it had been during Fedor's reign. Irina firmly rejected their pleas. She evidently had no interest in her brother's succession or in the founding of a Godunov dynasty. Ten days after Fedor's death, she left the Kremlin and entered the Novodevichy Monastery on the outskirts of Moscow, where she took vows under the name of Aleksandra. The monastery, founded to commemorate the recovery of the city of Smolensk by Grand Prince Vasily III, father of Ivan the Terrible, was a fortress, guarding Moscow especially against attacks by the Crimean Tatars from the south-west. It contained a special garrison of Streltsi, but the centre of the life of the monastery was the magnificent Smolensk Cathedral, where widows of the Grand Princes and Tsars were buried. Here Irina occupied a small building with its own chapel near to the cathedral.

Patriarch Iov as the most senior man in the land now headed the government, but he acted in the name of the Tsaritsa-Nun Aleksandra. The urgent problem was the election of a new Tsar. The Patriarch and the great majority of the people had no doubt that Boris Godunov should be chosen. He had exercised power during Tsar Fedor's reign in a way that had won him general popularity. He was immensely rich and powerful. Countless people had benefited from his patronage and had become his ardent supporters. He was the brother of the Tsaritsa and had stood close to the throne not only in the reign of Tsar Fedor but also of Tsar Ivan. There was no one else who could equal his record of service or rival him in ability.

The Patriarch with the church hierarchy, and representative boyars and citizens of Moscow went to the Novodevichy Monastery to ask the Tsaritsa to give her blessing to her brother as Tsar. Irina declined. The Patriarch and his party then approached Boris, who had himself also retired to a cell in the monastery, and asked him to accept the throne. Boris refused. He declared that he had never considered it possible that he might be elevated to such a position or could succeed a Tsar so saintly as Fedor, and that he was unworthy.[2] But in private consultation with the Patriarch he apparently made it clear that he would accept the throne if this was the demand of the Zemsky Sobor, the assembly of representatives of the people from all parts of the country.

The Patriarch then ruled that the election of the new Tsar should not take place until forty days after the Tsar's death, which was the period of formal mourning for a deceased sovereign.

But couriers were sent without delay to summon representatives to Moscow.

In this tense period of interregnum Boris acted with greatest caution. He was ambitious and confident in his ability to rule. But he had served two Tsars loyally, and had never shown signs of being a usurper. The possibility that the throne might come within his grasp apparently occurred to him no earlier than 1594–95. The death of the infant Tsarevna, Feodosia, in 1594 had been followed by a noticeable decline in the health and spirits of Tsaritsa Irina. Tsar Fedor, too, was then ageing. The possibility that they might have more children had become remote.

About this time Boris began to bring forward his own son, Fedor Borisovich, as joint ruler. The boy received envoys with his father and sometimes alone, and his name was joined with that of Boris in official documents. Indeed, it seemed that, looking ahead to the succession of his son and to the firm foundation of a new Godunov dynasty, Boris was starting the training of his son early. But he embarked on this course only after it was clear that Irina would not produce an heir to the throne and that she would not obstruct the succession of her brother and her nephew.

With such dynastic ambitions Boris was not prepared to accept election by the Patriarch, the boyars, and the people of Moscow. His election had to be the result of the will of all the people, formally expressed by their representatives, meeting in the Assembly of the Land. This was important, for he knew that his position as Tsar and his dynasty would be precarious and that enemies would be waiting to overthrow him and his son.

While Tsar Fedor was alive, the boyars had accepted him as ruler, but many of them were hostile to his election as Tsar. With vivid memories of their complete subjugation to the throne during the reign of Tsar Ivan, they were eager now to limit the power of the throne by some formal deed which would also secure their own powers and privileges. In Poland-Lithuania the nobility had succeeded in entrenching their position so that their kings had to respect their rights and privileges, and the throne was not hereditary. The boyars wanted a similar arrangement. The election of the first Tsar of a new dynasty offered a favourable opportunity to secure their position. It was all the more important to them, if Boris, a representative of the untitled Muscovite boyars, who as ruler had shown no favour towards the boyar class as a whole, was to be elected Tsar. Indeed, the boyars would probably have accepted him as Tsar, if he had been willing to agree some limitation of the absolute power.

Boris did not want the throne on such terms. He was evidently determined that he and his dynasty would not be shackled in this way. He had grown up under the absolute rule of Tsar Ivan and clearly believed that the principle of a centralised state under the unfettered rule of the autocrat was the right system for Russia. Like Tsar Ivan, he accepted the principle of absolute rule as enunciated by Peresvetov.

Soon after Irina's renunciation of the throne, the boyars attempted to gain power at least temporarily. Dyak Vasily Shchelkalov proposed to the people of Moscow that, instead of calling Boris to the throne, a government should be formed from members of the Boyar Council. The crowd rejected the proposal. They were generally hostile to the boyars as a class and feared above all a boyar anarchy such as the country had known in the first years of Tsar Ivan's reign. Now they insisted that they had already sworn allegiance to Irina. Many were demanding that Boris should mount the throne without further delay. In the face of popular opinion, the boyars could only await the decision of the Assembly of the Land.

Reports by foreigners in Moscow, which are valuable sources of information, are limited for this crucial period of interregnum. The reason was that, on the death of the Tsar, the Russians with their passion for secrecy and concern for security, went to great lengths to prevent news of their affairs reaching other countries. The frontiers were closed and no one could enter or depart from the country. Sentries, standing guard on all roads to the borders, turned back travellers without exception. Precautions were yet more stringent now when the new Tsar and dynasty had to be elected. Foreign merchants were detained under guard in Moscow, Pskov, Smolensk, and other towns. Garrisons were reinforced and special defences hurriedly erected. The country was placed virtually in a state of siege.

Foreigners for their part made every effort to find out what was happening. On learning of Tsar Fedor's death, Andrei Sapega, a Lithuanian official, managed to send his agents over the frontier and during the forty days of official mourning he obtained interesting, although not always reliable, information which he reported to the Lithuanian Hetman, Kristofor Radzivil.

In January, Andrei Sapega wrote that there were four candidates for the throne. They were Boris Godunov, Fedor Nikitich Romanov, Prince Fedor Ivanovich Mstislavsky, and Bogdan Belsky. He considered that Fedor Romanov was most likely to succeed because of his family relationship with the deceased Tsar. He added that the rivalry for the throne was intense and might give rise to bloodshed and civil war. In particular, Bogdan Belsky, who had been banished and had returned to Moscow with a large suite, intent on becoming Tsar, might provoke violence.

Ten days later, Andrei Sapega wrote that, as he neared death, Tsar Fedor had told Boris that he could not succeed because he was not of noble birth and that the throne should pass to Fedor Romanov. It was a most unlikely story, for the Romanovs were equally not of noble birth. He also reported a distorted rumour that Tsarevich Dmitri had been murdered and had not died from a self-inflicted wound. The letter was of interest in illustrating the stories that were being circulated in the campaign to prevent Boris's election. Closing his report, however, he wrote of the great popularity of Boris with all except the nobility. In a further letter, dated 13/23 February he referred to the bitter rivalry between Boris and Fedor Romanov and again mentioned the possibility of bloodshed.[3]

The Assembly of the Land met in Moscow on 17 February. It consisted of 512 delegates, representing the clergy, the boyars, senior officials, serving gentry, merchants and townspeople, as well as for this occasion the officers of the Streltsi. Patriarch Iov presided and, having opened the proceedings with prayers, he declared that, "For me, Iov Patriarch, for the metropolitans, archbishops, bishops, archimandrites, abbots, and for the whole of the holy oecumenical synod, for the boyars, lesser nobility, both civil and military, for all the people, for the merchants, and all Orthodox Christians, who have been in Moscow, the mind and counsel of all unanimously is that we do not wish to look beyond Boris Fedorovich for our sovereign."[4] The Patriarch then explained to the Assembly in detail the achievements and qualities which entitled him before all others to election to the throne of Muscovy.

On Saturday and Sunday, 18 and 19 February, the members of the Assembly and others gathered in the Uspensky Cathedral for prayers that God would bless their request and grant them Boris as their sovereign. On Monday, the Patriarch and members of the Assembly, followed by a vast crowd, made their way to the Novodevichy Monastery, where Boris was still in retreat. In response to their humble petition that he should become Tsar, however, Boris replied firmly that he could not entertain the thought of such high office.

The Patriarch and all with him were nonplussed. Many wept and prayed. The Patriarch returned to Moscow and on the following day he prayed with the members of the Assembly and the vast congregation which crowded into the Uspensky Cathedral and filled the outside square. It was resolved then that any Muscovite who recognised as Tsar any person other than Boris, his son, or their successors would be excommunicated from the Church and handed over to the state authorities for trial.

The Patriarch then led the members of the Assembly and almost the whole population of Moscow, including women and children, in a solemn procession with the most sacred miracle-working ikons and with banners to the Novodevichy Monastery. Boris was moved to tears by this procession which he met at the monastery gates. After praying in the chapel, the Patriarch, accompanied by members of the holy synod and ikon-bearers, went to the cell of the Tsaritsa-Nun. The meeting was emotional and marked by deepest piety. But again she and then her brother rejected the petition, presented by the Patriarch on behalf of the Assembly.

On the following day the Patriarch and holy synod again attended upon the Tsaritsa-Nun and on Boris. It had been decided that in the event of their continuing to reject the pleas of the Assembly, Boris would be expelled from the Church. It was a terrible threat which would also lie heavily upon Irina. This time she yielded to their pleas. Boris was present and, repeating once again that he had never had pretensions to the throne, he agreed to become Tsar.

Five days later Boris went to Moscow. The Patriarch conducted him into the Uspensky Cathedral and he joined with the congregation in a service of thanksgiving. Boris stood before the people in the cathedral, holding the hands of his son, Fedor, and of his daughter, Kseniya. They remained at his side during the great banquet that followed in which the boyars, clergy, and merchants and all the people feasted.

Boris then returned to his cell in the Novodevichy Monastery and remained there during Lent and Easter. Only on 30 April, some two months later, did he take up residence in the Kremlin Palace and then, as though still feeling unworthy, he declined to occupy the apartments of Tsar Fedor and resided in his sister's part of the palace, while a new building was erected. Furthermore, he postponed his coronation until 1 September, the first day of the new year in the Russian calendar.

Certain contemporaries and later historians were highly critical of Boris's conduct. They decried the hypocrisy of his repeated avowals that he had no thought of occupying the throne and of his persistent rejection of the popular pleas that he become Tsar. Rumours were to circulate later to the effect that, having poisoned Tsar Fedor, Boris procured his election by trickery. It was alleged that he sent agents, including priests and monks, throughout the country to persuade the people, by bribery and force if necessary, to demand his election, and that the procession of the people to the Novodevichy Monastery was organised by armed troops. Such rumours, spread by enemies, run counter to all that is known of the character and methods of Boris. At this time, in particular, he was seeking real, not coerced or bribed, support from the people.

This was a critical time for Boris. While ambitious for himself and his family and confident that he could serve the country more effectively than any other contender, he may well have had fears and second thoughts. He had known the savagery surrounding the throne in Tsar Ivan's reign and then the quiet years when he had been the ruler under Tsar Fedor. His fears were primarily for his children whom he adored. He knew that the savagery could erupt again at any time. Unlike Tsars Ivan and Fedor he would not have in support of his authority the strong dynastic tradition which had placed them beyond serious challenge. At times he appeared to be appalled by the dangers to which he and his family would be exposed when he became Tsar, and his worst fears were to be realised. In the weeks after Tsar Fedor's death he acted like a man who was moved by the fates towards a cruel and tragic end.

Boris was determined that his election to the throne should have the widest possible support. It could not rest on election, although apparently unanimous, of the Assembly of the Land. It had to be seen to be the will of the people. Moreover, his position as Tsar and founder of a new dynasty had to be entrenched and formalised so as to be beyond challenge. The oath of loyalty to a new Tsar was usually taken by the people kissing the Cross at the palace and in government offices. Boris sought to make the oath more binding by having it administered in churches and in Moscow in the Uspensky Cathedral. For weeks prayers and services in the Cathedral were disrupted by the people loudly intoning the oath. Moreover, the terms of the oath were stronger, threatening all who betrayed him and his family with anathema. Church authorities were ordered to include in the daily prayer for the sovereign special prayers for his wife and children, which was then unusual. An annual procession of the Cross to the Novodevichy Monastery was inaugurated to commemorate the election of Tsar Boris. The Deed of Confirmation of his election, composed by Patriarch Iov or under his supervision, was couched in a high-flown eulogistic style, but also it had to be signed by every member of the Assembly of the Land in duplicate. One copy was solemnly deposited in the sacristy of the Uspensky Cathedral and the other with state papers in the Tsar's treasury. The oath of loyalty was apparently administered twice, the first time soon after Boris's election and the second on 1 September on the occasion of his coronation. But these and many other devices intended to bind the people irrevocably in their loyalty to their chosen Tsar were to be in vain.

On 1 April, while Boris was still residing in the Novodevichy Monastery, Don Cossacks brought news to Moscow that Kazy Girei, the Crimean Khan, was about to launch a massive invasion. Boris gave urgent orders for the mobilising of the army on the banks of the Oka River. On 20 April, Don Cossacks reported further that advance detachments of Tatars had been seen in the steppelands and had attacked Russian border posts. Boris decided now to take command of the army. On 2 May he set out from Moscow for Serpukhov which he made his headquarters.

The Muscovite army, concentrated on the banks of the Oka River, was said to be the largest ever mobilised. It was even reported to be 500,000 strong. The military camp, covering an area of five square miles, was like "a whole town of tents" or a white-walled city with many gates and towers. On the petition of the Patriarch and the Assembly of the Land, which remained in session, Boris set aside *Mestnichestvo* for the campaign. This freed him from the obligation of appointing Prince Fedor Mstislavsky and other boyars to the high commands. He gave senior commands to serving gentry of ability and also to certain loyal Tatar Tsarevichi in the Muscovite service.

On 10 May two fugitives from the Crimea brought news that the Khan with his main army had begun his advance northwards. No further reports were received for some time. Boris devoted himself to inspecting his troops and the defence positions, and launched a flotilla of barges on the Oka. But on 18 June a courier rode into Serpukhov with the message that the Khan's envoys were coming to propose peace terms. The envoys arrived on 29 June. They were well received and lavishly entertained. Every effort was made at the same time to impress them with the military might of the Tsar. Boris accepted the offer of peace and sent his own envoys to the Khan.

The threat of war removed, Boris entertained his troops and rewarded them generously. Critics in Moscow alleged that there had never been a genuine Tatar threat and that the Muscovite army had been mobilised so that the Tsar could ingratiate himself with his troops. It seems certain, however, that the Khan was planning a major campaign and that he was deterred by reports of the prompt and massive build-up of the Russian defence forces. The Khan made no further attempts to invade Muscovy during Boris's reign. The Tatars wanted booty and captives, not pitched battles and casualties. Raids on Hungary, Moldavia, and Poland were less arduous and more rewarding. But Boris took full advantage of the concentration of his army round Serpukhov to gain popularity and support among the officers and men. In this he was apparently successful. The army was loyal to him. "And all of the warriors rejoiced and hoped for more favours in the future."[5]

On 29 June, Boris set out from Serpukhov in a great triumphal procession. He was welcomed with enthusiasm by the people of Moscow, as he entered the city. In a fulsome speech of welcome the Patriarch praised him for defending the nation. Indeed, all seemed united in their loyalty to him. But Boris knew that enemies were conspiring against him.

Andrei Sapega wrote in a letter dated 6 June (1598) that, according to his agents, Boris had been about to set out from Moscow for Serpukhov, when he learnt that certain boyars were planning to put forward Simeon Bekbulatovich as Tsar in his place. The boyars, who were now his active enemies, had formerly been his friends and allies. Foremost among them was Fedor Romanov, supported by his brother, Aleksandr. Nikita, father of Fedor and Aleksandr Romanov, had entrusted them to Boris's care. Bogdan Belsky had shared with Boris the favour of Tsar Ivan during the closing years of his reign, and the two young men had been friends. When shortly after Ivan's death Belsky had aroused the anger of the Muscovite people and had been banished, Boris had helped him, ensuring that he had essentials and could live in reasonable comfort. The outstanding Dyaki, Andrei and Vasily Shchelkalov, had also been the close allies of Boris. Andrei had been dismissed for reasons not known, but his brother, Vasily, had carried on his work.

During the reign of Tsar Fedor, the Godunov and Romanov and Shchelkalov had formed the powerful nucleus of the court nobility which had wielded authority. The fact that Boris was pre-eminent and, in fact, the ruler had caused no rift between them. As soon as Tsar Fedor died, however, the struggle for power put them asunder. They united in cruel enmity against Boris, whose title to the throne they would never accept. They provided the core of the opposition. The princely caste has always resented the rise of the untitled Muscovite boyars. It was noteworthy at this time, however, that no surviving member of the princely families of the Rurik and Gedimin lines laid any claim to the throne. These families had been so weakened by Tsar Ivan's persecution that they had remained in the background, accepting Boris's administration during Tsar Fedor's reign. In fact, they had no popular support. No one mentioned the names of the Princes Shuisky, Golitsyn, Kurakin, or others of this caste. Prince Fedor Mstislavsky was named as a candidate, but he firmly renounced all claims to the throne.

It was significant, too, that Boris's enemies could find as a rival candidate only Simeon Bekbulatovich, who was old and blind, and had never been more than a figurehead. He was the direct descendant of the last Khan of the Golden Horde. As Tsar or Khan of Kasimov he had sworn allegiance to Tsar Ivan and, embracing Christianity, had been baptised Simeon Bekbulatovich. Tsar Ivan had made him Grand Prince of all Russia for a time, but it had been merely a nominal appointment. He was next made Grand Prince of Tver where he exercised all the powers of an apanage prince. Soon after the death of Tsar Ivan, however, he was shorn of his wealth and power, and he also lost his sight, which enemies of Boris blamed on his use of witchcraft. He had fallen into disgrace when his father-in-law, Prince Ivan Mstislavsky, was banished. In promoting Simeon Bekbulatovich as a candidate for the throne, the boyars clearly expected that he would be no more than a figurehead and that they would wield power in his name.

Boris did not make an issue of this conspiracy. He had no fear that Simeon would prove a serious rival. The formal deed, recording his election, nevertheless threatened with excommunication any who dared to support rivals to Boris, his son and heirs. Moreover, the second oath of loyalty contained a specific clause, by virtue of which all had to swear that they would not befriend or correspond with Simeon or recognise him as Tsar. Simeon himself was required to swear that he would never lay claim to the throne or support opponents of Boris, and he was kept under constant guard.

Boris took no further action, but in this savage age he would have been wise to have acted as ruthlessly as his enemies behaved towards him. He was confident, however, that the overwhelming majority of the people supported his election and that he had been right to postpone his coronation until he had secured such support.

The coronation took place in the Uspensky Cathedral on 1 September, 1598, as appointed. It was an occasion of magnificence and solemn prayer. But the incident which apparently most impressed all present, happened when the new Tsar, having received the blessing of the Patriarch, declared in a loud voice: "Father, great Patriarch Iov! May God be my witness that there will not be a poor man in my Tsardom!" and, tearing the collar from his gown, he added: "And even to my last shirt I will share with all!"[6] It was a melodramatic gesture, which has been distorted and derided. It was, however, sincerely intended. Boris sought power and eminence for himself and his family, but he was also eager to rule with popular support and to rule justly.

Again when the awards, customarily made after the coronation of the Tsar, were declared, it was noteworthy that Aleksandr Romanov was made a boyar and that Bogdan Belsky was advanced to the rank of Okolnichy. The awards were intended no doubt to mollify them. But the awards also reflected Boris's anxiety to avoid the extremes of Tsar Ivan who would have had both men executed long ago.

Other awards revealed Boris's concern for the merchants, most of whom were exempted from payment of customs duties for two years. He also tried to ameliorate the hardships suffered by the peasantry. On patrimonial and service estates, their masters often exacted crushing obligations. A table of the maximum payments and services that could be required of peasants was issued in an attempt to protect them. Generous grants were made to other classes of the people. Boris was clearly indicating that his reign would be a time when all of the people were to be his concern.

Notes
1. Solovyev, IV, VII, p. 345.
2. *Ibid.* p. 347.
3. S. F. Platonov, *Boris Godunov* (Petrograd, 1921) pp. 124–5.
4. Solovyev, IV, VII, pp. 349–9.
5. G. Vernadsky, *The Tsardom of Moscow 1547–1682* (New Haven, 1969) p. 209.
6. Solovyev, IV, VII, p. 356.

CHAPTER XII

Tsar Boris : The Years of Promise,
1598–1602

AT THE OUTSET OF BORIS'S REIGN, MUSCOVY SEEMED POISED FOR AN era of peace, stability, and prosperity such as the country had never known. The first two years were acknowledged by one of Boris's most fervent critics to have been the finest years in the history of Muscovy since its foundation.[1]

One of the first triumphs for Boris was the final conquest of Siberia. Kuchum, the former Siberian Khan, had rejected Moscow's proposals for peace and continued to attack Russian settlements. While he was at large there could be no security for settlers. Indeed, the Tsar's rule in Siberia was threatened. In August 1598 the Tarsky military commander, Andrei Voeikov, with a force of only 397 Cossacks, Lithuanians, and others advanced against the positions held by Kuchum on the banks of the Ob River. He attacked the Khan's camp and, after a day of fierce fighting, he defeated the Tatars. He took prisoner the eight wives, five sons, and eight daughters of Kuchum, who managed to escape by boat downriver. Voeikov sent envoys to find the Khan with the offer of security for himself and his family, if he would accept the Tsar's suzerainty. But Kuchum, now old and nearly blind and deserted by all but thirty faithful servants, stubbornly refused. He made his way farther south where, it was said, the Nogai Tatars murdered him.

In January 1599 Voeikov made a triumphal entry into Moscow with the remnants of his small force and his prisoners. The Tsar spared no expense in making it a magnificent occasion. The Muscovites were in a mood to rejoice. This time they were celebrating not the conquest of Siberia which Tsar Ivan had achieved, but the secure possession of this vast new land as an integral part of Russia. This had been brought about by the statemanship and administrative genius of Boris. During Fedor's reign he had erected the chain of strongholds and had peopled them with settlers and garrisons of troops and now he was responsible for the defeat of the last opposition.

Foreign policy underwent no change after Boris had become Tsar. It was the policy that Tsar Ivan had pursued, but Boris was more cautious, avoiding war and relying on diplomacy, astutely taking advantage of the weaknesses of his enemies. Livonia remained the chief objective in the west, but Boris's immediate purpose was to obtain security from attack, while Muscovy gathered stability and strength and he established himself on the throne.

The conflict which had erupted between Poland-Lithuania and Sweden favoured this policy. Disagreements between Sigismund III, King of Poland, and his uncle, Karl, whom he had appointed to rule as regent in Sweden during his absence, had become critical. In 1598 Sigismund landed an army in Sweden in an attempt to expel Karl. He was defeated, however, and in the following year the Swedish Diet deposed him, appointing Karl as governing Crown Prince and later as Karl IX, King of Sweden. In 1600 Sweden and Poland-Lithuania went to war over possession of the whole of Livonia. Boris was careful to avoid being directly involved, but he watched for the chance to regain Narva and ultimately to claim Livonia. It was with this policy in mind that in 1599 Boris invited Prince Gustavus to Moscow.

Gustavus was the son of the Swedish King, Erik XIV, who had been overthrown and imprisoned by his younger brother, Johann, in 1568. The new king gave orders for the young Prince Gustavus, his nephew, to be drowned. Friends carried the boy off to Poland, however, and there he had been brought up by Jesuits and converted to Catholicism. He was an able scholar, learned in chemistry and the master of four or five languages. He had lived in several countries, supported by the meagre allowance granted by his brother, Sigismund. Tsar Fedor had invited him to Moscow, but he had declined. Now he accepted Boris's invitation.

Boris saw in Gustavus a useful political weapon against both Sigismund and Karl. His plan was to instal him as vassal ruler of Livonia as a step towards annexing the province. He had been cultivating the goodwill of the nobles and merchants of Narva, Dorpat, and Riga, promising that under the Tsar's rule their freedoms, religion, and laws would be guaranteed. The plan miscarried, mainly because the Livonians harboured deep mistrust of the Russians and did not believe that the Tsar's promises would be honoured. Moreover, since both Sigismund and Karl had troops stationed in parts of Livonia, they knew that they would face swift reprisals if they sought to transfer allegiance to the Tsar.

During these months Boris had entered into separate negotia-

tions with Sigismund and Karl. Both were eager for peace with
Russia. Boris had sent the customary embassy to inform Sigismund
of his election to the throne. In return the king appointed as his
ambassador Lev Sapega, the Lithuanian chancellor who, like his
brother Andrei, was experienced in Russian affairs. Sapega's embassy was exceptional in size and opulence. In addition to diplomatic staff, it included 400 attendants and 700 servants. On its
arrival in Moscow the embassy was allocated accommodation and
there it was confined for nearly six weeks. Sapega fumed with
impatience and offended dignity, but was merely told that the Tsar
was unable to receive him in audience because he had gout. In fact,
Boris was in no hurry to start negotiations, preferring to wait in the
hope that Sigismund would find himself tied down in a major war
with Sweden and compelled for this reason to concede Moscow's
demands.

On 16 November, 1600, Sapega was at last received in audience.
Negotiations with senior boyars began in the following week. They
were constantly bedevilled by bitter quarrelling. The Poles refused
to use Boris's title of Tsar, calling him Sovereign and Grand Prince.
The boyars countered by refusing to recognise Sigismund's claim
to be called King of Sweden. Sapega nevertheless put forward his
main proposal for an "eternal peace" on the basis of the union of
Poland-Lithuania with Russia with equality of rights and movement for all subjects of both countries. This proposal had first been
made in Moscow in 1586 by Garaburda, the envoy of Stefan
Batory, and the Tsar had rejected it. Boris did not favour this
solution. Negotiations on conditions and guarantees reached dead-
lock, which was broken apparently as a result of the direct intercession of Fedor Borisovich, the son of Boris. Agreement was then
reached on a twenty-year armistice.

Meanwhile Karl, who had not yet been elected King of Sweden,
was seeking alliance with Moscow against Poland-Lithuania. Boris
considered sending troops to expel the Poles, but then decided to
try to secure his purpose by diplomacy. In the course of discussions
the Russians pointed out that the armistice agreed in 1597 had to
be reviewed and confirmed, for it had not been ratified by Sigismund at that time and a new Tsar had since ascended the Russian
throne. Further it was claimed that Narva should be surrendered
to Moscow under the revised agreement. It was even alleged that
Sigismund had already conceded part of Livonia in return for
military aid against Sweden. The bluff did not work. The Swedish
envoys indignantly rejected the proposal and Boris did not press it
further. He was careful to avoid any action that might unite Poland-
Lithuania and Sweden against Muscovy. He continued to maintain

friendly relations with Karl and was the first to recognise his election as King of Sweden.

In welcoming the Swedish Prince, Gustavus, to Moscow in 1599, Boris had in mind the Livonian plan which proved abortive. But he had also another purpose. He was desperately eager to establish a dynasty by the marriage of his children with royal families in the West. He could never forget that the Godunov family, while highly respected, was not of noble origin. It may be, too, that he was reluctant to accept a Russian prince or princess, since to be worthy of marriage with the Tsarevich or the Tsarevna it would have to be someone chosen from one of the old noble families, who might overshadow the Godunovs in the eyes of the people, and in time might take over the dynasty. Intermarriage with ruling houses in the West would bring prestige, while furthering Russian interests. He saw such advantages in the marriage of Kseniya, his daughter, with Gustavus.

Kseniya was about seventeen years old at this time and renowned for her beauty. She was of medium height, full-figured and shapely. Her complexion was "milky white" and her hair black and thick, reaching in curls to her shoulders. Her eyes, too, were large, dark and expressive. She was, moreover, gentle and submissive, and by Muscovite standards well educated, loving books and music. She was, indeed, an exemplar of Muscovite womanhood.

Gustavus, a prince of Sweden and highly educated, seemed a desirable husband. In other ways, however, he proved unsuitable. He refused to serve as an instrument of the Tsar's policy against Sweden. He would not change his religion, as was necessary for marriage with the Tsarevna, and he would not be parted from his mistress. At one stage, when excited by wine, he spoke against the Tsar and threatened to set fire to Moscow, if he was not allowed to leave the country. When this was reported, Boris was extremely angry. He at once confiscated the estates that he had settled on the prince and had him held under house arrest. He relented, however, and bestowed upon him the ruined apanage of Uglich. There he lived quietly, devoting himself to the study of chemistry. He died in the nearby town of Kashin in 1607.

The obstinate refusal of Gustavus to comply with the conditions for marriage with Kseniya was a severe disappointment to Boris. Evidently this was noted at court. Sir Anthony Shirley, writing to Sir Robert Cecil on 10 June, 1600, from Archangel, proposed that Queen Elizabeth might offer to Tsar Boris "any gentleman of spirit whom she might vouchsafe to call cousin" as a husband for the Tsarevna.[2]

Boris turned meanwhile to Denmark, the traditional enemy of

Sweden. King Christian III was keenly interested in securing an alliance with the Tsar. His brother, Duke Johann, who was unmarried, also expressed interest. He seemed eminently suitable, and he raised no objection to joining the Russian Orthodox Church and becoming an apanage prince under the Tsar's suzerainty.

In August 1602 Johann arrived at the mouth of the Narova River and travelled by land to Moscow. His journey was a triumphal progress. He was shown the greatest respects at every halt, and he made a favourable impression on the Muscovites. On 18/28 September in the midst of magnificent ceremonial he was presented to the Tsar and the Tsarevich. Boris was apparently delighted with the good-looking young Dane, whose illustrious background, dignity, and charm made him an ideal son-in-law. Kseniya was said to have fallen in love with him on sight. She could not meet him, according to Muscovite convention, until the betrothal and then the marriage ceremony, which were appointed to take place in the winter. She had been able, however, to glimpse him from behind a screen.

Johann was eager to learn Russian and to prepare himself for baptism according to the Orthodox rite. He was escorted to the Troitsa Monastery by the Tsar and Tsarevich and the whole court. They remained there for nine days, praying at the tomb of the greatly venerated St Sergii, and asking God's blessing upon the union of the young couple.

Boris was travelling back to Moscow when couriers overtook him with the news that Johann had fallen ill. At first it had seemed to be some minor ailment, but suddenly it had become more serious. Boris travelled on to Moscow, but on 7 October, accompanied by the Patriarch and leading boyars, he again made the forty-four-mile journey to the Troitsa. He was amazed to see the young prince so weak and wasted. The doctors, including a Dane from the prince's suite, had already given up hope. At 6 p.m. on 18 October Johann died. He was just twenty years old. He was accorded a full state funeral which Boris, the court, and all Moscow attended. The young prince was mourned throughout the country, and there were rumours that he had been poisoned by enemies of the Godunovs.[3]

Relations with the Crimean Tatars remained peaceful, although overclouded by mistrust, threats, and petty disputes. Khan Kazy Girei was under pressure to provide troops for the Sultan, his suzerain and, striving to maintain his independence, he was anxious for peace with Moscow at this time. Moreover, he had not forgotten the military might which Boris had concentrated at Serpukhov on the Oka in 1598. The new Russian defence lines and strongholds, erected against Tatar attacks, were a further deterrent. In 1600

Boris ordered the building of Tsarev-Borisov, a new fortress-town on the lower Oskol, near to its outlet into the Donets River. He entrusted this important project to Bogdan Belsky, who had a reputation as a military expert. The town, which was close to the Crimea, was intended to serve not only for defence but also for offensive action against the Tatars when the time was ripe.

At this stage, however, the Khan was more disturbed by the continued raiding of the Don Cossacks. This was one reason for his tardiness in formally concluding the peace treaty, agreed in Serpukhov. He complained, too, that the Tsar's gift of 14,000 rubles was far below the amount expected. When in 1602 he finally ratified the treaty, he demanded a further 30,000 rubles. This was refused, but the Khan was in no position to embark on war.

The Turkish Sultan, Mehmet III, and his successor, Ahmet I, were preoccupied with the Long War on the Danube and also by internal unrest and Persian advances in the Eastern Caucasus under the able leadership of Shah Abbas I. The Turks made no attempts at this time to recover Astrakhan or to act directly against Moscow. Boris carried on discussions with the Austrian ambassadors concerning the formation of an alliance against the Turks. He knew that the Sultan had ordered the Crimean Khan to lay waste Russian territory. He therefore encouraged the Emperor in his war against the Ottoman Porte. Indeed a series of envoys were exchanged between the two courts in the years 1598 to 1604. Emperor Rudolf expressed appreciation of Boris's offers of help, but requested money rather than troops, and subsidies were paid into the imperial treasury. Boris also discouraged the Crimean Khan from attacking Austrian territory. Meanwhile Russia remained at peace with the Crimean Khanate and with the Ottoman Porte.

In his efforts to extend Muscovite influence in the Caucasus, however, Boris had to recognise that he did not possess the military and economic power to maintain the Tsar's authority so far from Moscow, especially in a region which Persia and the Ottoman Porte considered to be their sphere of influence.

Alexander, King of Kakheti in Georgia, had been taken under the Tsar's protection in 1586. His envoy arrived in Moscow in July 1599, however, bearing bitter complaints that he had received no support from the Tsar's army during the past twelve years. In 1601 Boris sent two envoys, Ivan Nashchokin and Ivan Leontyev, to the king with renewed assurances of the Tsar's protection and the promise that he would send an army against the Shevkal of Tarku in Daghestan. Meanwhile Alexander was under pressure from Shah Abbas, who demanded that Kakheti should come completely under his rule. In an attempt to mollify the Shah, Alexander had

agreed that his son, Constantine, should become a Moslem, but this
was not enough. The Shah instructed him to kill his father and
brother and, having carried out this order, Constantine became
King of Kakheti. He received Boris's ambassadors and assured
them of the friendly feeling of the Shah and himself for the Tsar.
It was clear, however, that Muscovite influence counted for little in
Kakheti or indeed in Daghestan where a force of some 7,000
Russian troops was wiped out in 1605.

Relations between Russia and England continued to be friendly.
News of the death of Tsar Fedor apparently reached London at the
beginning of May 1598. Elizabeth wrote promptly, expressing
pleasure "that one professing goodwill to us should receive so great
honour as by general opinion of the whole nation to be thought
worthy to be their Lord and Sovereign".[4] Then suddenly the har-
mony which seemed assured between the two courts was threatened by misunderstanding, provoked by Muscovite mistrust and a
lapse in English diplomacy.

Moscow's suspicions that England had helped the Sultan against
his Christian enemies had been assuaged. By the end of 1598, however, rumours were circulating in Moscow to the effect that the
queen was actively supporting Sigismund, King of Poland, against
his uncle, Duke Karl, in the struggle for the Swedish throne.
English merchant ships, it was alleged, had taken part in Sigismund's invasion of Sweden. The invasion was unsuccessful, but
the Tsar and the Muscovite court were incensed by the reports that
the queen was helping their enemies.

Francis Cherry, an officer of the Muscovy Company, who was
experienced and skilled in dealing with the Russians, had managed
to satisfy the Tsar that the queen was not aiding the Turks. But on
his return to London in March 1599 he brought from the Muscovite Foreign Office demands for explanations and assurances that
she was not supporting the King of Poland in any way. In his report
Cherry urged that the queen should send a special envoy to Moscow, bearing her warm congratulations to Boris on his accession
and also her formal denials that she had given any help to Poland.

At this time the queen's Principal Secretary, Sir Robert Cecil,
was concerned with recruiting a physician to attend on the Tsar.
Dr Mark Ridley was eager to leave Moscow after the death of Tsar
Fedor and had invoked the help of influential friends with the
result that the queen herself wrote asking Boris to release him. Dr
Joseph Jessop, who was well qualified both as a physician and a
diplomat, agreed to go to Moscow, but died soon after his appointment. In his place Dr Timothy Willis was chosen. It was an unfortunate choice. The lapse in the judgment of Cecil and Cherry,

two of the queen's most able servants, was presumably due to their desperation in the search for someone to fill this unattractive post.

The medical qualifications of Timothy Willis were slight. He had been expelled from Oxford and had been denounced at St John's College, as "the corrupter of all the scholars . . ." He had failed an examination at the Royal College of Physicians in 1586. Indeed, his sole qualification for the appointment of physician to the Tsar was that he was eager to go to Moscow where, presumably, he thought he would make his name and his fortune.

On 24 June, 1599, the queen nevertheless signed a letter recommending "an especial choice amongst our learned physicians of him to be used in your service; being in degree a Doctor of Physic and of great experience, not only in that profession but in all liberal sciences, fit for any Prince's service".[5]

Already in March it had been decided to appoint Richard Lee as the queen's ambassador to Moscow. One of the main purposes of his mission would surely have been to convey assurances that the queen had not given any support to Sigismund of Poland. His departure was delayed, however, presumably because it was thought that Dr Timothy Willis could perform this task. It was a regrettable decision. He was not only inadequate, but also he was not properly briefed.

Francis Cherry had had for his mission in the previous year a set of instructions, attested by four Privy Councillors and drafted with special care for presentation to the Muscovite government. It was well understood that the Russian officials would examine such documents with great care and, seizing on any flaws in the drafting, would demand detailed explanations.

The unfortunate Willis was not equipped in this way. He carried only for his own information a copy of a memorandum by George Carew, the queen's envoy in Poland and Sweden, who had recently returned to England. This memorandum showed convincingly that thirteen of the English ships which had sailed in support of Sigismund's invasion of Sweden had been forced into the Polish service. Two other ships had been fitted out for the purpose by English merchants in Elbing, who probably feared that the ships would be requisitioned in any case. Certainly no ships had been provided by or with the knowledge of the queen. Sir Robert Cecil was disturbed by the reference to the two ships, for he wrote in the margin of the report that Willis should inform the Russians that they were both "taken by constraint". Timothy Willis thus had a strong case to present and it was thought that, relying on the advice of John Merrick, the experienced senior agent of the Company in Russia, he would be able to satisfy the Tsar and his ministers.

Timothy Willis arrived in Moscow on 4 September after a difficult journey which can only have aggravated his irascible temperament. He was quite unprepared for the interviews with Vasily Yakovlevich Shchelkalov, the Dyak of the Foreign Office who was strongly anglophobe, or for his probing examination of every statement made.

Willis presented the queen's letter and, when questioned, admitted that he was empowered to make a statement concerning the allegation of English aid to Poland. Shchelkalov then extracted the further admission that he had a copy of the Carew report, although he insisted that it was "only for my memory". He was ordered to fetch the document forthwith. The Russians apparently believed that the report was part of Willis's instructions and intended for them to see, and they bitterly resented Willis's apparent reluctance to part with the document.

The inexperience and flustered bad-temper of Willis and the deep suspicion of Shchelkalov and the Russian Foreign Office provoked further misunderstanding. Willis was cross-examined about the Carew report and then about his medical qualifications. For safety he had travelled to Russia as a merchant and had left his books, drugs, and equipment in Lubeck. But Shchelkalov seized on this lack of basic equipment and began to tear to shreds his pretensions to be a physician, competent to treat the Tsar. Willis became more angry and truculent. Then in a third interview Shchelkalov returned to the Carew report which he had had time to study in translation. Dwelling on the reference to the two ships he stated bluntly that the queen's protestations were clearly false. Willis made a spirited defence of her honour, but apparently did nothing to present the English case.

By this time it was evident that Shchelkalov regarded Willis not only with deep suspicion but also with active dislike. He vented his long-standing anglophobia upon him. He raked up all the grievances that the Russians had held against the English from the time of Ivan the Terrible. The unhappy Willis was not equipped by ability, temperament, or experience to counter such an assault. He was dismissed ignominiously and dispatched from Moscow after a stay of just three weeks.

In September of the following year Grigori Ivanovich Mikulin arrived in London as the ambassador of Tsar Boris. He was warmly welcomed and every effort made "to receive him royally".[6] The special attention shown to him was certainly intended to repair the damage and erase the ill-feeling caused by Willis's mission. In a closed meeting of the Privy Council, Mikulin made a devastating attack on Willis especially on the ground that he had "varied from his commission" or departed from his instructions, and that, having arrived in Moscow without drugs and books his competence as a physician was questionable. Mikulin's denunciation concluded with the plea:

> Therefore that hereafter it will please the Queen's most excellent Majesty to give charge to her Worthy Counsellors to have care in sending unto our great Lord, King, and great Duke Boris Fedorovich, of all Russia, such messengers and directions as things be not mistaken. But that both their Commissions and speeches may be agreeable the one to the other: to the end that hereafter between our great Lord and the Queen's Majesty of England there may not be any occasion given of breach.[7]

Already in June 1600 Richard Lee, now knighted, had sailed for Archangel at the head of a lavishly equipped embassy. He was elaborately documented for his mission. He carried the queen's commission as her "true and undoubted Attorney, Procurator, Legit, and Ambassador", a Letter of Credence, and full confidential instructions, carefully checked by Sir Robert Cecil. These instructions empowered Richard Lee to make a virtual repudiation of Willis and to deliver a final categoric denial that the queen had ever aided Sigismund of Poland. He was also to counter Russian suspicions about Carew's mission in Poland by explaining that its purpose was "to expostulate injuries offered by the Polonian". At last Moscow was apparently satisfied and their complaints about English aid to Poland no longer figured in diplomatic exchanges.

Mikulin contributed to this improvement in Anglo-Russian relations. He was gratified by his treatment in London and by the respects shown to him as ambassador of the Tsar. Moreover, he acquitted himself well and made a good impression on the queen and her court. Indeed, he greatly distinguished himself during the rebellion of the Earl of Essex on 8 September, 1601, when he took up arms in defence of the queen. She wrote to Boris that, "Upon an occasion of some rebellious attempt against the peace of our government . . . [Mikulin] was ready to have come forth and to have put himself in danger against the undertakers thereof." She added graciously that she could "not but take it in very kind and thankful part of him and think it worthy of Your Majesty's knowledge".[8]

In the course of his discussions, Mikulin referred to the possibility of English marriages for Boris's two children. The matter may have been raised informally earlier. Sir Richard Lee apparently promised the Tsar during his mission in Moscow that the queen would provide suitable spouses for both Tsarevich Fedor and Tsarevna Kseniya. It may be that Lee had no authority to give such an undertaking. But the Muscovy Company in London was disturbed by reports that the Tsar had sent an envoy to Emperor Rudolf II to negotiate the marriage of Kseniya to Archduke Maximilian. The merchants of the Company were afraid that such a marriage would mark the first step in a movement whereby German merchants would supplant them in the Russian trade. The Company was also concerned at this time to get a favourable reply to a request for its agents to be permitted to travel through Russia to trade with Persia. The queen's advisers, too, were disturbed by the friendly attitude of the Tsar and his court towards Austria, and also concerned about trade with Persia. For these reasons, some effort was apparently made to find suitable partners for the Tsar's children.

Boris welcomed Sir Richard Lee's promise. He announced at once that he would call off all other marriage negotiations and requested details of the queen's proposals. She informed him in due course that one of the daughters of the Earl of Derby would provide an excellent wife for the Tsarevich, but that she had then discovered "to our great grief" that she was five years older than Fedor. She concluded that, since she could find no other suitable young people, "We think it our part no longer to hold you in expectation."[9]

The Company's agents in Moscow knew what importance the Tsar attached to the marriage of his children. In August 1601 they wrote to Sir Robert Cecil, urging that the queen should make further proposals, even if unsuitable, for this would show at least that she was taking the matter seriously.[10]

Under pressure from the Company, Elizabeth wrote to Boris and the letter was accompanied by pedigrees of several noble families "near a kind unto her by her mother".[11] The courier chosen to take this letter was John Merrick, one of the Company's senior agents, who spoke Russian.

Merrick arrived in Moscow on 9 February, 1602. Three days later he was conducted to a private interview with Boris who, probably suffering from gout, sat "having his feet placed on a footstool covered with sables".[12] He presented Elizabeth's letter and the pedigrees, which Boris ordered to be translated without delay. Merrick had a further interview on 22 June, 1602. By this time Boris had studied the documents. He was gratified to note that

Elizabeth had chosen only families close to her in blood. In his letter of reply he expressed his pleasure on finding "Your Majesty so sincerely affected towards us and our children" and regretted that she had "not any persons fit or equal to match" with his son and daughter.[13]

In October 1602, still under pressure from the Company, Elizabeth wrote to Boris. This time she stated that she had found a "young lady, being a pure maiden, noble descended by father and mother, adorned with graces and extraordinary gifts of nature, of convenient years between eleven and twelve".[14] The identity of this maiden remains a mystery. Boris wrote on April 1603, asking for details of her pedigree and in particular her relationship with the queen. By this time, however, Elizabeth had died and there was no further action concerning the English marriages.

Boris now turned his attention to Georgia. He had learnt that the Kakhian King, Alexander, had grandchildren, Prince Teymuraz, aged seventeen, and Princess Helen, aged twelve, who might prove acceptable. On 6 May, 1604, Mikhail Tatishchev and Andrei Ivanov, set out on a mission to Kakheti and Kartli "with a view to selecting a prince and princess of the Georgian royal house, suitable for his (the Tsar's) son and daughter . . ."[15] The envoys found conditions troubled and confusing in the Caucasus. They managed, however, in May of the following year to interview both the prince and the princess. By this time, however, Boris was dead and Russia in turmoil.

Boris was undoubtedly deeply disappointed by the failure to arrange marriages for his children in the West. He was a good father, devoted to both of his children. He was also strongly attracted to Western countries, recognising that in industry, education, and even in social life they were ahead of his own country. He had a lively curiosity about everything that happened in the West and was eager to attract to Russia all who possessed special knowledge and skills. In this he shared the outlook of Tsar Ivan during whose reign the *Nemetskaya Sloboda,* the Foreign Quarter, had become established on the banks of the Yauza River outside Moscow.[16] Here doctors, engineers, soldiers, and other trained men settled in increasing numbers, attracted by the rewards that service with the Tsars offered.

Boris showed greater enthusiasm in bringing foreigners to Russia than any previous ruler. At one stage he extended a special welcome to everyone from Livonia, paying them special subsidies to help them settle, granting them estates and, if they were merchants, allowing them interest-free loans. In like manner he promoted Western trade. He surrounded himself with Western doctors and would discourse with them for hours about his own health and health generally, and on other subjects. His enemies, some of whom, like Bogdan Belsky, were rabidly xenophobic, strongly criticised this partiality for foreigners.

Boris was also concerned to encourage education among his people, the vast majority of whom were illiterate. He ensured that his own children had a broad education. His son, Fedor, was said to be learned in the sciences. An interesting memorial of Fedor's interests was a map of Russia which he commissioned and which was published in his name in 1614 by the German cartographer, Gerard. Kseniya, Boris's daughter, received an education unusual for a Russian princess, for it was Muscovite custom to keep girls of noble families immured in the *Terem* or women's quarters, leading ignorant slothful lives.

Boris planned to establish schools and universities. In 1600 he sent a German in his service, named Ioann Kramer, to the West to engage professors and doctors who would found a university in Moscow to teach Russians languages and the sciences. The project alarmed the church hierarchy, who maintained that Catholic and Lutheran teachers, foreign languages, and Western knowledge generally would lead to the corruption and even the apostasy of young Russians. Under pressure from the Church, Boris had to abandon the idea for the time being. But he went ahead with a kindred plan. This was to send Russians abroad to study. When John Merrick, the Russia Company's agent, left Moscow in July 1602 he took with him at the Tsar's request four "Russe young gentlemen" who were to study English, Latin and other subjects. In all, eighteen Russians were sent abroad to study. None returned. It was nevertheless an experiment which showed vision. In more stable political conditions it might have developed to the benefit of Russia. Exactly a century later, Peter the Great revived the scheme on a greater scale.[17]

Boris was, in fact, a reformer, not only in the field of education but also in the social field. He waged a constant struggle to suppress corruption, to discourage drunkenness, and generally to raise standards of behaviour. His reign might have been a time of remarkable achievements. It was, however, cut short.

Notes

1. Karamzin, XI, I, Col. 55.
2. E. Denison Ross, *Sir Anthony Shirley and his Persian Adventure* (Hakluyt Society, London, 1933) p. 246.
   See also W. E. D. Allen, "The Georgian Marriage Projects of Boris Godunov" and N. Evans, "Queen Elizabeth I and Tsar

this episode has been described by historians as the first battle in the long peasant war which continued into the twentieth century.

Boris sent a force of regular troops under the command of Okolnichy Ivan Basmanov to disperse the brigands. They fought a savage battle near Moscow. Basmanov was killed, but the brigands were defeated, many escaping south into the Ukraine. Khlopko himself was wounded and captured, and brought to Moscow where he was hanged. But, although this army of fugitives had been broken up, the southern lands continued to be plagued by lawless bands of peasants and Cossacks.

Famine and brigandage presented challenges against which Boris could take positive action. But the subversive activities of enemies, who conspired and spread evil rumours, surrounded him with nebulous threats against which action was difficult. Rumours attributed to Boris all manner of crimes and increasingly denounced him for the murder of Tsarevich Dmitri. The campaign, blackening his character, aimed at destroying the loyalty of the people and making them question his right to the throne. Many of these rumours began in the Kazan region and in western Siberia, where the Nagoi and other political exiles had been sent. But the sources of the rumours were impossible to track down. Believed and repeated by credulous people, these tales gathered strength and spread rapidly to all parts of the country.

Boris found himself isolated on the throne. The friends and allies who had surrounded him when he was the ruler under Tsar Fedor had become his enemies. He found that he could not rely on members of his own family. The Godunovs were not popular, and Semen Nikitich Godunov, who was head of security, was feared and hated. Dmitri Ivanovich Godunov, the uncle of Boris, had been widely respected and had been granted the rank of boyar in 1578, but he was now an old man. Ivan Ivanovich Godunov, a third cousin, had married Irina, daughter of Fedor Romanov, and he was later to join the enemy camp. Indeed, although members of his family formed the customary informal privy council of the sovereign, Boris could not turn to them for real support and counsel.

It was also the practice for the autocrat to have about him several chosen men, many of whom he raised to boyar rank and treated as favourites. But Boris created very few boyars and apparently had no favourites. The Basmanov brothers, Peter and Ivan, came closest to this relationship. They had been orphaned in the reign of Tsar Ivan, who had banished their father to Beloozero where he had died. The Tsar had taken the two boys under his protection and had granted them their father's estates.

Boris: Five Letters 1597–1603" in *Oxford Slavonic Papers*, XII, 1965.

3. Karamzin, XI, I, Cols. 31–33; Solovyev, IV, VII, p. 367.

4. N. Evans, *op. cit.*, p. 52.

5. For this account of the mission of Dr Timothy Willis I am indebted to the illuminating article by N. Evans in *Oxford Slavonic Papers*, New Series, II (1969) pp. 39–56.

6. T. S. Willan, *The Early History of the Russia Company 1553–1603* (Manchester, 1956) p. 236. See also N. Evans, *op. cit.*, p. 56.

7. N. Evans, *op. cit.*, p. 54.

8. T. S. Willan, *op cit.*, p. 238.

9. N. Evans, *op. cit.*, p. 62.

10. *Ibid.* pp. 62–63.

11. T. S. Willan, *op. cit.*, p. 240.

12. *Ibid.* p. 241.

13. *Ibid.* p. 242

14. *Ibid.* p. 243.

15. W. E. D. Allen, *op. cit.*, p. 71.

16. The Foreign Quarter or *Nemetskaya Sloboda* was sometimes called in English the German Quarter, because *nemets,* from the Russian word meaning "dumb", was the name by which Russians described Germans, but the word early came to mean all European foreigners.

17. The four young Russians, taken to England by John Merrick in 1602, were forgotten during the Time of Troubles. In 1613 representations were made concerning the return of the Tsar's subjects. The Russian Ambassador who arrived in London in 1621, Isaak Samoilovich Pogozhevo, pursued the matter actively. He ascertained that two of the Russians had died, while a third had gone to Ireland and vanished. The fourth was Nikifor Alphery who had joined the Church of England, after taking his degree at Cambridge, and had been Rector of Woolley in Huntingdonshire since 1618. Several attempts had been made by Russian envoys to persuade him to return to Russia. Pogozhevo brought every persuasion and pressure to bear. Alphery insisted, however, "that he believed in the doctrines of the Church of England and did not wish to hold to our (Orthodox) Christian faith . . ." Pogozhevo insisted during an audience with the king that Alphery should be forcibly returned to Russia, but this demand was firmly rejected. Alphery married an Englishwoman and died at Hammersmith in 1668. S. Konovalov, "Anglo-Russian Relations 1620–4" in *Oxford Slavonic Papers*, IV, (1953) pp. 80–82.

CHAPTER XIII

Tsar Boris : The Calamitous Years, 1602–1605

THE PROMISE OF THE FIRST YEARS OF BORIS'S REIGN WAS CRUSHED by the sudden calamity of severe famine and by the subversive activities of his enemies. The wise and humane policies which had given Russia peace and had arrested the economic decline of the 1580s were nullified. The country moved rapidly towards the period of anarchy, known in Russian history as *Smutnoe Vremya*, the Time of Troubles.

In the spring of 1601 heavy rains began to fall and continued for ten weeks. The grain could not ripen and grew tall and green like grass. Then in mid-August the country was gripped by severe frosts which killed the crops in the fields. Grain stocks were soon exhausted and by the winter of 1601–2 the people were starving. They ate grass and hay like cattle. Driven to desperation they became cannibals. Fathers and mothers ate their children. Human flesh was sold in the markets and used in pies.[1]

Profiteers and landowners, including churchmen, intensified the crisis by hoarding grain or buying up what was available and holding it until prices soared. In districts which had been less severely affected, profiteers prevented peasants from bringing their grain to market, seeking in the midst of the general suffering to push their profits yet higher.

Boris acted promptly. He opened the granaries in Moscow and other towns, and grain was distributed to the most needy. He launched a massive building programme to give employment to the people in Moscow. The programme included the erection of new public offices, two new palaces, and a conduit for water to flow to the Kremlin from the Moskva River. He brought pressure to bear on landowners to keep down the price of their grain. He issued a series of ukazi, designed to stop abuses, but the profiteers continued to exort high prices from the starving people. He then ordered distributions of money from the treasury. Four enclosures

were erected by the outer walls of Moscow. Silver coins were laid out in each enclosure and distributed daily to the poor. But grain prices had been so inflated that the coins could buy too little to assuage the general hunger.

Meanwhile the news of the free distributions of grain and money in Moscow spread through the countryside. Peasants with their families streamed into the city, aggravating the terrible conditions there. Adding to this flow were the peasants, many of them slaves or bondsmen, whom landowners evicted from their estates to avoid the obligation of feeding them. These unfortunates were declared to be emancipated, but most landowners failed to provide them with emancipation deeds. Boris tried to remedy their misfortune and to discourage this practice by an ukaz in August 1603, enabling all evicted bondsmen to claim deeds of emancipation from the Office of Slave Affairs. But, like other measures intended to relieve the suffering of the people, this ukaz was only partially effective. It remained almost impossible for the evicted bondsmen to find work and food, and in growing numbers they fled southwards. In the north-western regions the suffering and the death rate were appalling. Boris sent 20,000 rubles for the relief of the poor in Smolensk, and cartloads of grain, which had to be closely guarded by troops, were despatched to centres of greatest hardship. In fact, no town or region was left without aid of some kind.

Conditions in Moscow worsened. The people in the city, weakened by lack of food and eating noisome substances, fell ill and died. The stench of rotting corpses choked the city. Boris ordered burials at state expense, for proper burial was a matter of tremendous significance to the people. Wrapped in the white shrouds and shod in the red boots, which were so important to Muscovites in death, 127,000 bodies were buried by the State. In the period of two years and four months during which the famine raged, 500,000 people were said to have died in Moscow alone and the death rate was far higher outside the city. The famine and plague ended only in 1604, when an exceptional harvest provided food in plenty for all, and the price for a quarter of grain dropped from three rubles to ten kopecks, a thirty-fold decrease.

Famine had given rise to large-scale brigandage. Starving peasants, evicted bondsmen, and malcontents formed robber bands which marauded at will and threatened a complete breakdown of order, especially in the regions south of Moscow. One band of brigands, led by a Cossack ataman, called Khlopko Kosolap, grew to the size of a small army and its advance, which threatened Moscow, was like a peasant rebellion against the State. Indeed

Boris had shown them affection and special attention. But Ivan Basmanov lost his life in the battle against Khlopko's brigands and Peter Basmanov was to go over to Boris's enemies at the first opportunity.

The sense of isolation and the fear that he was surrounded by enemies began to undermine Boris's confidence. He became withdrawn. He did not appear before his people to hear complaints or receive petitions with his own hands, as was customary at certain established times. When he did appear in public, it was with such magnificence that he seemed remote and unapproachable. In his isolation he began to harbour suspicions of all about him, fearing plots to kill him by use of poison or sorcery. Increasingly he turned to agents and informers as a means of protecting himself and his children.

The devil gave Boris the idea that he must know all that was happening in the Muscovite State, so wrote one chronicler.[2] Contemporaries and historians accused him of building up a monstrous network of informers, who stifled society with suspicions and fears. The accusation amounted to gross exaggeration. Delation had long been part of the Muscovite system. It was not his personal invention, but as his sense of security on the throne was undermined he undoubtedly made greater use of informers. Moreover, his cousin, Semen Nikitich Godunov, who was in charge of all security, devoted himself to his task with a zeal which was at times excessive. On one occasion he publicly rewarded a bondsman of Prince Shestunov for informing against his master, although it was shown that the information was false. Encouragement and rewards brought a mounting stream of informers to Semen Godunov's office. Bondsmen and peasants, living in misery and ill-treated, had little to lose in denouncing their masters, and they coveted the rewards.

The increase in the number of informers did not lead, however, to the terror and bloodshed that had stained the reign of Tsar Ivan. Boris was always slow to shed blood. He punished conspiracy by banishment and then only after investigation and trial. Allegations that those who were banished were executed secretly far away from Moscow were unsupported by evidence and questionable.[3] If innocent people suffered as a result of malicious informing, they must have been few in number. Those who really incurred the Tsar's anger and punishment were Bogdan Belsky and the numerous Romanov family, and there could be no doubt that they were his most implacable enemies.

Detailed information about the activities of Belsky and the Romanovs is lacking. It is not possible to establish that they were

the main authors of the deliberate campaign to circulate the
rumour, which became widespread early in 1600, that by a miracle
Tsarevich Dmitri had been rescued before Boris's henchmen could
murder him in Uglich. But there is strong probability that Fedor
Romanov, supported by his brothers and by Bogdan Belsky, was
the mastermind behind this campaign, and in particular that he
devised the plan to destroy the Godunov dynasty by presenting a
pretender, the False Dmitri.

Tales that Tsarevich Dmitri was alive were reported soon after
the death of Tsar Fedor. In part, such rumours reflected the
deep anxiety of the people over the extinction of the Rurikid
dynasty. They regarded themselves as the children of their Tsar.
On the death of Tsar Fedor they became orphans, and the word
sirota (orphan) recurs in the documents and folk stories of this
period.[4]

One of the earliest reports of this rumour was recorded at the
time of Boris's election. Andrei Sapega, governor of Orsha near
the Russian frontier, wrote to the Lithuanian Hetman that Dmitri,
whom he described wrongly as the son of Tsar Ivan by his second
wife, Maria, was said to be alive. He added that Boris had taken
the Tsarevich under his protection, intending to put him forward
as a candidate for the throne, if he himself were not elected.
Another rumour, reported from Tobolsk in Siberia in July 1598,
accused Boris of the murder of Dmitri. Three brothers, sons of a
banished boyar, were arraigned for saying publicly: "Imagine
whom they want to be Tsar—the man who exterminated the real
tsar dynasty by murdering Tsarevich Dmitri in Uglich and by
strangling Tsar Fedor."[5] Such reports revealed that gossip, passed
on by people in different parts of the country, was already
preparing the way for the legend of the miraculous survival of the
Tsarevich.

By early 1600 the rumour had hardened in its final form. The
enemies of Boris whispered in every part of Moscow that Dmitri
had escaped the attempt by Boris's agents to murder him and that
he would come to claim the throne of his father, Tsar Ivan. At
this time the Romanovs and their supporters were at liberty, and
active in their clandestine plans to destroy the Godunovs. At this
time, too, the great embassy from Poland-Lithuania, headed by
Lev Sapega, was in Moscow. There may well have been secret
discussion between the Romanovs and Sapega, for both parties
evidently had the idea of resurrecting the dead Tsarevich.
Certainly by this time a young man was being trained to play the
part. He was present incognito as a member of Sapega's embassy
in Moscow and returned with it to Poland.[6]

Boris must have known of the rumours that were circulating. The network of informers in the households of leading boyars and in the market places of Moscow and other towns would have brought frequent reports of the talk about Tsarevich Dmitri. But to counter or suppress such tales, disseminated in hushed voices by people of all classes, was impossible. Boris knew that the Romanovs and Belsky were dangerous enemies, but evidently he had not penetrated their secret plans. He decided, however, that the time had come to take action against them.

Towards the end of 1600 Bogdan Belsky was summoned to Moscow for interrogation. He had been sent early in the year to take charge of the building of the new fortified town of Tsarev-Borisov on the Donets River. A wealthy and powerful landowner, Belsky took with him a large force of retainers and enlisted more men locally among the runaway peasants who had taken refuge in this wild steppeland region. The building of the town progressed rapidly with ample living quarters and with towers and other fortifications against Tatar attack. Belsky made himself popular with all in the district, whom he feasted and treated generously. Reports began reaching Moscow of his boasts that Boris might be Tsar in Moscow, but he was Tsar in Tsarev-Borisov, a boast with insulting implications. Another report was that Belsky had repented having killed Tsars Ivan and Fedor on Boris's instigation. That was, however, merely an illustration of the vicious tales that were circulating.

Whether solely because of his boasting or also because he still had designs on the throne and was involved in conspiracy, Belsky was interrogated and found guilty. The extent of Boris's anger was demonstrated by the fact that he ordered one of his doctors, a Scot, to pluck out Belsky's beard. This was a fearful humiliation. Orthodox Russians tended their beards with almost religious fervour. In the case of Belsky the humiliation was all the greater because he had a passionate hatred of foreigners. He was then knouted and deprived of all rank. His estates were confiscated and his army of retainers was disbanded. He was imprisoned in a settlement in the lower Volga region.

About this time Boris was seeking firm evidence that would justify charges against the Romanovs. Semen Godunov called on the household servants to give information against their masters. But their evidence was not considered sufficient for a prosecution. Then a certain Bartenev, who was the treasurer of the estates of Aleksandr Nikitich Romanov, went secretly to Semen Godunov and reported that his master was hiding baskets of poisonous herbs and practising sorcery. Boris sent Okolnichy Saltykov to Aleksandr

Romanov's house, where he found the baskets and brought them to the palace. There the boyars and others denounced the Romanovs so loudly that they could not make themselves heard.

Sorcery was one of the most serious and feared crimes. The church and civil authorities paid earnest attention to all charges of sorcery. The oath of loyalty to Boris, sworn by all, had contained a specific reference to "poisonous herbs and roots" which no one should handle with the motive of harming the Tsar and his family.[7] The oath also bound Russians "not to invoke witches or witchcraft to harm in any way the sovereign".[8]

Aleksandr and his four brothers, the sons of Nikita Romanov, were arrested and also those who were part of the Romanov circle, including the Princes Cherkassky, Shestunov, Repnin, Karpov, and Sitsky, together with their servants. All were accused of plotting to kill the Tsar by sorcery and poison. They were closely interrogated and, following Muscovite practice, this involved knouting and other gruesome tortures, but on this occasion they were not burnt by fire.

The Council of Boyars conducted the trial and in June 1601 pronounced sentences. Boyar Fedor Romanov, the most energetic and able member of the family, was compelled to become a monk, which meant that he could never be a contender for the throne. Under the name of Filaret, he was banished to the Siisky Monastery in the far north. His wife became a nun and was banished to the Onega region. Their children, Mikhail and Tatiana, together with the family of Aleksandr Romanov, were sent to Beloozero, Aleksandr himself being sent to a settlement by the White Sea. The others were scattered to distant parts of Siberia and the north. Of the Romanov brothers, only two, Filaret and Ivan Nikitich, survived. Accusations were to be made that Boris had them secretly murdered. But records showed that he displayed constant concern for their welfare. He sent numerous instructions to their guards that they were to be well treated and fed and clothed suitably. As early as May 1602 he allowed Ivan Romanov to live in Nizhni Novgorod and in September to return to Moscow.

Boris was neither vindictive nor malicious. Indeed, it seemed that, unlike the Romanovs, he could not forget that they had once been close friends. But he had made the mistake of trying to rule humanely and with justice. To survive in sixteenth-century Russia demanded ruthlessness of the kind that he had witnessed in Tsar Ivan's rule and which he had always refused to apply. Now when he struck against the Romanovs, he acted too gently and it was already too late.

Notes

1. Karamzin, XI, I, Col. 66; Solovyev, IV, VII, pp. 399–400.
2. Solovyev, IV, VII, p. 393.
3. *Ibid.* pp. 394–9; S. F. Platonov, *Boris Godunov* (Petrograd, 1921) p. 184.
4. See, for example, p. 131 above.
5. G. Vernadsky, *The Tsardom of Moscow 1547–1682* (New Haven, 1969) I, p. 220.
   Stories of the murder of Tsarevich Dmitri by Boris had also become part of the folklore of the age. Several *byliny* or folk legends in verse, which were recited in peasant villages and in market places, bore witness to the wide popular acceptance of the story. N. Kershaw Chadwick in *Russian Heroic Poetry* (Cambridge, 1932, pp. 216–17) gives a translation of one of these *bylina*.
6. Solovyev considered that this is the most probable explanation, namely that the Pretender was chosen and trained by the enemies of Boris in collusion with Sapega and the Jesuits. Solovyev, IV, VII, pp. 404–5.
7. S. F. Platonov, *op. cit.*, p. 138.
8. *Loc. cit.*

CHAPTER XIV

The False Dmitri

IN THE SUMMER OF 1603 A YOUNG MAN, RECENTLY TAKEN INTO THE service of Prince Adam Vishnevetsky, astonished his master by declaring that he was Tsarevich Dmitri, the youngest son of Tsar Ivan IV. He displayed a jewelled cross which he said had been given to him by his godfather, Prince Ivan Mstislavsky, at his christening.

Impressed by his bearing and eloquence, the prince was inclined to accept his story. He also saw political advantage in befriending the claimant to the Muscovite throne. His estates were in Bragin in Belorussia on the then Polish side of the Dniepr River, which had been threatened often by the Russian armies. If this young Pretender became Tsar, he would be able to look to him for protection and greater rewards.

Vishnevetsky sent a report to the king on the sudden appearance of the Tsarevich Dmitri. Sigismund responded cautiously. He could not risk violating the twenty-year peace recently concluded with Tsar Boris. He gave orders nevertheless for the young man to be brought to Krakov. Vishnevetsky took him by way of Sambor, the king's estate of which Mnishek, the Sandormirsky governor, was steward. Mnishek was a wealthy, flamboyant, and dissolute Polish nobleman who saw at once the profits to be made from espousing the Pretender's cause. At Sambor, too, Dmitri appeared to fall genuinely in love with Mnishek's younger daughter, Marina, who at the age of fifteen was already renowned for her beauty and, calculating the advantages of being Tsaritsa, she did not rebuff him. In March 1604 he arrived in Krakov.

The identity of this young man who claimed to be the son of Tsar Ivan has been debated endlessly. Some of his contemporaries believed him and the Russian people were persuaded at first by the magic of a miraculous reappearance of a member of the Rurikid dynasty. But in Poland-Lithuania and in Russia most people suspected that he was an impostor. The fact that he himself appeared to have convinced himself that he was truly the Tsarevich lent conviction to his protestations and strengthened his appeal, but did not make him any less of an impostor. In fact, there can be no doubt that Tsarevich Dmitri Ivanovich died in Uglich in May 1591. The question remained, who was this remarkable young man?

All surviving evidence suggests that he was a Russian, chosen and put up to serve as Pretender to the throne.[1] Boris himself had no doubt on this score. Hearing for the first time that the False Dmitri had appeared in Poland, he turned to the princes and boyars at court and said to their faces, "This is your doing!"[2] From the investigations, carried out by Patriarch Iov and Semen Godunov, he was evidently satisfied that the Pretender was a certain monk by the name of Grigori or Grishka Otrepyev.[3]

The father of Grigori was a minor nobleman, named Bogdan-Yakov Otrepyev, who had served as captain of a detachment of Streltsi or Musketeers, and whose throat had been cut by a drunken Lithuanian one night in the streets of Moscow. The boy had served in the households of the Romanovs and of Prince Boris Cherkassky. He learnt to read and write and showed promise as a scholar. But, resenting his humble position in life and seeking greater freedom and security, he became a monk. For a time he wandered from one monastery to another and finally reached the renowned Chudov Monastery within the Kremlin. There he came under the supervision of his own grandfather who had been a monk in the monastery for many years. Patriarch Iov himself noticed this young monk who displayed great ability, especially as a scribe, compiling lives of the saints. He raised him to the office of deacon and attached him to his personal staff. On occasion Grigori accompanied the Patriarch to court and there evidently his restless imagination was inflamed by the magnificence which surrounded the throne.

The young deacon studied closely the chronicles of Russian history, preserved in the monastery. On several occasions he remarked to other monks that one day he would be Tsar in Moscow. They merely laughed, but certain monks spat on him for unseemly talk. Metropolitan Iona learnt of his boast and reported him to the Patriarch who did not take the matter seriously. The Metropolitan then reported to the Tsar "that the unworthy monk, Grigori, wants to become the vessel of the devil", and that the Patriarch had treated his denunciation lightly.[4] Boris ordered that Grigori should be sent to the Solovetsky Monastery on an island in the White Sea to repent his heresy. Warned by a friend,

Grigori fled from the Chudov Monastery with two other monks, Varlaam and Misail Povadiny.

Wandering monks were a feature of Russian life in the sixteenth and later centuries. They could always count on the charity of the people, who looked upon them as holy men, and the numerous monasteries all over the country readily opened their gates to them. Grigori and his two companions made their way to Novgorod Seversky and thence to Kiev which was in Polish territory. From there Grigori set out secretly and alone. It was reported that the Archimandrite of the monastery where he lodged in Kiev found after his departure a note which read: "I am Tsarevich Dmitri, son of Ioann, and I will not forget your kindness when I sit upon the throne of my father."[5] The Archimandrite was so terrified that he told no one about it.

For a time Grigori was at the court of Prince Konstantin Ostrozhsky who was a well-known patron of Orthodox churchmen. He wandered next to the estate of a Polish nobleman, Gavriil Goisky, who was also sympathetic to Orthodox believers. There he laid aside his monkish robes and enrolled in an Arian college in Goshchi where he studied Latin and Polish. About this time, too, he became proficient as a swordsman and horseman and acquired something of the veneer of a young Polish nobleman. The Goisky were friendly with the Princes Vishnevetsky and in the summer of 1603 Grigori, no longer a monk, joined the retinue of Prince Adam Vishnevetsky and to him he declared his claim to be Tsarevich Dmitri.

In Krakov the arrival of the Pretender had aroused special interest. The Roman Catholic Church saw in him a means of promoting its influence in Russia and in particular of pursuing the cherished policy of uniting the Eastern and Western Churches. Pope Clement VIII had been informed about Dmitri. He was inclined to dismiss him as an impostor. He was easily persuaded, however, that the Church should take advantage of the situation to weaken the Orthodox regime in Russia and to spread Roman Catholic interests there. He agreed therefore to sponsor Dmitri's efforts to seize the throne in Moscow.

Dmitri himself recognised that he must embrace Roman Catholicism if he was to gain Polish support for his claims. He knew, too, that marriage with Marina would be possible only after his conversion, for the Mnishek family purported to be fervent Catholics. He wrote twice to the papal nuncio, Rangoni, asking for his aid and blessing. When received soon after his arrival in Krakov, he was told by Rangoni that the king would help him only if he joined the Church of Rome and sought the Pope's

protection. Dmitri agreed readily. The Jesuits were entrusted with
his indoctrination and in the following month he was received
secretly into the Roman Catholic Church. He then wrote to the
Pope, declaring "before your Holiness, supreme pastor and father
of all Christianity, my obedience and submission. I do this
secretly and I humbly pray your Holiness for weighty reasons to
guard the secret. Executed at Krakov the 24th April of the year
1604. Your Holiness' most humble servant, Dmitri Ivanovich,
Tsarevich of Great Russia and Heir to the States of the
Muscovite Monarchy."[6]

On 15 March, Dmitri was granted private audience with King
Sigismund. Unconvinced by his claims and anxious to avoid war
with Russia, the king refused to give him official support. He had
to heed, too, the opposition of the powerful Grand Chancellor,
Jan Zamoisky, as well as of other leading Polish nobles who
openly derided Dmitri's pretensions. Indeed, none of the Poles,
including Mnishek, who surrounded and aided Dmitri, believed
that he was truly the son of Tsar Ivan. Nevertheless Sigismund
could not resist the opportunity that offered to weaken Russia and
for him to seize the western regions on Poland's frontier. In
refusing to give official support to Dmitri, he therefore promised
him privately an annual grant of 4,000 florins and, which was
more important, he gave permission for all nobles who wished to
do so to use their own troops and any other Polish volunteers in
the Pretender's campaign to secure the Russian throne.

Mnishek, whom the king appointed to take charge of this
unofficial operation, made haste to secure his own personal interests. As soon as Dmitri had been received into the Roman
Catholic Church, he sought the hand of Marina formally in
marriage. This was promptly agreed by father and daughter on
the condition that the wedding could take place only after he had
been crowned Tsar. The other condition of the betrothal was that
Dmitri should pledge himself in writing to pay Mnishek one
million zlotys (100,000 florins) on becoming Tsar and further that
he would transfer to Marina to hold in her own right the cities of
Novgorod and Pskov and their surrounding regions. Carried away
by his greed, Mnishek extorted from Dmitri some three weeks later
a further written pledge that on his accession he would grant to
Mnishek both Smolensk and Severia, half of which would be
transferred to the king with further compensation being paid to
Mnishek.

Dmitri's cause appeared to make some progress in Poland, but it
was a result of the sordid cupidity of the Polish nobles and of the
Roman Catholic hierarchy rather than of belief in the justice of his

campaign. It was nevertheless remarkable that this young Russian of apparently humble origins should have gained any support among the proud and wealthy Polish nobility. Physically Dmitri was unprepossessing. He was of medium height, broad-chested, with reddish hair, a swarthy complexion and a large broad nose. His eyes were blue and his expression generally dull. He had beneath his right eye and on his forehead large warts, although one observer described these blemishes as birthmarks. Certainly descriptions of the Pretender portray him as being utterly unlike his father, Ivan the Terrible, who was tall and majestic in appearance.

Dmitri had, however, a lively mind and an impressively eloquent tongue, which apparently more than compensated for his un-inspiring appearance. He possessed also a self-confidence which enabled him to bear himself proudly as befitted the son of an autocrat. The papal nuncio, Rangoni, saw him for the first time at a banquet on 13 March and described him in a letter to Clement VIII. "He is a young man of good presence, brown of complexion, with a large birthmark on his nose by his right eye, with long white hands, so shaped as to indicate noble extraction. He is spirited in speech and in his behaviour and manner of treating others he has true grandeur."[7]

In Moscow, Boris was alarmed by the reports of the sudden presence of Dmitri in Poland and even more by the support which he was gaining there. Apparently Boris himself began to wonder whether the Tsarevich had really died in Uglich. Early in April 1604 he had Marfa, the banished mother of the Tsarevich, brought to Novodevichy Nunnery, where in the company of the Patriarch and, according to certain sources, also his own wife, he questioned her. The young Dutch merchant, Massa, who believed Dmitri's claim to be genuine, wrote a dramatic and colourful account of the confrontation. Massa was not, however, an eye-witness and was merely reporting the gossip of the marketplace. In fact what happened at this meeting, if it took place, is not known.[8]

The action taken by Boris to counter the claims and activities of the Pretender were confused and belated, displaying none of the sagacity and efficiency which usually marked his dealings with foreign courts. At this time he was in poor health, and this may provide some explanation. But also the enmity of the Romanovs and others and their clandestine activities against him had clearly undermined his confidence. The appearance of the Pretender in Poland gave proof that their sinister work continued even after they had been banished. The tragedy of the great famine, followed by this political challenge, may well have caused him to lose heart. He may have begun to feel that no matter how he struggled to rule moderately and humanely, he and his dynasty were still doomed.

One of the steps taken to denounce the Pretender was to send messages to commanders of Polish frontier posts, explaining that Dmitri was none other than the unfrocked monk, Otrepyev, and that the true Tsarevich had died in Uglich. But these messages were full of errors of fact concerning the date of death and place of burial. Supporters of Dmitri seized on these mistakes and cast scorn on Moscow's crude attempts to destroy confidence in his just claims. Then the monk, Varlaam, who had been Otrepyev's companion, and Yakov Pykhachev, who had known him, arrived in Poland to denounce him as an imposter. Dmitri at once stated that both men had been sent by Boris to kill him. Varlaam was cast into prison and Pykhachev was executed.

Smirnoi Otrepyev, an uncle of the Pretender, was sent to Poland in the name of the Boyar Council. But he arrived without documents establishing his credentials and without any indictment of the False Dmitri. It was said that other envoys were despatched from Moscow and they proved equally ineffective in influencing the Poles. Posnik Ogarev was sent in the Tsar's name to King Sigismund, bearing a document protesting that an unfrocked monk and "such a criminal had been received and believed in your kingdom without sending to us for true information. Even if that criminal were truly Prince Dmitri Uglitsky, risen from the dead, he is not legitimate, being of the seventh wife."[9] Boris apparently believed in the possibility that by witchcraft or by the miraculous intervention of God, Dmitri might have been resurrected.

Ogarev was informed in the king's name that Dmitri was receiving no help from the Polish government and that those who were assisting him would be punished. Patriarch Iov sent his own envoy to Prince Ostrozhsky, begging him in the name of Orthodoxy not to support an unfrocked monk. The prince merely sent the envoy back without reply. Another envoy, sent by the Patriarch, was held at Orsha near the frontier. In response to these clumsy protestations the Pretender addressed a detailed statement to Boris, condemning him for his crimes, including the attempt to murder him in Uglich, and exhorting him to repent.[10]

In Moscow the people were growing restive. Patriarch Iov and Prince Vasily Shuisky assured them that the Tsarevich had died in Uglich and that the unfrocked monk, Grishka Otrepyev, was using his name. Vasily Shuisky recounted that he himself had buried the Tsarevich and could not be mistaken. Both admonished the people not to believe evil rumours. But they remained unconvinced. Tales of the miraculous survival or resurrection of Dmitri continued to spread not only in Moscow but throughout the country. It was not until January 1605, however, that the Patriarch sent an encyclical to all priests that they should offer prayers in their churches that God might turn away his wrath from the Tsardom and not allow the people to become the victims of pagan Lithuanians and Latin heretics. Priests were ordered to read out to their congregations an official statement, giving the facts about the False Dmitri. These and other operations, designed to discredit the Pretender, should have been undertaken far earlier, and even before he made his appearance in Poland, for the widespread rumours had insidiously sown seeds of doubt about Boris and had prepared the way for Dmitri. At the time that the Patriarch's encyclical was being read in the churches, he had already marched from Poland.

Mnishek had managed to enlist some 2,000 volunteers among Poles and Ukrainians for Dmitri's march on Moscow. It was a small enough response and it reflected the general lack of faith in his cause. But during the summer of 1604, working from Sambor, he had been building up support in the Russian Ukraine and had made invaluable contacts with the Don Cossacks. In this vast area where malcontents, fleeing from their landowners and from famine, had gathered in their thousands, he was able to rally men to his cause.

In August 1604 Dmitri set out from Sambor with his 2,000 volunteers. Near Kiev he was joined by some 2,000 Don Cossacks. With this army he crossed the Dniepr in October and advanced northwards. Thousands joined him on the march until he had a force of 10,000 men by the time that he reached Chernigov. The people of these frontier regions were not carried away by any conviction that he was the true Tsarevich. They seemed confused and moved to support him out of opposition to Boris. In this they apparently took their lead from the boyars and military governors who were hostile towards their Tsar and took every opportunity to hasten his defeat. The military governors of Putivl, Rylsk, Sevsk, Kursk, and Kromy, for example, surrendered their fortresses to Dmitri without firing a shot. Others behaved in the same way and the local people followed their lead.

At Novgorod-Seversky on 21 December, Dmitri gained a victory over the Tsar's army, commanded by Prince Fedor Mstislavsky. He then set up his headquarters at Sevsk, where more Cossacks rallied to his banner. Indeed, the support of the Cossacks and not a general uprising among the Russian people had made his advance possible.

Boris had mobilised a new army after the defeat at Novgorod-Severesky, and he entrusted it to the command of Prince Vasily Shuisky. It was noteworthy that he felt that he could rely on the princely families at this stage and not on his own boyar class. Shuisky's army joined battle with Dmitri's forces near Dobrynichi and on 21 January, 1605, completely routed them.

Dmitri fled with the remnants of his army to Putivl. His predicament was so critical that he hardly expected to escape with his life. But again the Don Cossacks came to his rescue with some 4,000 men. Meanwhile Vasily Shuisky had not followed up his victory by destroying the remainder of Dmitri's force. Boris was angered by the inactivity of his commanders and their failure to capture the Pretender. His orders stirred them to reluctant action. They laid siege to the important stronghold of Kromy where the Don Cossacks and other supporters of the Pretender were concentrated. The defences of Kromy were shattered and its walls on fire. All was ready for the final assault. At this point Mikhail Saltykov, commanding the artillery, withdrew the cannon. Kromy was saved and Dmitri narrowly escaped a second, and probably decisive, defeat. But even with Cossack support and with the disaffection within the Tsar's army, especially among its commanders, his campaign was foundering. It was saved because suddenly on 13 April, 1605, Boris died.

Notes

1. S. F. Platonov, *Boris Godunov* (Petrograd, 1921) pp. 144–5; Solovyev, IV, VII, p. 405.

2. *Loc. cit.*; Solovyev, IV, VII, p. 406.

3. The Muscovite government consistently maintained not only while Boris Godunov was on the throne but also during the brief reign of Shuisky and the long reign of Mikhail Romanov and subsequently that the Pretender was the Muscovite, Grigori Otrepyev. Solovyev could find no grounds for seriously questioning this identification. He did not accept the theory advanced by some, that the monk, Grigori Otrepyev, was merely in attendance upon the Pretender and not the same person. But this monk had originally been called Leonid; if he had been Grigori Otrepyev then surely he would have been produced in Moscow to discredit the statements made by Tsar Boris and his officials.

   Philip Barbour in *Dimitry: Called the Pretender* (London, 1967, pp. 321–7) has examined the various hypotheses concerning the identity of the Pretender. He appears to favour without endorsing the explanation, based on slight circumstantial evidence, put forward by A. S. Suvorin (*Concerning Dmitri the Pretender,* St Petersburg, 1906).

Suvorin's theory was that Tsarevich Dmitri did not die in Uglich in 1591 but was rescued by the Nagoi. Subsequently this child was adopted by the Otrepyev family and given the name Grigori, so that the Tsarevich Dmitri and Grigori Otrepyev were in fact the same person. Thus the Pretender was truly the Tsarevich and heir to the Muscovite throne while at the same time the official account that he was Grigori Otrepyev was equally correct. The theory is ingenious but, lacking any real evidence to support it, it is fanciful.

4. Karamzin, XI, I, Col. 73.
5. *Ibid.* Col. 74.
6. Philip Barbour, *op. cit.,* p. 42; P. O. Pierling, *Lettre de Dmitri dit le Faux à Clement VIII* (Paris, 1898).
7. Philip Barbour, *op. cit.,* p. 34; P. O. Pierling, *Rome et Démétrius* (Paris, 1878).
8. Philip Barbour, *op. cit.,* p. 64; Solovyev, IV, VII, p. 411.
9. Solovyev, IV, VII, p. 412.
10. *Ibid.* p. 413.

CHAPTER XV

The Death of Tsar Boris
and his Dynasty

BORIS HAD BEEN IN POOR HEALTH SINCE 1602. HE PROBABLY suffered from dropsy and from heart trouble. It was said that in 1604 he had a stroke which caused him to drag one leg and for some time he did not leave the palace. His sudden death at the age of fifty-three was nevertheless unexpected. As usually happened when any prominent person died suddenly in Russia, rumours were soon circulating that he had been poisoned or had taken his own life. But he died apparently from natural causes.[1]

On the day of his death Boris had appeared to be in reasonable spirits. He attended a council meeting and received certain eminent foreigners. At 1 a.m. on 13 April he dined with them and members of the court in the Golden Palace. He was rising from the table when he staggered. Suddenly blood began to gush from his nose, mouth, and ears. His doctors who were always in attendance could do nothing to staunch the blood. He was in agony, but managed to give his blessing to his son, Fedor, as his successor on the throne. Then he lost consciousness and, after lingering for some two hours, he died. During this time following ancient Muscovite custom, he was consecrated as a monk under the name of Bogolep. A few days later he was buried in the Arkhangelsky Cathedral.

The people of Moscow swore allegiance to Tsar Fedor Borisovich without question or disturbances. Fedor was a handsome and intelligent boy and, at the age of sixteen, well developed both physically and mentally. Boris had loved his son and had taken pains to give him a broad education and, by involving him directly in state affairs, to fit him to rule. The oath of loyalty, administered in Moscow and elsewhere, was, however, to the Tsaritsa Maria as well as to Tsar Fedor, for the Tsaritsa was acting as regent at this stage. The oath contained specific references to the "criminal who calls himself Prince Dmitri

Uglitsky".[2] All swore that they would neither aid nor accept him in any circumstances.

One of the first acts of the new Tsar was to recall to Moscow Princes Fedor Mstislavsky and Vasily Shuisky, who commanded the main army and were proving unable or unwilling to crush the Pretender and his forces. Tsar Fedor was probably also recalling these princes to be at his side, for like his father he knew that he must trust them rather than the Muscovite boyars. In their place he appointed Peter Fedorovich Basmanov, the able military leader whom his father had trusted and rewarded. Basmanov could be appointed only second-in-command because of the rules of *Mestnichestvo,* and Prince Ivan Katyrev-Rostovsky was made nominally commander-in-chief.

The new commanders set out with the Novgorod Metropolitan, Isidor, to administer the new oath of loyalty to the army. The troops swore the oath, but they were confused and looking to their commanders to give them a lead. Peter Basmanov found that the brothers, Princes Vasily and Ivan Golitsyn, and also Mikhail Golitsyn, were ready to go over to the Pretender. Any gratitude and loyalty that he might have felt for Tsar Fedor's father were forgotten, together with the oath he had so recently sworn to the Tsar. Peter Basmanov apparently did not hesitate to join with the Golitsyns in declaring that Dmitri was the true Tsar. On 7 May, only three weeks after the death of Boris, the oath of loyalty to Tsar Dmitri was administered to the army. Only a few officers and men rejected the new oath and with Prince Katyrev-Rostovsky they fled to Moscow.

In Moscow the people were bewildered. Numerous couriers, bearing proclamations from the False Dmitri, arrived in the city. They were seized and done to death. Then Naum Pleshcheev and Gavril Pushkin brought a declaration which they took first to the Red Village where the wealthy merchants and craftsmen lived. They had always been hostile towards Boris and now they welcomed the Pretender. In a crowd they escorted the two couriers into the city. A force of Streltsi was sent to arrest them, but unsure who was in authority and fearing punishments, they turned back. On the Red Square the proclamation of the False Dmitri was read out to the people and it was now stated to have the support of Princes Mstislavsky, Vasily and Dmitri Shuisky, and other leading men in the land. It recounted in detail the Pretender's title to the throne and the alleged crimes of the Godunovs. It promised rewards to all who recognised him promptly, and those who resisted his claims were threatened with the anger of God and of himself as Tsar.

The Muscovites were now completely unsettled. A crowd was said to have asked Prince Vasily Shuisky to reveal the truth about the Tsarevich and whether he had in fact buried him in Uglich in 1591. Shuisky now stated, falsely as he admitted later, that the Tsarevich had been saved from his assassins and that a priest's son had been buried in his place.[3]

On 3 June a mob broke into the Kremlin Palace and seized Tsar Fedor together with his mother and sister. They were held under close arrest in the house which Boris had occupied before his accession to the throne. From Tula, Dmitri sent to Moscow Princes Vasily Golitsyn and Vasily Mosalsky, and Dyak Sutupov to dispose of the Godunovs. They began their task by seizing Patriarch Iov, Boris's most consistent supporter. Iov was conducting the service in the Uspensky Cathedral when they broke in and took him away. Clad as a simple monk he was sent to the distant Staritsky Monastery. Next they placed under arrest all members of the Godunov family and those related to it, and dispersed them to distant prisons. Semen Godunov, who as head of the security service had made himself hated, was sent to Pereyaslavl and strangled on arrival.

Princes Vasily Golitsyn and Vasily Mosalsky, were joined by Vasily Molchanov and a court official named Shelefedinov and three Streltsi. They went to Boris's house. On instructions they took Tsarevna Kseniya away and kept her under close guard. Dmitri, learning of her beauty, had ordered that she should be kept for him, and soon after he arrived in Moscow he raped her and then made her his mistress.

The assassins, sent by Dmitri, quickly strangled Tsaritsa Maria. But Tsar Fedor, who was unusually strong for his age, proved a difficult victim. He knew that he was fighting for his life and he struggled furiously with them for some time. In desperation one of the assassins reached under his caftan and, grasping his genitals, tore them away. Fedor cried out in agony. The others beat him with cudgels and strangled him to make sure that he was dead. The Muscovites were told that mother and son had committed suicide, but the bodies bore clear marks of struggle and strangling.[4]

The body of Boris was disinterred from its tomb in the Arkhangelsky Cathedral, where the Muscovite sovereigns were buried. It was encased in a simple wooden coffin and taken secretly to the nunnery of St Varsofonie, and from there to the Troitsa Monastery. There in the special *Usypalnitsa* or burial vault, erected close by the entrance to the Uspensky Cathedral, his body was laid to rest finally on 1 May, 1605. The bodies of his wife and son were laid beside him on 10 June in the same year. Seventeen years later the body of his beloved daughter, Kseniya, long known as the Tsarevna Nun Olga Borisovna, was joined with them in the vault. Boris and his family were thus finally reunited in death after suffering the "punishment of Heaven" for his alleged crimes.

Notes

1. S. F. Platonov, *Boris Godunov* (Petrograd, 1921) p. 152.
2. Solovyev, IV, VII, p. 421.
3. *Ibid.* p. 424.
4. Karamzin, XI, I, Cols. 118–20 and Notes 347 and 348.

CHAPTER XVI

The Time of Troubles

ON 20 JUNE, 1605, THE FALSE DMITRI ENTERED MOSCOW, GREETED by the pealing of church bells and the acclaim of the people. But his popularity was shortlived and he reigned for less than a year. The widowed Tsaritsa Maria, who was now the nun, Marfa, acknowledged him as her son, admitting later that she had been in fear of her life when she did so. He was crowned Tsar on 21 July. He married Marina and she soon put an end to his cruel self-indulgence with Kseniya Godunova, who was forced to become a nun under the name of Olga.

Dmitri did not lack ability and he tried to rule as Tsar. But he could not resolve the critical problems of the day and particularly the conflicting class and factional interests. Peter Basmanov and Bogdan Belsky became his chief Russian advisers, but they could not help him. Muscovites were quick to resent his large retinue of Poles and Jesuits and to criticise his scant observance of Orthodox practices. The boyars who had promoted him as a means of removing Boris from the throne schemed to get rid of him.

In the early hours of the morning of 17 May, 1606, the boyars, headed by Vasily Shuisky, acted. A detachment of Novgorod troops, loyal to him, closed the Kremlin gates. All the church bells in the city then rang out the tocsin. The people rushed to the Red Square where Shuisky and other boyars inflamed them against the Poles. In a mob they began breaking down and looting the houses occupied by Poles. While the people were thus distracted, the boyars and a band of their men entered the Kremlin and after a short struggle they killed Peter Basmanov and Dmitri. The body of Dmitri was later burnt. The ashes were mixed with gunpowder and fired from a cannon in the direction of Poland, whence he had come.

There followed a period of chaos and disasters such as the

Russians had never known in their troubled history. Vasily Shuisky
was hurriedly elected Tsar by the boyars. As a representative of a
senior branch of the Rurikid dynasty he was acceptable to many,
but the numerous gentry class, the townspeople and peasants, and
the Cossacks opposed him as the boyars' Tsar.

Unrest became more widespread. A certain Ivan Bolotnikov
emerged as the leader of a popular movement. Proclaiming that he
would restore Dmitri as Tsar and bring about a revolution in which
peasants would take over the estates of the landowners, he massed
a large army and advanced on Moscow in October 1606. He held
the city under siege for two months, but was then forced to retreat.
In the following year, Shuisky defeated him and dispersed his
army.

Rumours were already circulating that Tsarevich Dmitri was
still alive and would come to claim his father's throne. To prevent
such rumours spreading further, Shuisky decided to have Tsarevich Dmitri of Uglich canonised as a martyr. The remains of the
Tsarevich were brought to Moscow on 3 June, 1606, and with
solemn ceremonial interred in the Arkhangelsky Cathedral in the
Kremlin. In a proclamation, distributed to all parts of the country,
Shuisky declared to the people that the true Dmitri had been
murdered by the agents of Boris in Uglich and that he himself had
buried the sacred infant. The declaration also condemned the False
Dmitri as a secret apostate and on other grounds.

Such measures were not enough, however, to exorcise this
particular ghost. In June 1607 a second False Dmitri appeared in
Poland. In the spring of 1608 he advanced to Tushino with trained
Polish troops and strong forces of Don and Zaporozhsky Cossacks.
The identity of the new Pretender is not known, but he fought
as the people's Tsar against Shuisky, the boyars' Tsar. During the
next two years their struggle caused untold suffering and devastation.

Shuisky ceded to Sweden the territories on the Gulf of Finland,
so recently recovered by Boris, in return for military aid. The re-
inforcement of 15,000 Swedish, English, Scotch, and French
mercenaries enabled him to dislodge the Pretender from Tushino.
But then King Sigismund invaded Russia and laid siege to Smolensk. In June 1610 the Poles defeated the Russian army at
Klushino and advanced on Moscow. At this time the Pretender,
again reinforced by Cossacks, was also advancing on the city.

In July the people of Moscow rebelled and demanded the abdi-
cation of Shuisky, who became a monk. The Boyar Council provided such government as there was. The Polish army was at the
gates of Moscow. The boyars hastily negotiated an agreement

whereby Vladislav, son of King Sigismund of Poland, would become Tsar. This expedient would, they hoped, unite Russia and
Poland as equals. They found, however, the Sigismund himself
wanted to be Tsar and that the Poles, far from regarding the
Russians as equals, behaved arrogantly, treating them as inferior
subjects. Russian resentment mounted. A national militia *(opol-
chenie)* was mobilised, which forced the large Polish garrison to
take refuge within the Kremlin in the spring of 1611. But even
now attempts to form a national government and to give some
leadership to the country, which was in a state of chaos, failed because of the conflicts of interests, especially between boyars, gentry,
townspeople, and Cossacks.

By 1612 Russia was on the point of disintegrating. The administration had collapsed completely. The country was being
devastated by rival armies and by brigands. At this point an up-
surge of national feeling united the people. Kuzma Minin, a
butcher who was the mayor *(Starosta)* of Nizhni Novgorod and a
remarkable leader, rallied the upper Volga region. A second
national militia was organised under the command of Prince Dmitri
Pozharsky, a provincial noble. Together Minin and Pozharsky
cleared the Poles and other foreign troops from Russia. The Cossacks, who had inflicted so much suffering on people, now joined
in the task of finding a new Tsar. Early in 1613, the Assembly of
the Land elected Mikhail Romanov, the son of Filaret, Boris's
most bitter enemy, and he was the first Tsar of the dynasty which
was to endure for three centuries.

Bibliography

THE FOLLOWING ARE THE MAIN SOURCES AND STUDIES CONSULTED. I have not included all the relevant articles, published in the *Oxford Slavonic Papers, Voprosy Istorii, Istoricheskie Zapiski,* and other journals, which have been of value; references to such articles will be found in the notes to chapters.

Allen, W. E. D., "The Georgian Marriage Projects of Boris Godunov" in *Oxford Slavonic Papers,* XII, 1965 (Ed.) *Russian Embassies to the Georgian Kings 1589–1605.* Translated by Anthony Mango. (Hakluyt Society) Cambridge, 1970.

Bain, N. Nisbet, *Slavonic Europe,* Cambridge, 1908.

Bakrushin, S. V., *Ivan the Terrible,* Moscow, 1945; "The Chosen Council of Ivan the Terrible" in *Istoricheskie Zapiski,* XV, Moscow, 1945; with others, *History of Moscow* Vol. I. *Period of Feudalism,* Moscow, 1952.

Barbour, P., *Dimitry: Called the Pretender. Tsar and Great Prince of All Russia 1605–1606,* London, 1967.

Blum, Jerome, *Lord and Peasant in Russia,* New York, 1964.

Bond, E. A. (Ed.), *Russia at the close of the 16th Century,* (Hakluyt Society) London, 1856.

Cherepnin, L. V., *The Formation of the Russian Centralized State in the 14th–15th Centuries,* Moscow, 1960.

Eckardt, Hans von, *Ivan the Terrible.* Translated from the German by C. A. Phillips. New York, 1949.

Fennell, J. L. I. (Ed. and Trans.), *The Correspondence between Prince A. M. Kurbsky and Tsar Ivan IV of Russia 1564–1579,* Cambridge, 1963; *Ivan the Great of Moscow,* London, 1961; *The Emergence of Moscow 1304–1359,* London, 1968.

Graham, Stephen, *Boris Godunof,* London, 1933.

Grekov, B. D., *Peasants in Russia from earliest Times until the XVII century,* Moscow/Leningrad, 1946.

Grey, Ian, *Ivan the Terrible,* London and New York, 1964;

Ivan III and the Unification of Russia, London and New York, 1964.

Grunwald, Constantin de, *La Vraie Histoire de Boris Godunov,* Paris, 1961.

Hakluyt, Richard, *The Principal Navigations, Voyages and Discoveries of the English Nation* (J. M. Dent edition), London, 1927.

Hamel, J. V., *Russia and England,* London, 1854.

Herberstein, Sigismund von, *Notes upon Russia.* Translated and edited by R. H. Major, (Hakluyt Society) London, 1851–2.

Karamzin, N. M., *History of the Russian State,* 5th ed., St Petersburg, 1842–43.

Klyuchevsky, V. O., *Course of Russian History,* Moscow, 1956–59.

Kurbsky, Prince A. M., *History of Ivan IV.* Translated and edited by J. L. I. Fennell. Cambridge, 1965.

Margeret, J., *Estate de L'Empire de Russe et Grand Duche de Moscovie,* 3rd ed., Paris, 1821.

Massa, Isaak, *Short Account of Muscovy at the beginning of the XVII century,* Moscow, 1937.

Morgan, E. D. and Coote C. H. (Eds.), *Early voyages and Travels to Russia and Persia,* (Hakluyt Society) London, 1866.

Novoselsky, A. A., *The Struggle of the Muscovite State against the Tatars in the first half of the XVII century,* Moscow/Leningrad, 1948.

Oman, C., *The English Silver in the Kremlin 1557–1663,* London, 1961.

Palitsyn, A., *The Story of Avraam Palitsyn,* Moscow/Leningrad, 1955.

Parker, W. H., *An Historical Geography of Russia,* London, 1968.

Pierling, P. O., *La Russie et le Saint-Siège,* Paris, 1896.

Platonov, S. F., *Boris Godunov,* Petrograd, 1921; *History of Russia.* Translated by E. Aronsberg. London, 1925; *Ivan the Terrible,* Berlin, 1924; *Essays on the History of the Troubled Times on the Muscovite State in the XVI and XVII centuries,* Moscow, 1937.

Ross, Sir E. Denison, *Sir Anthony Shirley and his Persian Adventure,* (Hakluyt Society) London, 1933.

Smirnov, I. I., *The Uprising of Bolotnikov 1606–1607,* Leningrad, 1949.

Solovyev, S. M., *History of Russia from earliest times,* Moscow, 1959–66.

Staden, Heinrich von, *Concerning the Moscow of Ivan the Terrible: Notes of a German Oprichnik.* Translated by I. Polosin. Moscow, 1925.

Tikhomirov, M. N., *Russia in the XVI century,* Moscow, 1962.

Tolstoy, G., *The First Forty Years of Intercourse between England and Russia 1553–93,* St Petersburg, 1875.

Timofeev, I., *Annals.* Edited by V. P. Adrianova-Peretts. Moscow/Leningrad, 1951.

Ustryalov, N. G., *Tales of Contemporaries about Dmitri The Pretender,* St Petersburg, 1831.

Vernadsky, G., *Kievan Russia,* Yale, 1948; *The Mongols and Russia,* Yale, 1953; *Russia at the Dawn of the Modern Age,* Yale, 1959; *The Tsardom of Moscow 1547–1682,* Yale, 1969; "The Death of the Tsarevich Dmitri" in *Oxford Slavonic Papers,* V, Oxford, 1954.

Waliszewski, K., *Ivan the Terrible.* Translated by Lady Mary Lloyd. London, 1904.

Willan, T. S., *The Early History of the Russia Company 1553–1603,* Manchester, 1956.

Wipper, R., *Ivan Grozny.* Translated by J. Fineberg. Moscow, 1947.

Zabelin, I. E., *The Domestic Life of the Russian Tsars and Tsaritsas,* Moscow, 1862–9; *History of the City of Moscow,* 2nd ed., Moscow, 1905.

Zimin, A. A. (Ed.), *The Works of I. Peresvetov,* Moscow/Leningrad, 1956; *I. S. Peresvetov and his Contemporaries,* Moscow/Leningrad, 1958; *The Reforms of Ivan the Terrible,* Moscow, 1960.

Index

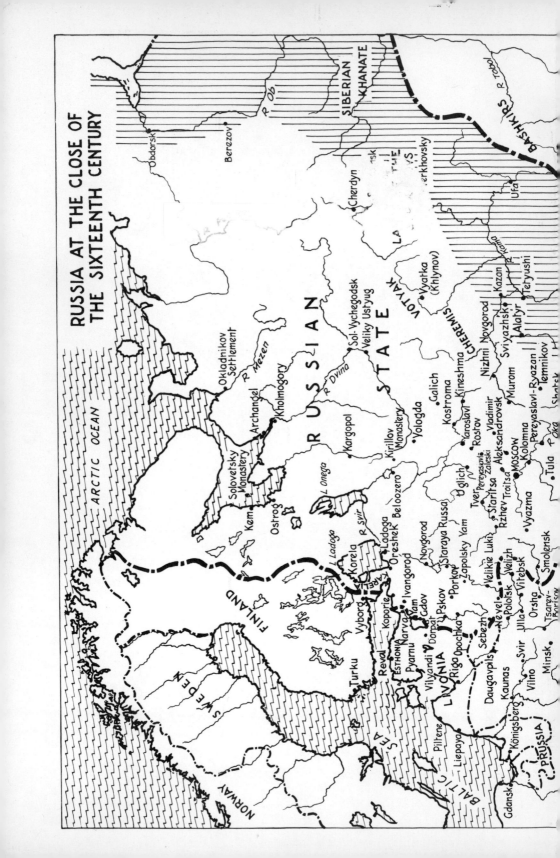

RUSSIA AT THE CLOSE OF
THE SIXTEENTH CENTURY